IVAN BUNIN

Ivan Bunin

A Study of His Fiction

By James B. Woodward

The University of North Carolina Press

Chapel Hill

© 1980 The University of North Carolina Press

All rights reserved

Manufactured in the United States of America

ISBN 0-8078-1394-X

Library of Congress Catalog Card Number 79-12790

Library of Congress Cataloging in Publication Data

Woodward, James B

  Ivan Bunin: a study of his fiction

  Bibliography: p.

  Includes index.

  1. Bunin, Ivan Alekseevich, 1870–1953—
Fictional works.

PG3453.B9Z93   891.7'8'309   79-12790

ISBN 0-8078-1394-X

To my wife

Contents

Preface

Ivan Alekseyevich Bunin (1870–1953) has claims to be recognized as perhaps the greatest Russian prose writer of the twentieth century. Certainly his position in the history of modern Russian literature is unique. Not only was he the last major Russian artist to emerge from the ranks of the landed gentry, the class that had raised Russian literature to its eminent position among the literatures of the world; he was also the only postrevolutionary exile whose continuing development as an artist was not seriously impaired by emigration. He was the only significant Russian poet of the early twentieth century who was not associated with the symbolist movement and its successors. And he was the first Russian writer to win, in 1933, the Nobel Prize for Literature. Above all, however, he is distinguished from his contemporaries by his apparent immunity to both the literary and the political pressures of his time and by the persistence with which he steered his completely solitary course of development. His hostility to symbolist art is well known; his early association with the "realists" concealed an almost comparable estrangement.

Bunin's literary career exceeded in length that of any other Russian writer. His first works were published in 1887, and he was still writing when he breathed his last. In the course of these sixty-six years, his art obviously underwent a considerable evolution, and he was already in his forties when he began to develop the type of short story that ultimately brought him his greatest success. Till 1909, his reputation rested mainly on his achievements as a poet, and he continued to write poetry throughout his career. But even though he himself would have disputed the view, his poetry is of far less importance than the long succession of prose works that began in 1909–10 with the publication of his short novel *The Village* [Derevnya]. As a poet, he never really transcended the traditions he inherited, but as a prose writer, while displaying a similar respect for tradition, he developed a medium for the expression of his highly personal conception of life that in a very real sense is more "poetic" than even the best of his verse and achieved, mainly in the genre of the short story, an originality that is quite as distinctive as that of Chekhov. Bunin will be examined in this study, therefore, solely as a prose writer.

With the passage of time, it has become increasingly evident that the reputations acquired in their lifetime by numerous Russian writers of the early twentieth century were somewhat inflated and that their success was largely dependent on, and coterminous with, a specific combination of cultural, social, and political conditions. The reputation of Bunin, conversely, probably stands higher now than ever before. Indeed, it is only in the last fifteen years that his art has at last begun to receive the attention it merits. In general, his fate at the hands of the critics has not been a happy one. Before the Revolution, his apparent insensitivity to the Zeitgeist and his anomalous position in relation to the main literary movements of the period obviously precluded the kind of acclaim that was accorded to Maxim Gorky or Aleksandr A. Blok, and although his skill as a craftsman was invariably acknowledged, few serious attempts were made to grapple with the main issues raised by his fiction. After his emigration to France in 1920, the study of his works in his homeland ceased almost entirely, and for nearly thirty years he was consigned to oblivion. Almost everything of importance written on Bunin during this time was contributed by his fellow exiles, who produced the only monograph on him that existed till 1962,[1] and a number of essays, notably those by F. Stepun[2] and V. Weidle,[3] that still provide the most illuminating comments on his art and personality. Given, however, the status Bunin enjoyed in the émigré community, this body of criticism falls far short, at least in quantitative terms, of what one might have expected, and it is also frequently vitiated by a recurrent and predictable tendency to compare his prerevolutionary works unfavorably with those he wrote in France and to dismiss the former as reflecting a degree of relative immaturity.

With Bunin's restoration to grace in the Soviet Union in the "thaw" of the fifties, this distortion was rapidly superseded by its opposite. It became, and remains, the common objective of Soviet commentators to emphasize the relative superiority of his prerevolutionary fiction. Moreover, although foreign students of Bunin owe a considerable debt of gratitude to these scholars—above all for the abundant primary materials they have brought to light[4]—even the most substantial of their works[5] tend to raise more questions than they answer and to present a curiously fragmented picture of the development of his fiction that tends to obscure rather than to illuminate the mainsprings of his art.

Bunin studies in the West are still in their infancy and have thus far contributed notably only to the elucidation of meaning in individual works. The first monograph on him in English, which is still the only book on his works in any language other than Russian, appeared only in 1971,[6] and its pretensions are strictly limited. Indeed, Western criticism in general has thus far proved no more successful than Soviet criticism in resolving the fundamental problems posed by Bunin's art—above all, the problem of whether or not his fiction expresses a coherent view of life and the human condition to which the dominant characteristics of his art may be plausibly related. Until this problem has been convincingly resolved, significant progress in the study of Bunin's fiction is difficult to envisage, and it is accordingly posed as the major problem in the present study. After the two introductory chapters, which are devoted to his life and to those aspects of his art that are most amenable to generalization, his responses in his early works to the processes of social change in Russia in the late nineteenth and early twentieth centuries are examined in detail. The main emphasis, however, is on the relation of these responses to a general conception of life that lies, I will argue, at the basis of all his art and invests his fictional portraits of the disintegration of prerevolutionary Russia with implications no less universal than those of the love stories that are studied in the later chapters. And it is precisely this conception of life, my argument continues, that explains the most distinctive attributes of the Bunin short story. The result, it is hoped, is a more searching examination than criticism has yet provided of the relationship in Bunin's fiction between content and style.

The edition of Bunin's works used in this study is the nine-volume edition published in Moscow in 1965–67, which is the most complete that has yet appeared.[7] References to the edition are included in the text, and in footnotes it is referred to as *Sobr. soch.* All translations from the Russian are my own, and prerevolutionary dates are given in Old Style.

I would like to express my gratitude to Gleb Struve of the University of California at Berkeley for his most helpful comments on the manuscript. My thanks are also due to the editors and publishers of the *Modern Language Review, Scando-Slavica, Die Welt der Slaven, Canadian Slavic Studies*, and *Forum for Modern Language Studies* for their permission to use in this book material from my articles on Bunin which are indicated in the Bibliography.

J. B. Woodward

IVAN BUNIN

1. The Biographical Background

The art and personality of few Russian writers have been so obviously and decisively influenced as those of Bunin by their family background and by the conditions in which they spent their childhood and early youth. He was born in Voronezh, in central Russia, on 10 October 1870 into a line of landed gentry that could be traced back to a Lithuanian knight of the fifteenth century and whose name was recorded in the exclusive Sixth Book of the Russian hereditary nobility. His paternal ancestors included the poets Anna Bunina and Vasiliy Zhukovsky, but they had chiefly distinguished themselves over the centuries as administrators, and through the family of his mother (née Chubarova, 1835–1910), which had lost its princely title only a century before, he could also boast kinship with an officer in Peter the Great's army who had suffered the same penalty for rebellion as so many of his hapless subordinates.

Although Bunin claimed complete indifference to his "blue blood" (9:254), his pride in his lineage cannot be doubted, and some of the more conspicuous features of his personality may plausibly be attributed to it—in particular, the unusual self-assurance he displayed from an early age, the arrogance and intolerance for which he later became renowned, and the acute sensitivity to time and history to which many of his writings bear witness. Even physically he seemed to personify the popular notion of an aristocrat,[1] and he was not unaware of the fact. It is not difficult, therefore, to appreciate the effect on him of the rapid economic decline of his family during his childhood. By 1870, the disintegration of the "nests of the gentry," which had been greatly accelerated nine years earlier by the emancipation of the serfs, was already well advanced, and the process was further quickened by the spread of industrialization to the provinces in the following three decades. Like many of his class, Bunin's talented, energetic, and magnanimous father, Aleksey Nikolayevich (1824–1906), was psychologically incapable of adjusting to the situation. By 1874, his addiction to the traditional way of life of the landed gentry had effectively reduced the family's possessions to two small estates in the province of Oryol—Butyrki, which was Bunin's home from 1874 to 1886, and Ozerki, where he spent the next three years. The rest suffered the fate later symbolized and immortalized by Chekhov's famous "orchard."

The economic plight of Bunin's family explains, in part, the meagerness of his formal education, but it was not the only reason. His enlightenment began, appropriately, under the supervision of an eccentric and versatile tutor named Romashkov, who played a notable part in stimulating his imagination and developing his taste for the arts. At the age of eleven, on passing a travesty of an examination, he entered the *gimnaziya* in the local town of Yelets. The pleasure of the experience was extremely short-lived. After an auspicious beginning, his academic progress ground swiftly to a halt, and the completion of a second stint in the third form was enough to convince him that his time could be better spent elsewhere. Accordingly, he left abruptly in the winter of 1886. His fees had not been paid, and he was therefore condemned to expulsion in any case, but the decision, it seems, was taken entirely on his own initiative in response to a situation he no longer found tolerable. It was an early indication of the resolute independence of spirit that was to remain the most salient trait of his character. It also reflected his nostalgia for the simple rural delights of Butyrki, from which the necessity of lodging in Yelets had parted him, and the distaste for urban life he was never to lose completely.

The prominence of the countryside and rural life in Bunin's art distinguishes him from almost every major Russian writer of his generation and is explained as much by his love of Butyrki as by his concern with the social changes of which he was a melancholy witness. He refers to the estate, in his "autobiographical note" of 1915, in the following terms:

"Here in the profound silence of the fields—in summer amid the corn that came right up to our doors and in winter amid the snowdrifts—passed the whole of my childhood which was filled with a unique and sorrowful poetry" (9:254). A vivid impression of this "poetry" may be obtained from many of his early writings and from the appropriate sections of his autobiographical novel *The Life of Arsen'yev* [Zhizn'Arsen'yeva], which he wrote in emigration (1927–29, 1933). Butyrki gave him a knowledge of nature's sounds, scents, and colors, of its flora and fauna, with which perhaps not even Ivan S. Turgenev could have competed, and there, under the combined influence of his surroundings and Romashkov, he initially aspired to become a painter. But the influence of his environment in the wider sense of the term, reinforced again by that of Romashkov and also by that of his mother, eventually ensured that his creative urge would express itself in language rather than color. Even as a child, Bunin was profoundly conscious of the rich literary associations of his native region[2] —the region to the south and southeast of Moscow, which was the birthplace of Lev Tolstoy, Turgenev, Mikhail Lermontov, Ivan Goncharov, Fyodor Tyutchev, Afanasiy Fet and Nikolay Leskov.[3] Kroptovo, the derelict estate of Lermontov's father, was in the immediate vicinity, and after the move to Ozerki he found himself within seventy miles of Yasnaya Polyana. Given his sensitivity to the tradition created by this exalted company of novelists and poets and his tendency to regard writers in general as "beings of a higher order" (9:259), it is not surprising that his first story—an unpublished piece entitled "An Infatuation" [Uvlecheniye]—had been written by the time he was sixteen or that by 1888 his first poems and short tales had appeared in print.[4]

At Ozerki, Bunin's education was under the more disciplined control of the elder of his two brothers, Yuliy, who was thirteen years his senior.[5] A man of wide cultural interests and a *kandidat* of Moscow University, Yuliy Bunin had been arrested in 1884 for disseminating revolutionary literature under the pseudonym "Alekseyev."[6] After a short period of exile he was committed to his parents' charge at Ozerki and confined there under police surveillance. Lacking creative ability himself, he quickly recognized his younger brother's potentialities and devoted himself for the next two years to the task of broadening his knowledge and encouraging his literary activity. He also endeavored to prepare him for the certificate of maturity that would make him eligible for admission to a university. The close relationship that developed between the two brothers during this period was not to be broken till 1920, when Yuliy rejected the idea of emigration.

When, in 1888, the restrictions on Yuliy's freedom of movement were finally lifted and he departed to Khar'kov in the Ukraine, Bunin abandoned his thoughts of a university education and decided that the time had come for him to lighten the burden on his parents and spread his wings. Thanks to Yuliy, his knowledge of Russian and European literature by this time was extensive, but he had still seen no town larger than Yelets. The pretext for departure came in January 1889 in the unexpected form of an offer of the post of assistant editor of the newspaper *Orlovskiy vestnik* [Oryol herald]. He accepted it gratefully, but did not take up the post at once. Feeling the need for the fraternal advice to which he had become accustomed, he set off for a two-month sojourn in Khar'kov, which was chiefly memorable for the first dispiriting acquaintance that it gave him, through Yuliy's Populist friends, with the "radical" mentality. Appalled by the puerile superficiality of their reasoning, he embarked in April on a whirlwind tour of the Crimea, Smolensk, Vitebsk, and Moscow, and after returning for the summer to Ozerki finally presented himself for duty in Oryol.

He worked for the paper for two hectic years in the capacity of general factotum—as creative artist, editorial writer, theater critic, and proofreader. In effect, he ran the paper and received for his pains a pittance. Even more exhausting than his diverse responsibilities was the atmosphere created by the rivalry between his employers—the actual editor, B. P. Shelikhov, who was forbidden for political reasons from presenting himself as such, and the nominal editor, his common-law wife N. A. Semyonova. Appeals for financial assistance alternated in his letters to Yuliy with lurid accounts of their incessant petty intrigues. But his most painful sufferings during this period were caused by his affair with Varvara Pashchenko, a junior member of the paper's staff, who forty years later inspired the conception of Lika in Book V of *The Life of Arsen'yev*. The affair lasted five years, and it is doubtful whether the scars it left ever healed completely. From the beginning, their hopes of marriage were frustrated by the implacable opposition of Varvara's parents, who took exception to his penury and limited prospects, and in despair they left Oryol in August 1892 and moved to Poltava. There Yuliy, who was now in charge of the statistical bureau of the provincial *zemstvo*, found positions for him, successively as librarian and statistician, which at least offered the possibility of a more peaceful existence. In fact, they offered much more —opportunities for reading and writing such as he had not known since leaving Ozerki and, in addition, the chance to indulge further his passion for travel. His duties as statistician involved frequent data-hunting expeditions to different parts of the province from which he derived a knowledge of the Ukraine and its people that is reflected in several of his early stories. He witnessed at first hand the withering effects of the famine of 1891 and the cholera epidemic of 1892 and the wholesale migrations of peasant communities that could no longer maintain themselves on the lands tilled by their ancestors. In the vicinity of Poltava, he also made his first acquaintance with a colony of "Tolstoyans" and in 1893–94 experienced a brief infatuation with their master's philosophy of "simplification," even schooling himself in the skills of the cooper's trade and winning a sentence of three months' imprisonment for selling without a license pamphlets issued by the Tolstoyan publishing house in Moscow, Posrednik [Mediator]. Unhappily, he was cheated of his martyrdom by the inopportune death in October 1894 of Alexander III and the amnesty of his successor, Nicholas II.

Nine months earlier, Bunin had met Tolstoy at Yasnaya Polyana. The perceptive sage, it seems, instantly recognized the unsuitability of the material before him and clearly im-

plied in their conversation that in his case excessively scru-
pulous observance of the creed would be unwise. Certainly
Bunin's temperament, his egotism, and his addiction to the
pleasures of life ensured from the start the brevity of his
dedication to the cause. But the source of his eventual disenchantment, as his stories "At the Dacha" [Na dache] (1895)
and "In August" [V avguste] (1901) confirm, was more the
practice of Tolstoyism than its theory or ideals—the divorce
between word and deed that he detected in the colonists'
behavior, their uncompromising self-righteousness, the artificiality of their asceticism, their disrespect for beauty, and
their pathetic inefficiency—and soon after his ineffectual
brush with the law he severed his ties with them forever.
Perhaps a more compelling reason, however, for his disaffec-
tion was the crisis at this time in his private life, which finally
came to a head in November 1894 when Varvara left him to
marry a more eligible writer and journalist, his friend A. N.
Bibikov. But for the intervention, it seems, of his brothers
Yuliy and Yevgeniy, he may well have taken his life, but in the
end he allowed them to escort him to the more tranquil atmosphere of Yevgeniy's estate Ognyovka, which fifteen years
later served him as a blueprint for Durnovka, the estate of the
Krasovs in *The Village*.[7]

Although "At the Dacha" was rejected by the editors of
the "thick journals" *Novoye slovo* [New word] and *Russkaya
mysl'* [Russian thought], presumably because of its ambiguity
and inconclusiveness, by 1895 Bunin had already achieved a
number of minor successes. A volume of his poetry, criticized
for its echoes of Fet,[8] had been published in 1891 by *Orlovskiy
vestnik*, and the first appearance of his name in the "thick
journals" had already been registered with the publication in
1894 of his story "Tan'ka" (1892), under the title "A Rural
Sketch" [Derevenskiy eskiz], in *Russkoye bogatstvo* [Russian
wealth], the Populist journal edited by the "dean" of contemporary Russian criticism N. K. Mikhaylovsky, who promptly
predicted for him a rosy future. In the meantime, his verse
had attracted the attention of the venerable poet A. M. Zhemchuzhnikov, who assisted in securing the publication in 1894

of several more poems in *Vestnik Yevropy* [The Herald of Europe]. The time seemed propitious for his first visit to St. Petersburg, and in January 1895, having abandoned his job in Poltava, he completed a round of the city's editorial offices, introducing himself to the luminaries, including Mikhaylovsky, with whom he had thus far merely corresponded. Repeating the process the following month in Moscow, he returned for the spring and summer to Ognyovka to continue the study of English that had been claiming his energies for some years and to complete a translation of Longfellow's *The Song of Hiawatha*, on which he laid considerable hopes. He was not disappointed, for after appearing in 1896 as a supplement to *Orlovskiy vestnik* and undergoing a final revision, it brought him in 1903, together with his collection of poems entitled *The Fall of the Leaves* [Listopad] (1900), the first of the three Pushkin Prizes he received from the Academy of Sciences.[9] Resolving that henceforth he should endeavor to maintain himself by his writing alone, he returned to the capitals in the autumn of 1895, after a second sightseeing visit to the Crimea, with the object of extending his range of acquaintances. In December, he was introduced to Anton Chekhov, with whom he had been corresponding intermittently since 1891,[10] and his meeting a few days later with Valeriy Bryusov began a period of close association with the future *maître* of the symbolist movement and the poet Konstantin Bal'mont that lasted till 1901.[11] By this time, Bunin's popularity in more socially conscious circles had been notably enhanced by the appearance two months earlier in *Novoye slovo* of a short piece called "To the Edge of the World" [Na kray sveta], which persuaded the journal's publisher O. N. Popova that he had earned his right to the publication of his first volume of prose. Entitled *To the Edge of the World* and containing nine stories, the volume came out in January 1897 and established his reputation as a writer of promise.

The almost unanimous praise, however, that greeted the volume evidently provided him with little incentive to continue with the same kind of writing, for his output of prose in the next two years was extremely limited. Not only, it seems, was he still somewhat bemused by the conflicting views of literature he had encountered in the capitals, but there can be little doubt that his achievements thus far had fallen far short of his aspirations and that he was acutely conscious of having failed to make in his prose works the truly distinctive mark he craved. This dissatisfaction and his inability at this stage to perceive any outlet probably explain the remarkable restlessness that shortly afterward uprooted him from St. Petersburg and impelled him between 1897 and 1899 to maintain a state of almost perpetual motion between Moscow, the Ukraine, the Crimea (where Chekhov was in residence), and the estates of Ognyovka and Vasil'yevskoye[12] in the province of Oryol. In the course of his wanderings, his circle of literary acquaintances was increased by meetings in 1897 with Aleksandr Kuprin in Odessa and A. N. Teleshov in Moscow and by regular attendance, together with Yuliy, at sessions of the "Wednesday" [Sreda] group of writers formed by Teleshov in Moscow in 1899. His visits to Odessa also yielded two surprises—a new job and a wife—for in 1898 the editor of the Odessa newspaper *Yuzhnoye obozreniye* [Southern review] N. P. Tsakni, a celebrated Greek revolutionary, offered him the editorship of the arts section, and a few months later he married Tsakni's daughter, Anna Nikolayevna. The rashness of his action soon became apparent. Irreconcilable differences of temperament and problems resulting from his wife's insistence that they live with her parents created a situation that by the early months of 1900 had exhausted his patience, and he left her. Thereafter he returned only to see his son, who was born the following August, and when the child died five years later from meningitis he severed all contacts with the family.

Placing his faith in the healing powers of distance, Bunin embarked in October 1900 on the first of his many journeys abroad. Accompanied by the artist V. P. Kurovsky, curator of the Odessa museum, he visited Berlin, Paris, Switzerland, Munich, and Vienna and returned to Moscow in late December with his appetite for work seemingly restored. A powerful new stimulus to resume work had already been provided by his association with Gorky that had begun soon after their first meeting in the spring of 1899 at Chekhov's house in Yalta. Gorky had lost little time in requesting a contribution for the new Marxist journal *Zhizn'* [Life],[13] which he edited with V. A. Posse, and Bunin eventually obliged with a number of poems and his most successful prose work to date, "Antonov Apples" [Antonovskiye yabloki] (1900). From this time forth, Gorky followed his progress with intense interest, and when *Zhizn'* was closed by government edict in June 1901, he offered on behalf of the new cooperative publishing house Znaniye [Knowledge], of which he was joint manager and an important shareholder, to publish a collection of Bunin's stories. Having failed, because of widening differences of opinion with Bryusov,[14] to persuade the symbolist publishing house Skorpion [Scorpion] to follow its edition of *The Fall of the Leaves*, issued earlier in the year, with the publication of a volume of prose, Bunin readily agreed to the terms suggested, and the collection of twenty-two stories appeared the following year. It was the first of the five volumes of his works Znaniye published between 1902 and 1909.

It should not be deduced, however, from Bunin's connections with Gorky, Znaniye, and the Wednesday group that he felt a particular sense of affinity with the predominantly "realist" writers with whom they brought him into contact. His total disregard for the literary or political persuasions of his associates is clearly attested by the wide variety of journals and miscellanies in which his works appeared and by his simultaneous negotiations in 1901 with Znaniye and Skorpion. He offered his works to Znaniye simply because after his break with Bryusov it was the logical alternative means of ensuring their publication. His indifference to the publishing house as an institution representative of specific literary and ideological attitudes is confirmed by the fact that of the prose works he wrote before *The Village* only two first appeared in Znaniye's famous miscellanies—"Black Earth" [Chernozyom] (1903)[15] in 1904 and "Poor is the Devil" [Beden bes][16] in 1909—and even these works were probably contributed simply because of the considerable material advantages that accrued from publication in the Znaniye volumes with their large circulation.[17] The rest he either offered in his customary fashion to any editor who showed interest or included in publications he edited himself.[18]

Despite his many new acquaintances and contacts, Bunin remained, in fact, at this time a profoundly lonely figure, and his sense of solitude is vividly reflected, as we shall see, in his writings of the period. The experience, of course, was not unfamiliar to him. Solitude had haunted him throughout his childhood and youth, and his entire education, although briefly assisted by his brother, had essentially been a solitary process of self-improvement. In the years ahead, his position in this respect changed little. Many, like Chekhov, fell under the spell of his mordant wit, his fitful charm, and the remarkable gift of mimicry inherited from his father that so impressed Stanislavsky that he tried to recruit him into the Moscow Art Theater,[19] but strong and lasting attachments were a rarity in his life. The reasons have already been indicated—his complete self-sufficiency and his uncompromising rejection of all who professed views different from his own unless, like Gorky, they could be of service to him.[20] Everything he said, wrote, and did proclaimed his unyielding independence—not least the distinctive way of life that from 1902 onward became a norm from which he seldom deviated. Spending the winter months in the capitals, he would proceed for the spring to Odessa or the Crimea and devote the summer and autumn either to writing in rural tranquillity or to travel abroad. Thus visits to Turkey, France, and Italy in 1903 were followed in 1907 by a protracted tour of the Middle East and by numerous visits in the next few years to western Europe. Further tours of North Africa and Turkey in 1910 and of Egypt, Lebanon, Ceylon, and Singapore in 1910–11 equipped him with a knowledge of the world beyond the confines of Europe that for a Russian writer was almost unprecedented.

Apart from his extensive peregrinations, the most notable events in Bunin's personal life in the first decade of the century were the death of his father in 1906 and that of his mother in 1910. In the seven-year period from 1904 to 1910 he lost the four people to whom he was most deeply attached —Chekhov, his son, and his parents. From early childhood, as *The Life of Arsen'yev* records, his sensitivity to death had been extreme,[21] and some indication of his state of mind after the death of his mother is provided by his failure to attend her funeral. Foreseeing his reaction, she herself, it seems, had advised against it.[22] The bereavements, however, did not leave him entirely alone, for a month before the death of his father he had acquired a companion who was to remain at his side for the rest of his days. In November 1906, he was introduced at the house of the writer Boris Zaytsev to Vera Nikolayevna Muromtseva (1881–1961), the daughter of a member of the Moscow City Council and a niece of Sergey Andreyevich Muromtsev, president of the First State Duma and one of the founders of the Constitutional Democratic party. Six months later she became his common-law wife. Prevented from marrying by Anna Tsakni's refusal to grant him a divorce, they were obliged to wait fifteen years before their marriage could finally be legalized in Paris.

Between 1903 and 1909, Bunin's most important literary achievements were in poetry, and it was primarily for his work as a poet and as a translator of poetry—of Tennyson and Byron as well as Longfellow—that in 1909 he was awarded his second Pushkin Prize, which he shared with Kuprin, and elected an honorary member of the Imperial Academy. Neither his poetry, however, nor his prose had yet made any significant impact on the reading public at large. At a time when traditional literary values were being belligerently "transvalued," his apparent dedication to the classical heritage seemed quaintly anachronistic. The turning point came in 1910 with the publication of *The Village* in the journal *Sovremennyy mir* [Contemporary world]. Certainly Bunin's central purpose in the work, if we may judge from contemporary criticism, was not generally recognized, but the powerful exposé of conditions of life in the countryside guaranteed an animated response. From this time forth his poetry was almost completely eclipsed by his prose. Although *The Village* is no masterpiece and far exceeds in size the type of composition in which Bunin was to excel, it may justly be viewed as the work that marks the beginning of the transition to the art of his maturity. It was followed in the next six years by a succession of tales on kindred themes, published either individually in journals or in volumes containing both prose and poetry, that eventually won him, if not the popularity of Chekhov, Gorky, or Leonid Andreyev, then certainly the reputation in most discerning quarters of Russia's most accomplished living prose writer. Characteristically, Gorky was one of the first to acknowledge the fact. "The best contemporary writer," he wrote in 1911, "is Ivan Bunin, and this will soon become clear to all who sincerely love literature and the Russian language."[23]

By 1915, when Bunin received his third Pushkin Prize, he had evolved a style and accent that were uniquely his own and achieved a consistency in his level of attainment matched by few contemporary writers. His themes were intrinsically compelling, and his craftsmanship was unanimously extolled. It remains, of course, debatable whether his art would have developed in a significantly different direction if his life had not been disrupted by the rising tide of events, but the evidence, as later chapters will confirm, suggests quite definitely that it would not, for even by 1916 the themes that dominated his later art were already gaining an ascendancy. Although, however, he could remain relatively immune as an artist to the collapse of the old order, as a man he reacted with predictable embitterment. In March 1917, he joined his brother Yuliy and other members of the Wednesday group in an attempt to organize a campaign against the Bolshevik antiwar policy[24] and in general lost few opportunities to declare his position. But by the summer, which he spent, as usual, in the country, he had lost all hope of Russia's survival and was resigned to the imminent realization of fears he had been expressing in his works for the last three decades.

Having endured eight months of Soviet rule, Bunin and Muromtseva left Moscow for the last time on 21 May 1918 and set out for the Ukraine, where the Germans, with the compliance of the Hetman and Rada, were in temporary control. After a brief stay in Kiev, they moved on to Odessa and remained there for almost two years. Not surprisingly, Bunin wrote little of significance during this period. His energies were chiefly devoted to journalistic support of the White cause in the newspaper *Yuzhnoye slovo* [Word of the South], which he edited, and to compiling the diary he published in 1925 under the title *The Accursed Days* [Okayannyye dni]. Both occupations were fraught with hazard, and in the five-month period from April to August 1919 the refugees experienced their second taste of Soviet rule before the city was retaken by the forces of General Anton Denikin. By January 1920, however, the Soviet victory was assured, and six days later they boarded the French ship *Patras*, which took them on the first stage of the arduous two-month journey that led via Constantinople, Sofia, Belgrade, and Czechoslovakia to France and permanent exile.

Rejecting the offer of a chair at a Bulgarian university,[25] Bunin at first took an active part in émigré politics. He briefly headed the Union of Russian Writers and Journalists that was quickly formed in 1920 in Paris, and, after relinquishing the position a year later to Pavel Milyukov, was a reliable and welcome speaker at anti-Soviet gatherings. But gradually his passion and indignation began to yield to demands for a tranquillity that would enable him to resume his writing. Even in the period from 1921 to 1923, his pen was by no means inactive, but only after settling in 1924 in Grasse in the Maritime Alps, the fragrant center of the French perfume industry, was he able to redirect his attention to the central issues of his art and reacquire the habit of disciplined creative endeavor. Thereafter his life bore a certain resemblance to the one he had been compelled to abandon. Once more he established a routine of regular alternations between town and country, spending his summers in Grasse and his winters in Paris, and the effect was instantly beneficial, for in 1924 and 1925 he wrote some of his greatest stories and two years later began *The Life of Arsen'yev*. The main difference, of course, was his inability in emigration, for financial reasons

at least, to embark on the sightseeing expeditions to distant
lands that had introduced into his earlier life so much color
and variety. In France his commitment not simply to his art
but to the actual business of writing was absolute, and the
character of his life is perhaps most graphically summarized
in a remark he made in August 1927 to the young writer
Galina Kuznetsova: "The life of a writer is a renunciation of
life. It is necessary to abandon everything, to think only of
work every day as if one were employed in some job and to sit
at one's desk and be patient."[26]

Although Bunin had no more in common with most of
his fellow exiles than he had with the writers who had remained in Russia, his ability not only to resume writing with
undiminished vigor but also to pick up again and retie the
threads of development that had been severed in 1917 gave
him an exceptional position in the émigré community. His
achievements were regarded by many as a kind of justification
for their own rejection of Soviet citizenship and as an implicit
indictment of the Soviet cultural desert. Hence the community's elated response to the announcement in 1933 that he
had at last been awarded the Nobel Prize for Literature.[27]
The award was seen in many quarters as a tribute to émigré
art in general,[28] and Bunin suddenly found himself riding on
a wave of unprecedented popularity. Almost overnight he
became a writer of international renown, and the demand for
new translations of his works rose abruptly.[29] His satisfaction
as he received the prize in Stockholm must indeed have been
immense. He had at last won the acclaim that the general
public, dazzled, he believed, and misled by the frivolous word
spinning of the modernists, had consistently withheld from
him, and with his faith in justice momentarily restored, he set
to work polishing his texts in readiness for the eleven-volume
edition of his works that was to be published in the next three
years by the Berlin publishing house Petropolis. But the sudden exposure to the footlights was of short duration. By the
late thirties he had returned to the relative obscurity to which
he was more accustomed, and his name was not to emerge
from it again till after his death. When his final volume of

stories entitled *Dark Avenues* [Tyomnyye allei], on which he had worked for ten years, finally came out in Paris in 1946, it was greeted with almost total silence.

Bunin spent the entire period of the German occupation in Grasse in conditions of gradually worsening deprivation. As a mark of his personal contempt for the invader, he refused to publish anything until the yoke had been lifted, and his income rapidly dwindled. In his first letter to Teleshov since leaving Russia, he wrote in May 1941: "I was 'rich' and now, by the will of fate, I have suddenly become a beggar like Job. I was an 'international celebrity,' but now no one in the world needs me. The world has no time for me." The letter ends with the postscript: "I am grey, wizened, and thin, but still venomous. I would very much like to come home."[30] This final statement was soon publicized and caused many eyebrows to be raised, and the impression that the war may have changed his attitude to the Soviet regime was reinforced both by the readiness with which he entertained in his home Russian prisoners of war who had been drafted to work in the vicinity[31] and by his unconcealed pride in the victories of the Soviet armies.[32] But the impression was completely false and could only have been formed by those who had little true knowledge of Bunin's character and little understanding of his attitude to Russia. Nor was there any cause for alarm when he accepted an invitation to visit the Soviet embassy in Paris soon after the promulgation in June 1946 of the Supreme Soviet's decree offering Soviet citizenship to all citizens of the former Russian Empire. His purpose was merely to clarify rumors about the impending publication of a collection of his works in Moscow, and when, after some twenty minutes, he did not receive an opportunity to raise the matter, he left.[33] The reference to him as "a Soviet citizen" by Konstantin Fedin in a speech of 1956 to the Second All-Union Congress of Soviet Writers[34] can only be ascribed to wishful thinking.

The Germans had withdrawn from Grasse on 23 September 1944, and after the liberation of Paris, the Bunins reinstalled themselves in their old apartment on the Rue

Jacques Offenbach, which the Germans had requisitioned. Now the publication of *Dark Avenues* could proceed, and the old pattern of life was quickly restored. In the remaining few years of his life, Bunin worked as energetically as ever, though mainly on nonfictional works—his uniquely vituperative *Memoirs* [Vospominaniya], published in 1950, and his reminiscences of Chekhov, which remained incomplete. He also revised his works yet again in preparation for a new complete edition and even considered writing a book on Lermontov.[35] But in 1951, soon after his election as the first honorary member of the PEN Center for Writers in Exile, he contracted a serious respiratory affliction and thereafter was almost permanently confined to his bed. The death he dreaded finally came to him in Paris on 8 November 1953—two years too early for him to witness the beginning of his "rehabilitation" in his native land and eight months after the death of the tyrant who had stood in its way.[36]

2. An Introduction to the Fiction

One of the first impressions the reader obtains from Bunin's works is that of an immense variety of characters and geographical locations. Russian peasants, landowners, urban dwellers, and émigrés, British empire builders, French settlers in North Africa, American capitalists, the poor of Ceylon —all are depicted in their appropriate settings. The variety, however, is merely the colorful mask of a striking uniformity, for the entire fictional edifice is underpinned by a conception of life that changed negligibly during the sixty-six years of Bunin's creative activity. His conception did not develop under the influence of philosophical systems, even though, like Tolstoy, he often turned to philosophical tracts for support and to the sacred texts of various, mainly oriental, religions.[1] It was simply a product of self-analysis, of his sensitivity as a child to his rural environment, and of the profound sense of personal affinity with nature expressed in his earliest writings. "Open to me your embraces, O nature," he wrote in a poem of 28 March 1886, "that I may merge with your beauty" (1:53). The need for the artist "to live at one in soul with men and nature" formed the central theme of one of his earliest pronouncements on art.[2] These statements of the adolescent poet provide an insight both into the philosophical basis of his art in its entirety and into the source of his wholly distinctive response to the death throes of czarist Russia, for the successive national disasters of the next thirty years were to be seen by Bunin as merely the superficial manifestations of deep underlying processes that raised the fundamental question of the relationship between nature and man.

Of the major social and political events of the late nineteenth and early twentieth centuries—the disruption of Russian rural life by the *ukaz* of 1861, the Russo-Japanese War, the revolutions of 1905 and 1917, the Great War, the Civil

War—only the first leaves an obvious mark on his works. The
rest are usually present more by implication, as part of an inferred background, than as significant elements of the fiction
itself. The study of man in the context of nation or society—
the fundamental preoccupation of nineteenth-century writers
—was entirely alien to Bunin and, in his submission, of sec-
ondary importance to more basic issues. Few Russians have
expressed a more profound attachment to their country, yet
he emerges from his works as perhaps the least nationalistic
of all Russian writers, for his overwhelming concern throughout is with those aspects of human experience that issue directly from the essential, biological nature of man's being. At
a time of accelerating social change, when the Russia of the
past was collapsing before his eyes, he turned as thinker and
artist to the timeless, immutable nature of existence itself and
viewed the march of history from the vantage point of an
inflexible conception of the human condition.

He remarked to his wife in 1929: "Since I came to realize
that life is an ascent of the Alps, I have understood everything. I have come to understand that everything is trivial.
There are certain immutable, organic things about which
nothing can be done—death, sickness, love—and the rest is
trivial."[3] To the category of "trivia" he consigns man's moral
conflicts, his struggles of the will, his pride in his intellect, his
pursuit of "family happiness"[4]—every attribute or preoccupation that differentiates him from the rest of nature. "In
their savagery and intelligence," he wrote in 1916 in his poem
"St. Prokopiy" [Svyatoy Prokopiy], "dogs and men are one"
(1:387). This does not mean that the struggle between will
and instinct is absent from his fiction. On the contrary, it is a
major theme of some of his most celebrated love stories, particularly of "By the Road" [Pri doroge] (1913) and *Mitya's
Love* [Mitina lyubov'] (1924). But the pathos of the struggle
is consistently less striking than the sense of its total futility.
The type of hero whom Bunin most favored exists in body
alone. His responses to life are entirely instinctive and sensual,
and his proximity to nature is the criterion by which his health
is measured. The pleasures and sorrows life affords him ema-

nate exclusively from physical or sensual forms of experience. His individuality is a purely biological phenomenon that owes little to the workings of intellect or conscience. Ideas are alien to him. He lacks the ability to formulate or conceptualize. His words and deeds are spontaneous reactions to stimulation of the flesh. He is a child of nature, and his capacity for contentment and self-fulfillment, insofar as it exists at all, is entirely dependent on recognition of the fact. The recurrent source of tragedy lies in the rarity of this recognition, in the inability of the overwhelming majority to attain to the self-awareness that would dictate the submissive attitude to life that accords with man's position in nature and prepare them for the experiences to which their position ineluctably condemns them. The result is the long succession of dramatic confrontations between individual human beings and individual aspects of the human condition that Bunin's works record, and this predominant concern with dramatic individual experiences chiefly explains his continuing preference for the genre of the short story.

Nature, therefore, is the point of departure in Bunin's portrayal of man, and observation of nature is the primary source of his art and metaphysical speculations. "For Bunin," writes Galina Kuznetsova, "the act of writing almost always begins with nature, with some scene that has flashed through his mind, often a fragment."[5] Nature is much more in his fiction than a harmonious or contrasting backdrop to the drama enacted by the characters. It dominates the proscenium, and even when the proscenium is removed and the characters are exposed to the footlights, its powerful presence is continually sensed in the wings. Nature is present in the fiction as the embodiment of the laws of existence that determine the human condition. It represents a reality to which man is wholly subservient and with which human consciousness is usually and unwittingly in fatal conflict. It is present as a rationally incomprehensible amalgam of beauty and horror, as a source of blind, implacable forces that demand man's submission and ruthlessly punish his resistance. By placing man in this position of total dependence, Bunin creates in his works a relationship between man and his environment that in Russian literature is without precedent. As Stepun has observed, the spiritualization or humanization of nature characteristic of Fyodor Dostoyevsky is replaced by Bunin with the naturalization of man, with the dissolution of man in nature.[6]

The fraternity of nature is Bunin's conceptual substitute for the brotherhood of man. Only in the experiences of the flesh, he argues, are men equal. "Yes, we are all brothers," proclaims the protagonist of "The Blind Man" [Slepoy] (1924), "but only death or great sorrows and misfortunes remind us of this with true, irresistible cogency, depriving us of our earthly ranks and prising us from the sphere of our commonplace lives" (5:148). The concepts of soul and spirit are invoked by Bunin merely to denote the universal life force that "performs its mysterious wandering through our bodies" (5:318) and implants in man the capacity for instinctive experience. The force of instinct, in Bunin's conception, is at once the bond between man and nature and the genetic heritage of every man, the ancestral link between the individual and his biological past. The consciousness of this link prompted him to write in a sonnet of 1916: "I say to myself on sensing the dark vestige of that which my ancestor perceived in ancient childhood: 'There are no different souls in the world and there is no time!'" (1:401). Hence the opening words of his story "The Dreams of Chang" [Sny Changa], written in the same year: "What does it matter of whom we speak? Everyone who has lived on earth deserves it" (4:370).[7] Reducing the concept of individuality to a complex of irrational drives and instincts, he methodically strips from his characters the outer layers of culture, nationality, and professional expertise and reveals the savage lurking behind the façade, ever ready to burst out and transport the personality to the heights of bliss or to the depths of despair. At such moments their control over their lives ceases abruptly. Their self-deceptions are starkly exposed. The rational philosophies or moral codes to which they normally subscribe crumble feebly. They are transformed into passive recipients of the stimuli from within or the blows from without—death, sickness, and love—and the penalty for resistance is pain and self-destruction.

It follows, therefore, that the concept of individual freedom has no place in Bunin's view of life. There can be no genuine freedom, he maintains, in a world governed by the impersonal forces of nature, and it is this belief that primarily explains his consistent indifference to the political causes espoused by his fellow writers and his reluctance to respond to Gorky's repeated appeals for support. The impression that he began his career as a socially committed writer bent on dedicating his art to the improvement of the lot of his fellow citizens is merely one of the many misconceptions that have been provoked by the prominence of social problems in his early fiction. His actual attitude is most clearly expressed in *The Life of Arsen'yev*: "I have never felt, nor do I feel now, any debt to the people. I have neither the ability nor the will to sacrifice myself for the people or to 'serve' the people or to play, in my father's words, at parties and issues at meetings of the district council" (6:159). The statement should not be attributed to the distorting memory of an embittered émigré, for the exposure of social misery in his prerevolutionary art was in no sense the gesture of a sympathetic heart or a wounded conscience. On the contrary, it was an act of indictment, a revelation of the unavoidable consequences of national insensitivity to the true nature of man and to the interdependence of human nature and the social structure. The social ills of Russia are regarded by Bunin *sub specie aeternitatis*, and by 1915, when the "interplay of the biological and social in the character of man"[8] in his works was gradually receding from view, the universal implications of his thought had become fully apparent. By this time Russia had ceased to be the exclusive setting of his stories or the exclusive homeland of his protagonists. Nationality, like all the other nonbiological attributes of personality, had begun to pale into insignificance, and even though the Russian setting was restored to its former dominance in the works written in emigration, its relevance to their thematic content is usually minimal. The reasons for its restoration were not thematic, but personal and aesthetic.[9]

The exclusion from Bunin's purview of virtually everything that differentiates men save the manner and setting in which their biological humanity expresses itself explains the relative narrowness of his thematic range, the "ordinariness" of most of his characters, many of whom are unnamed, and the violent contrasts of behavior and experience on which his mature works normally hinge. For life as experienced by the senses is a source alternately of overwhelming delight and unmitigated horror. It is summarized in the "two truths" of which the narrator speaks in "The Dreams of Chang": "The first is that life is indescribably beautiful, and the second—that life is conceivable only for madmen" (4:371). Almost every major work of Bunin is a translation of this statement into artistic images. Few of them fail to evoke a memorable impression of the beauty that is continually accessible to man, but fewer still omit the transition to the "second truth." Love is almost invariably experienced in the shadow of death, and the innocent beauty of nature coexists with its senseless cruelty and cold indifference. There is no struggle here between good and evil, for in the absence of genuine free will these moral categories are meaningless. There is only the struggle between the "natural" and the "unnatural." Hence the futility of attempting to draw parallels between Bunin and Dostoyevsky. There is no room in Bunin's fictional world for Dostoyevsky's "accursed questions," nor is there a God in whom these questions are resolved. God is contemplated and worshiped by Bunin only as the creator of nature and is usually inseparable from his sublime and terrifying creation.[10] No solution is offered to the great mysteries of life. Through his characters the author merely registers his wonderment and perplexity.

Although Bunin was occasionally disposed in his later prerevolutionary tales to state his views on life explicitly with the aid of a succession of eloquent "reflectors," he normally reserved such statements for his short lyrical compositions, which form an intermediary genre between his fiction and poetry and may be regarded in retrospect as diminutive stepping stones leading to *The Life of Arsen'yev*. The effect of such statements in his fiction is invariably discordant. Indeed, as though in recognition of the fact, Bunin rarely attempts to integrate them with the fiction proper, for on donning the reflective mantle the characters who voice them seem immediately to forfeit their role as *dramatis personae*. They are withdrawn, as it were, to the periphery of the fiction and obliged to gaze at it from without as though at a world to which access is no longer allowed them. Their directly expressed intellectual responses to life introduce a stylistic element manifestly at variance with an art that appeals directly to the reader's sensory imagination—with the art of a writer whose sight, in the words of the young Arsen'yev, "was such that I could see all seven stars in the Pleiades, while I could hear a verst away the whistle of a marmot in a spring field and become intoxicated on smelling the scent of a lily-of-the-valley or the odor of an old book" (6:92). Bunin's inspiration as an artist came from the sensations of the flesh, and for the evocation of sensual experience he developed a "sensual" style[11] incompatible with the conclusions of reason.

Again, however, his narrative art must be distinguished from his lyrical prose. In his early works the lyrical element is predominant and the convention of plot is little in evidence. His main object in numerous short sketches is simply to "infect" the reader, in his own words, with his personal responses to life.[12] Extended descriptions of nature are loosely connected by narrators from whom the author rarely detaches himself. Why invent, he asks implicitly, when everything that is most simple and yet most complex and wondrous in life may be conveyed by the intelligent observation and sensitive reproduction of physical reality? Why abbreviate descriptions of nature, Arsen'yev asks Lika, when "there is no nature which is separate from us" and when "every movement in the air, however slight, is a movement in our own lives" (6:214)? The remark makes clear the significant connection between Bunin's impatience with the conventions of fiction and his conception of life. But an equally important connection may similarly be perceived between his approach to life and those features of his mature narrative art that seem totally irreconcilable with the premises of his lyrical prose—the obvious element of control or restraint, the sense of balance and proportion, and his willingness to enlist the conventions, albeit on a limited scale. Here there is a perceptible distance between the narrator and his subject. The impersonalism of his thought is mirrored in the dispassionateness of his tone and the objectivity of his manner. The reveler in the experiences of the senses is held tightly in rein by the detached observer of the human tragedy, by the artist whose concern for man was less compelling than his conception of the human condition. Direct, personal responses are replaced by dramatized predicaments of universal relevance.

Thus two very different kinds of artistic prose were inspired by the same conception of life, and Bunin's prerevolutionary art is essentially a record of the fiction writer's gradual liberation from the power of the lyricist. But this does not mean, of course, that the two kinds of writing are hermetically sealed from one another and devoid of common features. Their common philosophical premise is revealed in many aspects of their style—above all, in his preference in both types of work for dwelling on externals. As an inalienable part of nature, man is likewise portrayed primarily in his physical aspect. The emphasis is on his appearance, his gestures, his mannerisms of behavior and speech, and his immediate environment, from all of which the reader is normally obliged to deduce his state of mind.[13] Although the heroes of Bunin's postrevolutionary tales are given a freedom to voice their emotional reactions to their experiences that is rarely extended to their prerevolutionary predecessors, even in these works the innermost recesses of the mind are seldom illuminated directly. The reason has already been suggested. Man is depicted by Bunin not as the author of moral and intellectual decisions but as the agent of forces beyond his conscious control. His actions are dictated not by readily discernible psychological processes but by his instinctive responses to stimuli that emanate either from the subconscious depths of his personality or from the external world of nature to which he is subconsciously related. The conventional procedures of psychological analysis, therefore, are rarely employed by Bunin to disclose the essential motives for action. He achieves this purpose by concentrating his attention wholly on the physical portraits of his characters and on the physical aspect of their way of life that are invariably an index of their relationship with nature, for it is precisely this relationship which determines the nature of their actions.

Bunin's preoccupation, therefore, with the external forms of life should not be regarded as a mark of superficiality. It is indicative simply of his concern with a level of psychological experience for which the normal techniques of analysis, he believed, were wholly unsuitable. The external façades are primarily reflections of the harmony or tension between his characters and the primitive forces that ultimately control the life of man, and in the constant, distinctly sensed presence of this powerful undercurrent in human affairs we perceive the counterpart in Bunin's narrative works of the direct, exclamatory responses to the mystery of life that punctuate his lyrical prose. Assertion and exclamation give way to the subtle connections between external reality and the human psyche that are forged by the elements of the fiction in their suggestive juxtaposition. In the fictional context, seemingly insignificant details are repeatedly transformed by repetition, by positional emphasis, or by their elusive interaction with other details into dramatic signals of the irrational, and this recurrent feature of Bunin's mature art more than any other gives his realism its distinctive character.

It is immediately obvious to the reader of Bunin that his language and technique owe much to the Russian realistic tradition. Unlike the symbolists, he felt no compulsion to reject the past. He saw no need, in his own words, for "revolutions" in "one of the youngest, freest, and most versatile literatures in the world."[14] But his conception of life, his central concern with the irrational, and, above all, his oblique manner of conveying the power of the irrational forces of nature over the mind of the individual entailed a certain departure from the aesthetic tradition of realism that relates him rather more closely than he himself would readily have acknowledged to writers of his own generation, both Russian and foreign, to whose aesthetic views and creative methods he was in most cases bitterly opposed. Certainly the term "realist" cannot be applied to him without qualification, and he himself rejected it completely. "If you call me a realist," he wrote to the émigré critic L. Rzhevsky two years before his death, "it means that you do not know me as an artist."[15] The statement confirms by implicaton that his lavish descriptions of the real, recognizable, physical world in which we live did not constitute an end in themselves, but rather were conceived as a means of illuminating a deeper reality, and it is consequently tempting to draw parallels with the romantic *Weltanschauung* and allusive techniques of symbolism. But, compared with the differences between Bunin and the symbolists, the similarities between them are of little significance. Above all, there is the crucial difference that the essential reality evoked by the art of Bunin is not a transcendental reality of which the physical world of nature is merely a distorted reflection; it is inseparable from nature and perceptible only through nature. Hence his distaste for the symbolist practice of transforming physical reality with the aid of metaphor, which he summarily condemned as "verbal fornication" (9:529). Although he was not averse, particularly in his early prose, to using such "poetic" procedures as syntactic parallelisms and phonetic "echoes," Bunin depicts the world as it presents itself to the senses in a language that is instantly comprehensible and totally free from lexical, syntactic, and phonetic curiosities. The suggestions of a deeper reality emanate from the fiction as a whole, from the reverberations of individual details in the context that is created for them, and the result is an extension of the bounds of realism which he himself evidently regarded as a transgression.

Bunin was never loath to proclaim his originality, but his conceit, to which he freely confessed,[16] should not be allowed to obscure the legitimacy of his boast. Certainly there can be no question of his susceptibility to the influence of any writer of his own generation. His attitude to the contemporary literary avant-garde was openly contemptuous. He responded with sadness, rage, and derision to the widely held view that the realistic tradition, which had yielded such a rich and abundant harvest, was outmoded and ill-suited to the age of "new aspirations." As his own art eloquently testifies, he was no proponent of stasis. He welcomed the evolutionary enrichment of realism, and no one paid greater tribute than he to the innovations and originality of Chekhov. But neither in the context of Russian literary development nor in the wider context of Russian social life could he perceive any valid justification for a "transvaluation of values." Hence his tendency to ascribe the genesis of Russian modernism to a single factor —to imitation of the West European movement which he regarded as a perfectly legitimate offspring of totally different literary and social conditions.[17] Symbolism, he contended, was devoid of natural roots in Russian soil. It was an imported, artificially nourished growth, and its art was consequently doomed to sterility. The "new values" it proclaimed, he declared in 1913, were an illusion, and the sole achievement of the movement was to initiate "the incredible impoverishment, stultification, and destruction of Russian literature"[18] that to him was merely one of the diverse manifestations of the general decline of Russia to which his prerevolutionary art is mainly devoted.

In general, it was Bunin's custom to judge writers as much by their knowledge of life—by their documented familiarity with nature and the "soil"—as by their ability to reproduce their knowledge in an aesthetically acceptable form. This chiefly explains both his unqualified praise of the minor realists Gleb Uspensky and Aleksandr Ertel'[19] and his high regard for such little-known peasant writers as Ye. Nazarov and I. S. Nikitin.[20] The symbolists incurred his wrath not only because of his congenital inability to respond to any art that did not derive its inspiration from the physical reality of life and from man's experience of that reality but, more pertinently, because he regarded their transcendental aspirations as merely a mask of ignorance. In this respect he recognized little difference between the symbolists and the radicals who were intent on reforming the country's social structure. Between his views on contemporary literature and his attitude to contemporary social developments there was a distinct similarity. Both symbolists and radicals were equally engaged in the task of disrupting the traditional modes and patterns that he valued for the simple reason that they were "natural," that is, deeply rooted in the time-honored reality of Russian life, and at the basis of this disruptive activity he perceived an ignorance of Russia and its people that precluded a proper appreciation of the past and explained, he believed, their peculiar susceptibility to alien influence. For Bunin, symbolism, socialism, and rampant capitalism were merely different manifestations of the attitude to Russia's past that he spent most of life combating. This does not mean that he may be classified as a latter-day Slavophile. Ideologies of whatever kind were consistently repugnant to him.[21] His contention, quite simply, was that symbolism and socialism were alike the cerebral inventions of intellectuals who were totally divorced from the reality of life in Russia and that the encroachment of these alien philosophies onto Russian soil was an unmistakable sign of Russia's fatal defection from the values of her glorious past. As early as 1894 he wrote of the symbolists: "They are consciously moving away from their people, from nature, from the sun. But for this nature wreaks a cruel vengeance. This should never be forgotten!" (9:506). The forms and effects of this vengeance were to become the main underlying theme of his prerevolutionary fiction.

Bunin's outbursts against intellectuals in general and symbolists in particular were frequently regarded by his contemporaries as expressions of aristocratic disdain by a scion of one of Russia's oldest families for lesser social breeds that had had the impertinence to challenge the honorable traditions bequeathed to them.[22] There may well have been some truth in the charge. Yet Bunin never invoked any higher authority for the justification of his views than his personal experience of life and the intimate knowledge of the average Russian peasant and small landowner which that experience had given him, and it was generally conceded, even by the symbolists,[23] that few contemporary writers could boast a comparable knowledge of Russian rural life. Thus, although the conclusions he reached on the basis of his knowledge were highly debatable, it would plainly be unjust to attribute them solely to narrow class prejudice. His knowledge was beyond question, and art that did not reflect a similar familiarity with the real conditions of Russian life inevitably incurred his criticism and hostility. The hierarchy of his literary sympathies, therefore, may easily be deduced.

With the conspicuous exception of Dostoyevsky, whose art was almost as alien to him as that of the symbolists,[24] every major Russian writer of the nineteenth century inspired him at various times to paeans of unstinting praise. But the two highest positions in his pantheon of literary deities were reserved for his elder contemporaries Chekhov (the story writer, not the dramatist[25]) and Tolstoy. To both of them he devoted substantial works toward the end of his career—his unfinished reminiscences of Chekhov and *The Emancipation of Tolstoy* [Osvobozhdeniye Tolstogo] (1937). His attitude to these two writers may be compared to that he adopts toward the aged peasant heroes of some of his earliest stories. He regarded them primarily as perpetuators of the traditions that had made Russia great, as living embodiments of the true spirit of Russia, as the last surviving beacons of light and sanity amid the gathering darkness of chaos and disintegration. For Bunin the publication of Tolstoy's *Hadji Murat* in 1911 was like the arrival of a *bogatyr'* armed with the power "to kill with a single blow all these modernists with their sweet, stupid words,"[26] and in his personal loyalty to its creator's legacy he perceived the most valuable contribution he could make to the cause of protecting Russia's unique culture from the forces that threatened its existence.

His declarations of loyalty, however, were by no means acknowledgments of influence. Like most other short-story writers of the period, of course, he was greatly impressed by Chekhov's art of brevity. In addition, he shared Chekhov's preference for "ordinary" heroes, his concern with the de-

cline of the landed gentry, and his disinclination to idealize
the peasantry. His tales reflect his concurrence with Chekhov's
view that the art of the short story is "as much an art of tone
as of incident."[27] But none of these similarities, which are in
any case wholly superficial, can plausibly be ascribed to influence. As artists, no less than as men, the two writers bear as
little resemblance to one another, in Chekhov's words, as a
borzoi and a beagle (9:195–96). The only really significant
features they had in common were their independence of
spirit, their abhorrence of pretentiousness, and their ven-
eration of Tolstoy. Commenting on Chekhov in his "autobiographical note" of 1915, Bunin confines himself to the
remark: "There was something in Chekhov that made an
impression on me—the cursory nature and spareness of his
writing" (9:260). But, however strong the impression may
have been, it clearly had little effect on his own writing, for
with the exception of some of the "miniatures" he wrote in
1930, his works rarely display either of the features that attracted his attention. At once more "earthy" and metaphysical
than the art of Chekhov, his stories are often distinguished by
a quality of compactness or "density" resulting from the sheer
abundance of descriptive detail which his contemporary, as
we shall see, found somewhat perplexing. In short, the brevity
of Bunin, which he himself attributed wholly to the discipline
of writing verse,[28] is of a totally different character from that
of Chekhov. It resulted from entirely different principles of
composition that in their turn were determined by his very
different approach to life.

The most obvious reflection of this difference of approach is the radically different status of the individual in the
works of the two writers. The Chekhovian hero is no vassal of
nature, no agent of impersonal forces. His individuality is no
mere biological phenomenon. He may be weak, but his weakness is no allegory of the intrinsic weakness of the human will.
It is his own weakness which his own individual will, if exer-
cised, is potentially capable of surmounting. His drama, therefore, is preeminently a personal drama rather than a scene
from some universal tragedy, and it is recorded with a sensi-

tivity to the foibles of human nature, a sympathy, and an intermittent humor that are seldom encountered in the fiction of Bunin. Yet this does not necessarily mean, of course, that Chekhov is the superior artist. It means simply that life is examined by Chekhov from a standpoint that provides for an intimate and subtle rapport between author and hero that is inevitably precluded by Bunin's external, impersonalistic approach to the life of the "body." The difference of approach explains why Bunin is immeasurably less successful than Chekhov in the creation of "living" characters. It also explains the absence from his tales of Chekhovian "moods,"[29] the greater boldness of his effects, and his generally less inhibited exposés of the extremes of human nature.[30] If, however, his approach had been different, he could not have conveyed with such unrivaled power that sense of the wonder and mystery of life and, in particular, that sense of the mysterious bond between man and the whole of creation that make his art unique.

The same difference of standpoint similarly explains the fundamental differences between the art of Bunin and that of Tolstoy, although it cannot be doubted that he had much more in common with the great novelist than he had with Chekhov. "If I am reproached," he once remarked to his nephew N. A. Pusheshnikov, "with imitating Tolstoy, I shall merely rejoice. All his alleged defects, which the critics talk about, are supreme merits. Other writers—Turgenev, for example—should not be imitated, but to imitate Tolstoy is a virtue: one loses the habit of talking nonsense."[31] Despite his rapid disenchantment with Tolstoyism in the nineties, Tolstoy the artist and Tolstoy the religious thinker continued to fascinate him throughout his life.[32] But above all he was intrigued by the tension between these two aspects of Tolstoy's personality, and in *The Emancipation of Tolstoy* he provides the following explanation for it: "The fact of the matter is that perhaps no one in world literature has been given such a keen sense of the flesh of the world for the predominant reason that no one has been given in addition such a keen sense of the doom and perishability of the flesh" (9:110). To the first

of these "senses" he traced the inspiration of the artist and to
the latter the inspiration of the religious philosopher, and his
lifelong interest in the conflict between them is explained
by the simple fact that the same two "senses" coexisted in
himself. Although, however, the thought of both writers was
dominated by the same dilemma, there is little resemblance
between the forms in which it expressed itself in their art, for
their common obsession with "the doom of the flesh" elicited
very different responses—rationalistic and moralistic in the
art of Tolstoy, aesthetic and metaphysical in the art of Bunin.

The natural inclination of both Bunin and Tolstoy as
artists was to portray man as a carefree child of nature responsive only to the promptings of his body.[33] The most
convincing of Tolstoy's fictional creations are precisely those
whose obedience to the demands of impulse and instinct is
totally uncompromised by moral or intellectual scruple, while
his "monumental" creations—Pierre, Andrey, Levin, Nekh-
lyudov—all reflect the artist's intermittent submission to the
rationalist and moralist. The interventions of intellect and
conscience deprive them of that "sympathy of the flesh"[34]
which was the instinctive gift of the artist. The conscience of
Bunin, by contrast, is never exposed to public scrutiny. To
refer to him, in the phrase of his friend and biographer K. I.
Zaytsev, as a "remarkable moralist"[35] is to convey a completely false impression of the premises of his art. There is no
conception in Bunin's fiction of man as a perfectible being.
Man is as he is by virtue of elemental forces that lie entirely
beyond his control. He may offer his gratitude to God for the
delights of existence, but he has no notion of a personal God
to whom he may ultimately be accountable, and the feeling of
guilt is consequently unknown to him. Death represents for
him merely the conclusive end of his individuality, its reintegration with the "single, universal Soul" of nature.[36] Men
differ from one another, in Bunin's depiction, only in the
degree of their self-awareness, and although the degrees he
distinguishes undoubtedly have certain moral implications,
they are invariably incidental to his basic concern with man's
dependence on nature's laws. His identification of God with

the amoral world of nature and his impersonalistic view of man as a totally subordinate part of that world and as merely an infinitesimal link in the chain of biological evolution inevitably precluded a significant concern for the moral aspect of individual conduct. His art was threatened not by the intrusions of morality, but rather by the element of abstraction that was inherent in this generalized view of man.

Unlike Tolstoy, therefore, Bunin was not distracted by his sensitivity to "the doom of the flesh" from his primary concern as an artist with the amoral life of the body. Although he was by no means blind to the tragic implications of his conception of life for the individual, in the absence of belief in a transcendent God he could do no more than simply register his horror and wonderment. He was neither impelled by his sensitivity to death to enter a sphere of inquiry that was intrinsically alien to his art nor deterred from passing in his portrayal of man as "primitive" far beyond the point at which Tolstoy is prone to halt in anxious trepidation. His conception of life ensured his undeviating commitment to those aspects of human experience that inspired the instinctive responses of the artist, and for a comparable example of aesthetic integrity in Russian literature one can refer only to Aleksander Pushkin, the constant companion of Arsen'yev's youth[37] and, in Bunin's words, "the embodiment of simplicity, nobility, freedom, health, intelligence, tact, moderation, and taste."[38] A fitting epigraph to his art would be his poem "The Compass" [Kompas] of 1916, the last quatrain of which contains the words: "No one will deflect me from my course. A certain North directs my soul, and it will not abandon me in my wanderings" (1:428).

3. The Decline of the Peasantry and Landed Gentry

For almost the first thirty years of Bunin's literary career the Russian peasant was the commanding figure in his fictional gallery. The most obvious explanation, of course, is the intimate knowledge of the peasant derived from his personal background, for a narrowing of the divide between masters and former serfs had been one of the most significant effects of the impoverishment of his family, and much of his childhood was spent in the company of peasant children.[1] There were clearly deeper reasons, however, for the dominant claim on his attention that the peasant was able to exercise for so long a period. First, Bunin never regarded the peasant as specifically a *social* type. Accounting for more than 80 percent of the population, the peasantry represented for him the Russian nation, and the individual peasant was the quintessential *national* Russian type. Hence the explicit identification of the village of Durnovka with the country as a whole in *The Village* and his remark in connection with the work to a correspondent of the newspaper *Moskovskaya vest'* [Moscow news] in September 1911: "I must point out that it is not the peasantry in themselves who interest me, but the soul of the Russian people in general."[2] The narrowness of range or vision, therefore, that is sometimes attributed to him in his early works is plainly more apparent than real. His studies of the peasantry are the vehicle of his judgments on Russian history, and it is clear that his pronouncements on rural life were intended to have a broad national relevance. It was his purpose, he claimed, to provide the first "genuine, serious study of the people" in Russian literature—a purpose, he alleged, which Dmitriy Grigorovich, Turgenev, and Nikolay Zlatovratsky had signally failed to fulfill.[3]

The second important reason for the enduring prominence of the peasant in Bunin's prerevolutionary fiction is his indissoluble connection with the author's general conception of life. To a significant degree, the view of man as a child of nature, which was ultimately to propel Bunin's art into spheres of human conduct and experience that his early public could hardly have anticipated, evolved from the impressions of peasant life that filled his childhood and youth. In the traditional, primitive way of life of the peasant he perceived the purest expression of the natural life, of the life spent in harmonious communion with man's native element. Since the commitment to such a way of life presupposed, in his contention, an instinctive awareness of man's essential nature, it follows that for Bunin, as for Tolstoy, the peasant is the supreme embodiment of intuitive wisdom.

The peasant, therefore, enjoys the status accorded him by Bunin not by virtue of his position in the social hierarchy but chiefly because of a fundamental attribute of his traditional way of life. Since this is Bunin's sole criterion for judgment, the relationship betweeen peasantry and gentry in his fiction is quite different from that in the literature of "critical realism," and in the context of his remarks of September 1911 on *The Village* he defended his views on this question at some length:

We know the gentry of Turgenev and Tolstoy. It is impossible to judge from them the Russian gentry as a whole, for both Turgenev and Tolstoy depict the upper stratum, the rare oases of culture. I believe that the life of the majority of Russia's gentry was simpler and that their souls were more typically Russian than they are in the descriptions of Tolstoy and Turgenev.... It seems to me that the soul and way of life of the Russian gentry are the same as those of the peasant. The whole difference is determined solely by the material superiority of the gentry class. In no other country is the life of the gentry so closely bound up with that of the peasants as in Russia. The souls of both, I believe, are equally Russian. (9:536–37)

Bunin's attention, therefore, is concentrated on the lower and middle strata of the rural gentry, who comprised the overwhelming majority of the class and whose way of life, like that

of his own family, allegedly differed in no significant respect
from that of the more well-to-do peasant. The class boundary
is virtually erased, and the traditional antagonism between
landowner and peasant is usually replaced by a harmonious
relationship based on common experience and a profound
psychological affinity that is attributed in the final reckoning
to their common proximity to nature. As a result, Bunin's
statements on either of the two classes individually usually
have a direct relevance to the other, and a distinct parallelism
can be detected between the successive judgments that he
pronounces on both.

His attitude, therefore, to the peasantry and landed gentry cannot be dissociated from the general philosophical belief
to which he came very early in life that man is an inalienable
part of nature and is consequently at his best when living in
conformity with its laws. The common "subtext" of his early
works are the seemingly trite sentiments that he expressed in
1900 in an article on the poet Zhemchuzhnikov: "Although
the educative importance of nature is great and beneficial in
our society, it is valued insufficiently. The influence of nature
on the emotional side of man is also beyond doubt. It purifies
and ennobles the soul. It brings peace and focuses man's attention on pure and selfless joys."[4] In this early period of
Bunin's development, the tragic and universal implications of
his conception of the human condition are much less in evidence than the tendency simply to elevate the "natural life" to
the level of a philosophic ideal which he equates with the
traditional way of life on the typical Russian estate.

How, then, do we reconcile the benign treatment of the
peasantry and landowners dictated by this philosophical angle
of vision with the "merciless" portraits for which he is best
known? Are we to conclude that he was acknowledging retro-
spectively the disruption of the continuity of his thought when
he wrote in 1934 in reference to *The Village*: "This was the
beginning of a whole series of works that harshly portrayed
the Russian soul, its peculiar complications, its light and dark,
but almost always tragic, foundations" (9:268)? Criticism has
generally tended to answer in the affirmative. It appears now

to be the unanimous view that *The Village* and the works that followed it were the product of a dramatic transformation in Bunin's attitude to the peasantry, and appearances would certainly seem to support this contention. The short novel undeniably presents Bunin, in D. S. Mirsky's phrase, "under a new aspect."[5] But a new aspect, of course, does not necessarily reflect a change of attitude. It may result simply from a different manner of affirming the same basic convictions or from an extension of the original subject, and the failure of criticism to consider these possibilities, which has led to serious misunderstanding, is primarily explained by its neglect of the indicated philosophical premise. In the light of this premise, the contrasting images of peasants and landowners in Bunin's works are perfectly intelligible in terms of a single, continuous line of thought.

The work in Bunin's early fiction in which ideal and reality are most clearly identified is perhaps the best known of the works he wrote before *The Village*—"Antonov Apples." Characteristically, the ideal is condensed in a sensation—in the lingering smell of a type of apple that, for the young narrator, a transparent mask of the author himself, is redolent of an entire way of life and symbolic of the shared contentment and well-being of landowner and peasant. But the realization of the ideal exists for the narrator as memory alone. The row of dots that begins the work eloquently conveys the immersion in reminiscence that prompts his opening words: "I remember an early fine autumn" (2:179), and the verb "to remember" (*pomnit'*) functions as a leitmotiv in the first paragraph, marking the stages by which this general recollection yields to the more specific and potent memory of the apples and their aroma. Devoid of a plot (in the conventional sense of the term), the work is essentially a collage of chronologically ordered scenes illustrating the transition from the realized ideal to its incipient destruction—from the harmony and prosperity of the past to the economic collapse of the present. The lyrically evoked scenes from the more recent past, particularly the scene of the hunt in chapter III, have the quality of a nostalgic charade. They are a game designed, in the narrator's words, to "maintain the waning spirit of the landowners" (2:186), to create an illusion of stability amid the unmistakable signs of change and decay. From the beginning, however, a shadow is cast over the resurrected scenes by the gray, autumnal landscape. By the time the final scene is reached, "the smell of Antonov apples is disappearing from the estates" (2:190) and Arseniy Semyonych, the colorful and vigorous leader of the hunt whom Bunin based on one of his own relatives,[6] has shot himself in despair.

The lyrical mode of narration in "Antonov Apples" vividly conveys Bunin's personal attitude to the transition the scenes record. Together with his "poem of desolation"[7] entitled "The Epitaph" [Epitafiya], written in the same year, the work is a survivor of a whole cycle of nostalgic "epitaphs" composed at the turn of the century[8] that express unequivocally his contention that for Russia the destruction of the rural estates was a historical tragedy and unmitigated disaster. "The Epitaph," which Bunin considered the best work he had written thus far,[9] is likewise a first-person narrative, and it is constructed in an identical manner, consisting of a succession of scenes linked by a central image—in this case, a white birch situated on the edge of a village that protects beneath its branches a cross supporting the Suzdal icon of the Mother of God. The village, like the estate in "Antonov Apples," is the stage on which the passage of time is concretely recorded in a sequence of "slides." Initially the narrator's attention is concentrated on its rhythmic life of the past, on the cyclic changes of appearance the seasons unfailingly brought in their wake. But this sense of movement duly motivates the transition to the transformed village of the present with its wizened crops and decimated population. The foliage of the birch has faded, the cross has fallen, and even the icon appears to have wilted. The peasants have dispersed to the towns and to Siberia in search of the livelihood the village can no longer provide because of the breakdown of its time-honored way of life, and from the towns an army of "new men" has arrived equipped with drills to extract its mineral wealth and to cover the earth with black heaps "like burial mounds" (2:198).[10] The narrator comments: "That which sanctified here the old life—the gray cross that has fallen to the ground—will be forgotten by all. . . . How will the new men sanctify their new life? Whose blessing will they call down on their cheerful and noisy toil?" (2:198).

A number of Soviet critics have claimed that Bunin's poetic evocations of the past in these epitaphs should primarily be related to the purely "aesthetic emphasis" on the intrinsic "beauty and joy of existence" commonly encountered in his early art.[11] Both works, however, contain abundant evidence that his treatment of the past cannot be explained solely in aesthetic terms and that his conception of a lost paradise is in no sense to be equated, as one critic has argued, with that of the early symbolists.[12] Not for nothing, it seems, did he delete the original opening of "Antonov Apples," in which he had written: "There are things that are beautiful in themselves but, above all, because they make us feel life more keenly" (2:505–6). The purpose of the excision was almost certainly to switch the emphasis from the intrinsic beauty of existence itself to the socially determined beauty of the past for which the two epitaphs in their present form provide a clear explanation. Bunin had little doubt about the force that "sanctified" the way of life that had collapsed under the impact of the emancipation of the serfs and before the disruptive advance of the industrialists. It was certainly not the cross or the icon in their conventional symbolic value, as the reader may deduce from his nostalgic references in "The Epitaph" to the pagan customs that had survived in the village. The dominant symbol is clearly the birch that overshadows them both—the symbol of all-powerful nature.[13] The cyclic rhythms of the "old life" were the rhythms of nature herself. "People were born," Bunin wrote in the early editions of the work, "they grew up, got married, joined the army, worked, and celebrated the festivals. . . . But the main thing in their lives was the steppe—its death and resurrection" (2:509). The men of the past lived in harmony with their native element; the "new men" endeavor to rape it, and in the form of the birch tree, which is endowed with almost human consciousness, nature withdraws its protection: "The birch did not answer the wind as it had done before. It weakly stirred its branches and fell again into a slumber" (2:197). The ancient communion is broken, and misery and desolation are the result.

Two main conclusions, therefore, may be drawn from the two epitaphs: that the contrast between past and present that lies at the basis of both is examined chiefly from the point of view of differing relationships between man and nature, and that the "beauty and joy of existence" are doomed to extinction with the widening of the gulf between them. In addition, both works expose, either directly or obliquely, the agents of disruption and thereby provide the key to most of the works written by Bunin before *The Village*.

Although they are inseparably related to the two epitaphs, the other early works devoted to rural life differ from them most obviously in that the main emphasis is placed on the present—either on various forms of disruption to which the present bears witness or on survivals in the present of the past. Among the earliest works that illustrate the former theme are those with which Bunin responded to the famine of 1891, "Tan'ka" and "News from Home" [Vesti s rodiny] (1893), and to the mass movements of starving peasants that followed the famine, "In Foreign Parts" [Na chuzhoy storone] (1893) and "To the Edge of the World." All these works are firmly based on Bunin's personal observations of peasant suffering in southern Russia and the Ukraine.[14] Like his two unsuccessful attempts in the nineties at a longer type of narrative, "The Teacher" [Uchitel'] (1894) and "At the Dacha," the two stories that directly reflect the famine display one of the most conspicuous marks of Bunin's immaturity—a primary concern with social contrast—and a similar determination to castigate the aloofness or ineffectuality of the provincial intelligentsia. Equally uncharacteristic of the mature writer is the hint of sentimentality that is particularly prominent in "Tan'ka" and "In Foreign Parts."[15] Even in these works, however, the various human situations depicted are repeatedly projected against the backdrop of nature. The scenes are repeatedly expanded to encompass a background that occasionally harmonizes with the human misery, as in the case of the blizzards that lash Tan'ka and the doomed peasant Mishka Shmyryonok in "News from Home," but more usually introduces a significant element of contrast. Indeed, in "To the Edge of the World," contrasting landscapes of this kind provide the principal structural link between the four scenes that divide the work. But this is not simply a structural procedure. The interlocking landscapes are the vehicle of the philosophical theme, and their prominence in the work is indicative of the predominantly philosophical angle of vision from which the social problem is regarded. The silent, impassive beauty of nature is a reproach to the folly of man, who has ordered his life in such a way that the peasant community of Velikiy Perevoz must uproot itself from its ancestral home and seek a new life in the alien Ussuri region of Siberia. Again the ancient bond is severed, and the inevitable outcome is human suffering.

Although, therefore, the relationship between man and nature is not an obtrusive thematic element in these works, the contextual force of the landscapes repeatedly suggests a direct connection between the human drama and the breakdown of this relationship. Only "To the Edge of the World" contains, in its opening section, an explicit reference to a contrasting past, but the implication throughout is that rejection of the past, its customs, and way of life is the ultimate cause of present misfortune.[16] A significantly different type of work results, however, when Bunin transfers his attention from the evolution of past into present and from the social consequences of this evolution and synchronizes the two layers of time by casting his narrators in the role of lonely wanderers or observers dedicated to the search for lingering vestiges of the old life among the ruins. The discovery of this formula marked an important stage in the development of his early art, for variations of it were ultimately to form the basis of some of the most outstanding of his prerevolutionary stories. Initially it assumes a very simple form. Each work concerned is dominated by a single isolated individual in whom the past lives on in the present. Again it is noteworthy that although they comprise a small minority in these tales, landowners—in such stories as "On the Farm" [Na khutore] (1892) and "In the Field" [V pole] (1895)—are portrayed in much the same manner as peasants. There is no suggestion here of social contrast.

The protagonists of both these stories are depicted amid the dereliction of their estates finding their only solace in memories and in contemplation of nature, and nature is again invested with the dual role of mentor and destroyer. For Kapiton Ivanych, the hero of "On the Farm," nature is the model on which his entire life has been based, and the attractive features of his personality are implicitly ascribed to the beneficial influence of this tutelage. In the first published version of the story, entitled "The Dreamer" [Fantazyor], he reflected: "Everything in my life has assumed a definite pattern. Everything is definite and tranquil like this nature of the countryside, like the village itself, its people and the relations between them, like its whole way of life" (2:491). And now, as his home slowly collapses about him, it is to the same mentor that he looks for spiritual support, resigned to the imminence of death and reaffirming in its shadow his lifelong philosophy: "I have lived peacefully and I shall die peacefully like the leaf that will eventually dry up and fall from this bush" (2:34). In "In the Field," however, nature reassumes the very different guise familiar from "Tan'ka" and "News from Home"—the symbolic guise of a blizzard assisting in the process of change by accelerating the disintegration of the past. The hero, Yakov Petrovich Baskakov, and his old friend Kovalyov huddle round the stove in the only room in the house that remains habitable, using the furniture for fuel and listening as they reminisce to the destruction of the world that feeds their memories and imaginations. Slowly the destroyer approaches, and by the end the tiles are being ripped from the roof. The old foundations of prosperity and contentment have crumbled, and in the world of nature the weak must perish.

It is significant that although the heroes of both works

are portrayed as hopelessly impractical individuals, no attempt is made to relate their misfortunes, in the Chekhovian manner, to this crucial weakness of character. The impracticality of the gentry, in fact, was to be adduced as an important factor in their decline only in 1911, when Bunin wrote *Sukhodol*, and even then his interpretation of its significance was quite different from Chekhov's. Kapiton Ivanych and Baskakov are respectively a dreamer and a spendthrift,[17] yet far from criticizing these vices, the narrator refers to them almost with warmth and admiration, for they are as redolent to him of the past as the Antonov apple. The strength of the past lay solely in the relationship with nature to which the social order was allegedly conducive, and the disruption of this order is the sole cause to which Bunin traces the misfortunes of his two impractical landowners. The emphasis throughout is on their solitude, their dedication to the past, and the imminence of their end, and in all these respects their situation is identical to that of the peasant heroes of such stories as "Kastryuk" (1892), "Meliton" (1900), and "The Pines" [Sosny] (1901). Each work may be regarded as a further episode in the serialized epitaph that comprises most of Bunin's early fiction.

Despite the continuing debate on the subject, it is now customary to accept the contention of the Soviet critic L. V. Krutikova that the attitude of the peasantry reflected in the short lyrical compositions with which Bunin began his career was largely determined by Tolstoyan and Populist influences.[18] It is manifestly plausible to trace to Karatayev (in *War and Peace*) the literary ancestry of Kastryuk, Meliton, and Mitrofan, the central figure of "The Pines," with their remarkable submissiveness, unpretentious wisdom, and endless capacity for self-effacement. The obliteration of self-interest, creative vitality, inflexible self-discipline, an inner harmony reflected in word and deed are the virtues of the natural life proclaimed by Bunin through the almost hagiographic portraits of these early peasant heroes. They are the living embodiment of Bunin's conception of the psychological consequences of harmony between man and nature. As he sits in solitude contemplating the freshness of spring and youth, the aged Kastryuk, compelled by his years to retire from a life in the fields spent tending the crops and herds, cannot resist the urge even to mimic nature physically as his imagination re-creates a typical scene: "He tried to imagine the rustling of the forest and the wavelike motion, the rustling and color changes of the rye on the hillocks in the wind, and he himself swayed slightly" (2:25). His body is weakening, but in spirit he remains at one with his environment. And even as he lies in his grave, the tracker Mitrofan seems to maintain the same communion with nature that has characterized his entire life. "The mastlike pines," we read, "raised their green crowns on high on their bare, clayey-reddish trunks and on three sides encircled the small mound like a compact entourage" (2:219). In life, his philosophy was succinctly summarized in his com-mandments: "Live like a farm laborer: do what is ordered and that's enough!" (2:214), and in practice this meant "liv-ing" and dying like the pines, adapting oneself to nature's cycle, and passively accepting the joys and sorrows of this primitive existence. The narrator makes little attempt to dis-guise his approval of this outlook, even though it occasionally eludes his understanding. Commenting on Mitrofan's death, he clearly endorses this philosophy of "natural" passivity which he shares with Kastryuk and Meliton: "He has died, he has perished, he could maintain the struggle no longer—so it had to be!" (2:214). His death, like his life, is viewed solely as an expression of the laws of nature, and in an early edition the passage continued: "The wind rages and covers us with snow, and this also has to be."[19]

But, on the symbolic level, the death of Mitrofan is the death of the past and its values, and once more the blizzard appears to sweep it irrevocably into oblivion, transforming the once peaceful settlement into the "barbaric village" (*dikar-skaya derevushka*) that was to become Bunin's principal symbol of the "new Russia," the antithesis of the sunlit world of "Antonov Apples." The recurrent symbol of the blizzard an-nounces the dawning of Russia's new ice age, and Bunin per-ceives no escape from the impasse. Like his lonely heroes, he finds his only relief from this spectacle of restored barbarism in reflection on "the eternal, majestic life" (2:220) of the universe that dimly reveals itself in the hum of the pines and the shimmering of the stars—on the mystery, as he puts it in "The Pines," "of the uselessness and at the same time the importance of everything on earth" (2:219). The precise implications of these reflections were not to be clarified for some years—not until he began work on his cycle of travel sketches entitled *The Shadow of the Bird* [Ten' ptitsy] (1907–11). For the moment, his meditations on the insignificance of earthly life may be regarded primarily as evidence of his intense feeling of alienation from the new Russia that was rising on the ruins of the old, the feeling that prompted him to ask in "The New Road" [Novaya doroga] (1901): "To what country do I belong as I wander in solitude? . . . What is there any longer in common between me and this god-forsaken land of dense forests?" (2:228). His spiritual exile may be dated from the posing of these questions.

Although critics have legitimately stressed the resemblance of Bunin's early peasant heroes to the peasants of Tolstoy and to the Populist ideal, they have failed to draw the necessary conclusion from their most revealing common feature—their old age. Either death is at hand or, as in the case of Mitrofan, it has already arrived. Bunin's later personifications of peasant humility—in "The Ancient Man" [Drevniy chelovek] (1911), "A Gay Farmhouse" [Vesyolyy dvor] (1911), "Thin Grass" [Khudaya trava] (1913), and "A Spring Evening"—are likewise placed on the verge of the grave as though to suggest by implication the incompatibility of humility and youth. Bunin creates no young Karatayevs. The statement of Muromtseva that his repeated preoccupation with old age in his early fiction was prompted by his reflections on the aging of his parents[20] is ludicrously inadequate. The crucial point is the marked social symbolism with which he invests the old age of his peasants. Its effect is simultaneously to identify the conditions conducive to the natural life with the social system of the preemancipation era and to signal the imminent demise of its last surviving practitioners. His early peasant heroes are proof incarnate that the backwardness of rural life in his later works on the peasantry is in no sense to be ascribed, as numerous critics have inferred, to the "habits and psychology nurtured by serfdom."[21] Kastryuk, Meliton, and Mitrofan are presented as living testimony to the virtues of a maligned social order. While the virtues of Turgenev's Khor' and Kalinych exist despite the social system under which they live, those of Bunin's aged peasants are implicitly ascribed to the beneficial influence of the same system, and now at every turn they are confronted with conclusive evidence of the present's indifference to these virtues. They pass their declining years in the shadow of the future's remorseless advance, bemused by the monstrous engines that shatter the rural calm and by the geometrical lines of telegraph poles that ruthlessly cleave the forest. "Everything indicated to him," we read of Kastryuk, "that he had outlived his time" (2:24), and nature resists in vain the onset of modernity. As the train forges on in "The New Road," the narrator comments: "The age-old pines enclose the railroad and seem to be unwilling to admit the train further. But the train fights. Beating time evenly with its heavy, jerky breath, it crawls up the slope like a gigantic dragon, and in the distance its head belches forth a red flame that flickers brightly under the wheels of the engine on the rails, and as it flickers it angrily illuminates the mournful avenue of still, silent pines. The avenue is closed in darkness, but the train advances stubbornly" [2:229]. In "The Gold Mine," the clatter of excavations again rings out as the present's harsh counterpoint to the life of harmony attuned to nature's rhythms. The estates are deserted and overgrown, the lands lie fallow awaiting their new masters, and the *kulak* makes his appearance on the rural scene. A hint of menace is now detectable in the attitude of the peasantry, and in "The Gold Mine" and "Dreams" the imminence of violence is clearly predicted.

Bunin's verdict on these developments is quite unequivocal. Since it emerges clearly from the works that follow *The Village*—from the portrait, for example, of the dying peasant Averkiy in "Thin Grass"—that the virtues that constitute, in his conception, the "light foundations" of the Russian soul are precisely those that he lauds in his portraits of Kastryuk, Meliton, and Mitrofan, it follows that the attribution of these virtues to the influence of a social order perpetuated only in the way of life of a disappearing generation is an oblique acknowledgment that the present and foreseeable future belong to the forces of darkness. Although Krutikova does not argue the point in these terms, it is precisely this indirectly expressed acknowledgment that justifies her reference to Bunin's earliest peasant stories as "the first steps toward *The Village*."[22]

Several points of fundamental importance for an understanding of Bunin's attitude toward the peasantry are consequently clarified. The allegations that he eventually came to reject the Tolstoyan peasant[23] and was intent on reversing the Populist tendency to idealize the peasantry[24] are now clearly exposed as misleading. It was simply his contention that Karatayev had regrettably become an anachronism. As the peasant "philosopher" Balashkin puts it to Kuz'ma Krasov in *The Village*: "Your Karatayev has been gobbled up by lice" (3:68). It is also evident once more that the source of the "lice" is traced by Bunin, at least at this point in time, specifically to the edict of 1861 that had inaugurated an era in which the ancient communion between the peasant and the soil was upheld only by the old generation whose attitude to life had developed under the old social system. By disrupting this communion, emancipation had irretrievably undermined the spiritual and psychological influence of the natural life implicitly associated with the "light foundations" of the Russian soul. Here, as always in Bunin's fiction, social developments are evaluated solely from the point of view of their effect on man's capacity for living the life that accords with his nature.

Having established these points, we may now examine more closely the argument that has recently been reiterated in the first English-language monograph on Bunin concerning his reaction to the events of 1905: "In his early stories Bunin tended to present his peasants in somewhat idyllic terms. The peasants' rebellions during the 1905 Revolution

apparently changed Bunin's view of them, and this drastic
change of mind manifested itself in *The Village*."[25] The argument is by no means confined to Western criticism. It is
encountered in the writings of even so sensitive a student of
Bunin as the Soviet scholar N. M. Kucherovsky, who asserts
that "the revolution of 1905 destroyed the ideal of the patriarchal 'order of life' in which Bunin still believed when on
the very eve of the revolution he wrote 'The Gold Mine.'"[26]
The impact on Bunin, therefore, of the 1905 revolution is
adduced as the crucial factor that allegedly impelled him to
compose the sequence of works—*The Village*, "A Nocturnal Conversation" [Nochnoy razgovor] (1911), "A Gay Farmhouse," and "A Spring Evening"—in which the peasant is
barely recognizable as a human being. The impact undeniably
was considerable, and its mark is no doubt discernible in the
thickening of colors and unrelieved gloom that distinguish
the cycle. But the claim that it destroyed Bunin's ideal is
plainly unacceptable, for the ideal was inseparable from the
social order that had created the conditions for its realization,
and his assignment long before 1905 of "spiritual light" almost exclusively to a generation nearing extinction testified to
his belief that resurrection of the past was already inconceivable. It was not the peasant's submission to the forces of
darkness that destroyed the ideal, but exactly the reverse: the
destruction of the ideal—the removal of the discipline of
nature—had unleashed the latent chaos of the peasant soul,
and this contention, as we have seen, is implicit in many of the
works that precede *The Village*. Bunin's concentration in these
works on the "fathers" implied his judgment on the "sons"
and to this extent prefigured his contrasting treatment of
the latter. No external event was required to motivate this
change of emphasis. The transition was potential from the
beginning. Indeed, it was directly anticipated in some of
his earliest stories and sketches, in particular, in the short
narrative "Fedosevna" (1891), first published under the title
"Dementevna." It may be assumed that only his later exclusion of these stories from his collected works prompted him

to refer to *The Village* in 1934 as the *beginning* of the series of works "that harshly portrayed the Russian soul."

"Fedosevna" introduces immediately the theme that was to recur in Bunin's later works on the peasantry of the postreform era—the Dostoyevskian theme of the splintered family, symbolic of moral decline and social disintegration. The aged heroine, whose patronymic provides the title, is the spiritual sister of Kastryuk, a humble and helpless relic of the past, reduced to the ultimate extreme of hunger and poverty and forced by her need to embark in search of aid on the long journey to the house of her married daughter. Her reward is a night's accommodation, after which she is unceremoniously expelled, and three days later her corpse is found by the wayside. Although the famine of 1891 was obviously in Bunin's thoughts as he composed the work, the import of the theme of hunger is undoubtedly more symbolic than literal. It is adapted to the projection of the author's conviction that by severing the peasant's contact with the soil, emancipation had destroyed the moral foundations of rural life. The rejection of Fedosevna by her daughter and son-in-law is a further symbolic representation of the present's defection from the values of the past, of the collapse of the "light foundations" of the Russian soul, and the same symbolic level of meaning is equally to be observed in the laments on their children and relatives of Kastryuk and Baskakov. Again the plight of the old gentry is identical to that of the old peasants. "Over there," cries Baskakov, "my nephew has a thousand desyatinas,[27] but does it ever occur to them to help an old man?" (2:99), and as Kastryuk pours a little milk into his mashed potato, he thinks with dread of his daughter-in-law's wrath (2:25). Again, one might be tempted to read these episodes against the background of the famine, but conclusive proof of the inadequacy of this narrow interpretation is provided by the expanded treatment to which Bunin subjected the same theme in 1911 in "A Gay Farmhouse," one of the most powerful works he ever wrote.

In "A Gay Farmhouse" the dependence of Bunin's treatment of the peasantry on his conception of the consequences of emancipation is perhaps most clearly revealed. Here the inhumanity of the former manor serf Miron Minayev is almost explicitly related, as effect to cause, to his acquisition of freedom. The notification of his change of status is followed immediately by references to the outbursts of uncontrollable violence to which he suddenly becomes prone, inflicting on his submissive wife Anis'ya the brutal beatings that ultimately result in her miscarriage. Like the failure of Tikhon Krasov to beget an heir in *The Village*, Miron's destruction of his unborn child is symbolic of the doom that, in Bunin's contention, threatens the emancipated peasantry, of the drive to self-destruction with which he endows his liberated serfs. Alienation from the soil is equated with alienation from the family and consequently from life itself. But even the violence of Miron cannot extinguish the love of Anis'ya in whom, as in Fedosevna, the past survives. Her predicament is briefly summarized: "Anis'ya had no one to love in her youth, but she was incapable of withholding her love. Unconsciously she was ready to give her soul to someone and she married Miron . . . , and for a long time she loved him patiently, for the miscarriage that resulted from the beatings soon after the marriage deprived her for a long time of the opportunity to transfer her love to her children" (3: 280). But with the birth of her son Yegor and the death of Miron the opportunity eventually arrives.

The birth of Yegor, however, serves merely to hasten the final disintegration of the "gay farmhouse" and to precipitate the destruction of Anis'ya and of all that she represents. In Yegor the violence of his father is refined into gross indifference—indifference "to family, property, and native land" (3:280). He aspires to a state of uninhibited "Cossack freedom," to emancipation from every human relationship. To the thought of marriage he reacts with horror, and this suppression of the reproductive instinct is clearly related on the symbolic level of the tale to his father's infanticide. It denotes the same subconscious desire for self-destruction that is ultimately realized in his violent suicide. The work concludes

with a graphic description of his mutilated corpse left behind
by the train under which he has thrown himself: "That which
a moment before had been Yegor now quivered in the sand,
and as it quivered it poured blood upon the sand and jerked
upward two fat stumps horrifying in their shortness. Two
other legs wearing bast shoes and wrapped in blood-stained
foot-cloths lay on the sleepers" (3:310). The legless body
of Yegor, which in the first redaction of the story was described in much greater detail, is Bunin's most grotesque symbol of the Russian peasant dehumanized by emancipation.
The causal connection is established unequivocally by the
positioning of events. The suicide at the end of chapter III
links up symbolically with the matricide—Yegor's fatal neglect
of Anis'ya—at the end of chapter I, which signifies his final
renunciation of the values that Bunin ascribes to the irrecov-
erable past. In other words, the suicide merely completes the
act of self-destruction implicit in the matricide, which is itself a symbol of the peasant's defection from nature. Through
the mother-son relationship, the peasant's emancipation from
serfdom is represented as an emancipation from the sources
of life.

Yegor's abandonment of his mother for work as a forest
guard in the neighboring village of Lanskoye is his culminating response to the same matricidal urge that prompts
him to buy the only present she ever receives from him, "a
funeral shawl bought in the monastery shop at Zadonsk—a
large, white, calico shawl strewn with black skulls, black cross-
bones, and black inscriptions" (3:283). For Anis'ya his rejection is consistent with the hatred and violence that have
surrounded her for most of her life and condemned her to
endless solitude. In the present her sole source of comfort is
her memory, her recollections of youth, of the time when
hope was still alive, and as she sets forth on her long death
march to Lanskoye in the naive and ironic faith that with
Yegor she will find salvation, her gradual submission to death
is paralleled by the lapse of her mind into the world of the
past. Her sustained sensory responsiveness to her environment vies with her progressive subconscious withdrawal from

it.[28] In the resurrected scenes from her youth she seeks refuge from the hostile present that ultimately confronts her, at
the end of her journey, in the symbolic form of the empty,
ramshackle hut of her son. The chill of the scene is accentu-
ated by the narrator's detachment: "The hut was unusually
small and dilapidated. Instead of a roof there were tall, pale,
silvery weeds growing across the ceiling area. . . . Dreamily
she looked at the rotten walls and the half-ruined stove. A
weak light entered through a small window above the table.
Further along there was another window without a frame,
stopped up with a fur coat and shreds of dirty sheepskin,
and there the dusk gathered. Small frogs were jumping about
in the dusk on the ground" (3:290). Such is the abode in
which Anis'ya achieves her final release, sinking slowly into
oblivion with a grace and humility that contrast sharply with
the violence and horror of the death of Yegor.

Essentially, therefore, "A Gay Farmhouse" develops further the contrast that lies at the basis of "Fedosevna" and of
which only one pole is examined in "Kastryuk," "Meliton,"
and "The Pines." The story summarizes Bunin's conception
of the moral and psychological legacy of emancipation and
synthesizes in a single structure the most significant motifs
that distinguish his treatment of the collision between "the
light and dark foundations of the Russian soul"—the motifs
that appear individually in other thematically related works
of the period from 1909 to 1914. Thus the treatment the
aged Taganok receives from his daughter-in-law in "The Ancient Man" presents yet another variation on the motif of the
starvation of the old. In "Thin Grass" the contrasting attitudes of the two generations to family relationships are briefly
highlighted with the introduction of the dying Averkiy's son-
in-law. In "A Prince among Princes" [Knyaz' vo knyaz'yakh]
(1912) the hut of Yegor, symbolic of the psychological chaos
and impotence that have resulted from the peasant's alienation from nature, is paralleled by the half-built house of
the *kulak* Luk'yan Stepanov. And in "A Spring Evening," in
which, as stated earlier, Bunin develops anew the plot of one
of his earliest short narratives,[29] the divorce between past and

present is externalized in the senseless murder of a symbolically blind beggar by a drunken peasant whom he meets in a
wayside inn. Such are the recurrent motifs that characterize
Bunin's treatment of the alienated peasant. But for his most
elaborate and provocative portrayal of the new Russia we
must turn to *The Village*, the work that made his first major
impact as a prose writer.

In the three main sections of *The Village*, which are devoted respectively to Tikhon Krasov, his brother Kuz'ma, and
the peasant community of the village of Durnovka ("Evilton"),
Bunin undertakes his most complex evaluation of the present
in relation to the past. Here for the first time he extends his
canvas to embrace the major events in Russian history of the
first decade of the twentieth century. Significant, however, is
the total failure of these events (in particular, the repercussions of the Russo-Japanese War and the revolution of 1905)
to inject any sustained sense of drama or action into the narrative or any sustained feeling of class solidarity into the
peasants of Durnovka. They briefly respond with relish to
the spirit of destruction in the air, brandish their pitchforks,
and commit an occasional act of violence or arson of the
kind Bunin witnessed in person in the summer of 1906 at
Ognyovka,[30] but the fever soon passes and its effects are
minimal. The impression conveyed by their rebellion is that
of a totally chaotic and apolitical convulsion—an impression
that, after 1917, Bunin sought to enhance by appropriate
excisions.[31] The deadening, aimless round of disorganized
daily activity is quickly resumed in the village, and this speedy
restoration of the lifeless status quo most conclusively invali-
dates the argument that the events of 1905 decisively influenced Bunin's portrayal of the peasantry in the cycle of
works to which *The Village* belongs. Tikhon aptly remarks
in the aftermath of the disturbance: "Everyone says revolution, revolution, yet all around there is the same humdrum
life as before" (3:25)—the gray, squalid, living death epitomized in the work in the existence of the peasant nicknamed
Seryy ("the Gray One"). In Bunin's depiction, the reaction of
the *durnovtsy* to the events of 1905 is not simply "a proof,"

in Kucherovsky's words, "of the destruction of the peasant world";[32] it is a symptom of the general malaise that
he traces to emancipation, a vivid manifestation of the alienated peasantry's complete incapacity for creative or construc-
tive endeavor. Reflecting simultaneously the partiality of the
durnovtsy for aimless violence and for the equally unproductive indolence that is again most conspicuously displayed by
Seryy,[33] it is neither more nor less important than any of the
other numerous symptoms that form the essential content of
the work. And it is precisely because the work is primarily a
catalog of symptoms coordinated solely by the author's personal verdict on history that it is so strikingly lacking in any
continuous narrative thread. Individually, the symptoms have
a distinct autonomy in the general structure of the work, but
they share a common function—to reinforce the cogency of
the author's diagnosis and the validity of his belief in the
imminence of a final catastrophe. Only by reference to the
historical judgments of the author himself can we explain
such episodes as the quarrel between the Krasovs and the
death of the peasant Rod'ka that are otherwise shrouded in
mystery.

Like "A Gay Farmhouse," *The Village* begins with a precise identification of the source of contagion: "The grandfather of the Krasovs succeeded in obtaining his freedom. He
went with his family to the city and soon achieved fame:
he became a celebrated thief" (3:12). In effect, this pair of
sentences comprises the text on which the rest of the work
is a commentary. In this highly condensed manner, Bunin
emphasizes yet again the causal connection between freedom, abandonment of the soil, and moral degeneration. The
grandchildren, the successful innkeeper and *kulak* Tikhon,
whom Bunin seems to have based in part on his brother
Yevgeniy, and the impractical idealist Kuz'ma, whose biography bears a certain superficial resemblance to that of the
author himself,[34] are at once the heirs to this legacy, living
out in their own wretched lives its consequences, and the
intermediaries or "reflectors" through whom the reader witnesses the general situation in Durnovka.[35] It is through the

convergence of the views on the peasantry of these two tem-
peramentally alien brothers, whose experience of life during
the years of a protracted feud is radically different, that Bunin endeavors to invest his chronicle with a semblance of
objectivity. Every facet of life in the village, like the tales
recounted by the peasants in "A Nocturnal Conversation,"
mirrors the dehumanization of the peasantry and loudly proclaims the approach of a culminating national catastrophe.
Here there is no hint of Grigorovich's sentimental humani-
tarianism or of the pathos that briefly illumines Chekhov's
pictures of rural darkness. In Durnovka, man is distinguished
from beast only by his greater capacity for savagery, hatred,
and squalor. Yet although he recognizes no moral constraints,
he is psychologically incapable of promoting even his own
self-interest. Abdicating all responsibility for his existence,
he prefers to vegetate in his gray, icy wilderness—a wilderness severed from the past, devoid of a future, and overshadowed by the twin specters of hunger and death. It is a
world peopled, in the words of Tikhon, with "such beggars,
fools, blindmen, and cripples that it is terrifying and sickening
to behold" (3:20). "At full speed," declares Balashkin, "we are
plunging back into Asia!" (3:68), and once more it is in the
breakdown of family relations that the moral implications of
this reversal of evolution are most dramatically illustrated.

On being informed that a few years after the death of
their father the brothers Krasov quarreled and "almost killed
one another with knives" (3:13), we are not unduly surprised
to learn of Tikhon's complete emotional estrangement from
his wife and of Kuz'ma's failure to marry. But their attitudes to women seem veritably civilized by comparison with
those of the peasants who work on their estate—the syphilitic
Men'shov, Akim, who offers the nocturnal attentions of his
wife for fifteen copecks,[36] and the apelike Rod'ka, whose
wife, Molodaya ("the Young One"), is the constant victim of
his sadistic beatings after her involuntary submission to the
heirless Tikhon.[37] And alongside the political pamphlet in
the pocket of the younger Seryy's overcoat nestle his other
cherished texts: "The Depraved Wife" and "An Innocent Girl

Enchained by Violence." In the person of Deniska Seryy, who proudly announces his espousal of the proletarian cause, the forces disruptive of national cohesion are thus identified with the forces disruptive of family relations. Graduation from the peasantry to the proletariat, in Bunin's submission, has precisely the opposite effect to that anticipated by Marx— it merely accentuates the alienated peasant's lack of social awareness and his indifference to the lot of his fellow man. It is not difficult, therefore, to interpret the symbolic import of Deniska's marriage to Molodaya at the end of the work—a marriage arranged by Tikhon, after the death of Rod'ka, ironically as an act of self-redemption.

As her name indicates, Molodaya is the main symbol in *The Village* of Russia's youth, of the past, of the Russia that Bunin now depicts in its death throes. Despite the marked differences of temperament and social environment, her symbolic role in the work has obvious affinities with that of Nastasiya Filippovna in Dostoyevsky's *The Idiot*. She is equally a personification of beauty profaned by a degenerate society, just as the homeless "old-fashioned peasant" Ivanushka, another victim of an intransigent daughter-in-law, embodies the buoyant but now scorned philosophy of Kastryuk and Mitrofan. In Durnovka it is her fate to endure the extremes of humiliation and brutality that foreshadow the tragedies of Anis'ya in "A Gay Farmhouse" and the beggar in "A Spring Evening." Her marriage to Deniska is thus the logical culmination of her biography and a vivid testimony to Bunin's unqualified historical pessimism. Like the blizzard that follows the ceremony and the nocturnal downpour, suggestive of the Flood, that overtakes Kuz'ma on his journey to Kazakovo, the wedding is a symbolic representation of impending national doom. The bonds of matrimony ironically symbolize the disintegration of society, and looming before the bride, symbolic of her future, is the tomblike hut of Seryy, the incarnation of Durnovka's malaise. Like the dilapidated hut of Yegor and the cellarlike shack of Fedosevna's son-in-law,[38] the roofless abode of Seryy and the coffin that is meaningfully placed before the eyes of the dying Ivanushka are eloquent symbols of the new Russia in which the past is doomed to extinction.

This summary of the ideas that lie at the basis of *The Village* shows that the work is directly related to the whole sequence of works on rural themes that Bunin wrote in the first twenty-five years of his literary career and that at no point is the continuity of his thought on the peasantry interrupted. The common premise of all these works, as we have seen, is a highly subjective interpretation of the moral and psychological repercussions of historical development founded on a utopian vision of the old social order. The widely held view that in *The Village* Bunin was subject to the influence of Gorky[39] hardly needs to be repudiated and is surely explicable only as the result of an excessively literal interpretation of his frequently unconvincing professions of respect for his contemporary in the first decade of the century.[40] Equally implausible are the attempts of critics to relate the pessimism of the work to the repressive climate and intellectual disarray that followed the collapse of the 1905 revolution.[41] Bunin's personal and family background, his innate conservatism, and, above all, his personal conception of life and human nature are the only factors worthy of serious consideration, and the result is a unique fictional record of the breakdown of the old order in which the humanitarian arguments for emancipation are implicitly challenged from the standpoint of an inflexible conception of the interdependence of the Russian national character and the social and economic organization of the state. It is a record in which the diverse external manifestations of social disintegration are related not so much to the political and economic effects of emancipation as to the psychological impact that Bunin ascribes to it. Between the cause and effect normally recognized by the economic historian and the political scientist, Bunin inserts an additional factor—the psychological breakdown of the peasantry to which he attaches a preponderant importance and which he presents as a portent of national disaster. And, despite the proliferation of dialogues on the pages of *The Village*, the issue is never really exposed to debate. There is no one to counter the claims of Balashkin that Russia's historical nemesis is at hand. The method is consistently one of direct or indirect categorical assertion. "Is Russia to live or is she to die?" is the question, according to Gorky, that the work poses,[42] but in fact the possibility of life is never seriously entertained. Hence Tikhon's increasing concern for the salvation of his soul, to which his brother responds with the words: "Our goose is cooked and no candles can save us. Do you hear? We are *durnovtsy*" (3:123).

Without wishing to impugn Bunin's honesty or sincerity in *The Village*, one might be tempted, like many contemporary critics, to challenge the veracity of his monochromatic portrait of the quintessential Russian village and to charge him with tendentiousness and excessive subjectivity. One might well subscribe to the view that *The Village* is most informative about Bunin himself—"about the author's thoughts and feelings," as the contemporary critic Ye. A. Koltonovskaya put it, "rather than about the essential nature of the phenomena depicted."[43] Our main concern, however, is not to adjudicate between conflicting assessments of what was typical or untypical in the rural life of prerevolutionary Russia, but to establish as clearly as possible the precise nature of Bunin's argument and to examine the manner in which this argument is expressed. This latter subject will be discussed further in chapter 5. For the moment, it may suffice to remark that in the two years before *The Village* made its appearance, a succession of works by minor writers had depicted rural life in equally unflattering terms,[44] and even critics who had reservations about *The Village* often felt obliged to concede the legitimacy of Bunin's indictment. Thus, despite her criticisms, Koltonovskaya wrote in 1912:

Perhaps I sympathize so strongly with Bunin's characters because I myself am now living in the country. . . . My village is remote, derelict, and devoid of roads and bridges. . . . Almost the entire population is illiterate. As in Bunin's village, the people here cannot perform the only task that is required of them—they cannot plow even though they have been plowing for thousands of years. Nothing is done without vodka. On holidays they sleep when they are not drinking and arrange cruel amusements. For example, they chase other people's cats and cut off their paws. Even the most uncivilized townsman could not imagine the confusion and unrelieved darkness which fill the minds of the local inhabitants.[45]

Whereas for Koltonovskaya, however, the guilt lay chiefly with the authorities, for Balashkin and Kuz'ma Krasov in their role as the mouthpiece of their creator, it lay with the people themselves, the *narod*, and with the endless succession of artists and radicals who had glorified the *narod* and made it the repository of their hopes for Russia's future.[46] "The Russian intelligentsia," Bunin observed in July 1912, "have remarkably little knowledge of their people,"[47] and five years later, in October 1917, he was to repeat the charge.[48] The effect of their misconceived idealism, he alleges, was the condemnation of Russia to darkness and death, and in the October Revolution he saw the ultimate justification of his viewpoint. "When I depicted Russia," he once remarked in the thirties, "I already experienced a vague premonition of the fate that awaited her. Is it really my fault if reality has justified my fears beyond all measure?"[49]

Representing in *The Village* his conception of the consequences of Russia's rejection of the past, Bunin appears to have meant by the past, as this survey has shown, the era that ended in 1861. But one of the most important aspects of the work is that it prompts one to question whether, in fact, the *ukaz* and the liberalism and radicalism of the intelligentsia were really the sole causes to which he ascribed the processes of disintegration, for occasionally we seem to detect new questions behind the critical remarks of his "reflectors." Why is it, he seems to be asking, that the disastrous transition in Russia had taken place so rapidly and given within such a brief span of time the results the work depicts? Why is it that the patriarchal society of the past had collapsed so easily and displayed such pitiful resistance in the face of social and economic developments? For the answers to these questions he turned to the same source as that to which he had traced the consequences of these developments—to the psychology of the individual peasant and landowner. It had become increasingly obvious to him that social and economic pressures alone could not conceivably explain so abrupt and comprehensive a transformation and that even before the edict the seeds of destruction must already have been sown. The effect of this realization was to impel him to extend the range of his inquiry and redirect his attention once more to the Russia of serfdom. The plan that he seems to have conceived for a sequel to *The Village*[50] was promptly abandoned, and the world of "Antonov Apples" was subjected to a new examination in a work that many commentators have declared his masterpiece and that Gorky referred to as "one of the most frightening of Russian books"[51]—his "poetic chronicle"[52] *Sukhodol* (often translated as *Dry Valley*), which he completed on Capri in December 1911 during the first of three consecutive winters that he spent there on the advice of his doctor.[53]

Indicative of his purpose in this work is his reversion to the first-person narrative he had abandoned in *The Village*. The mask he assumes is that of the last male descendant of the house of Khrushchov and heir to the family's now charred and derelict ancestral estate of Sukhodol, and in his portrayal of the estate itself and its last inhabitants he manifestly draws on the recent history of his own family.[54] From the vantage point of the present, he surveys the last years of life at Sukhodol in an attempt to uncover the reasons for its subsequent rapid decline in the wake of the Crimean War and the emancipation of the serfs. The first redaction contained in chapter II an explicit statement of the motives that prompt his inquiry:

Our youth coincided with the beginning of the great poverty of the landowners, and we were amazed at the suddenness with which it came. Can it really be, we thought, that the whole reason was the severing of the ties of serfdom that bound master and serf together? The rapidity with which the old nests of the gentry vanished from the face of the earth seemed incomprehensible. But now I wonder whether their antiquity, stability, and lordliness were not exaggerated. . . . In a few years—not centuries but years—the semblance of well-being on which our past so prided itself was completely destroyed. What was the reason for it? Is it not that instead of firm foundations there was only stagnation there? Is it not that the ruin of the degenerating *sukhodolets* corresponded to a need of his soul, to his craving for ruin, self-annihilation, destruction and fear of life? [3:426]

To these questions of the narrator the history of the Khrushchovs supplies an affirmative reply.

This does not mean, however, that the elegiac tone of "Antonov Apples" is no longer distinguishable. The narrator is far from immune to the magnetic lure of Sukhodol's past, to its indefinable atmosphere generated by the sense of history, to the age-old songs and legends in which its past is evocatively enshrined, and to the natural beauty of its setting. But now for the first time the forces of attraction are balanced by equally potent forces of repulsion as the transfigured reality of memory and legend is gradually pierced by the cold light of truth. From the very outset, the narrator's attitude to Sukhodol is strikingly ambivalent. In the early part of the work, comments on its irresistible fascination for all who lived there alternate with references to the death from fear of the mother of the former house serf Natal'ya, to the murder of the narrator's grandfather by his illegitimate son, the Smerdyakovlike lackey Gervas'ka, to the mental derangement of his aunt Tonya after an abruptly terminated love affair, and to the "insane" infatuation of Natal'ya for the narrator's uncle, Pyotr Petrovich, that culminated in her exile to the remote farm of Soshki. At this stage, however, the narrator makes no attempt to explain these curious events or to relate them to the questions that concern him. In the first three chapters, which form a kind of prelude, he is mainly preoccupied with recreating the atmosphere of Sukhodol, indicating its mysteries, and introducing the main characters. Occasionally interrupting his tale with exclamations of astonishment at the bizarre behavior of the estate's last inhabitants, he confines himself simply to cataloging his childhood memories and to repeating the stories about the past that he heard as a child from his parents. The amplification of the catalog is entrusted to Natal'ya, the last articulate survivor of the period concerned, whom the narrator and his sister visit at Sukhodol in chapter II, and her detailed and dramatic account of her life in chapters III and IV provides the narrator with the insights that he seeks into the psychology of the typical *sukhodolets*. Thereafter, extracts from Natal'ya's reminiscences are repeatedly inserted by the narrator into the record of his personal reflections.

It is evident, therefore, that structurally *Sukhodol* is an unusually complex work. But the structure was brilliantly conceived for the investigative purpose that inspired it. The last years of Sukhodol are examined from three different angles of vision represented by Natal'ya, the narrator as child, and the narrator as adult. Chronological exposition is replaced by a latticework of interacting narrative strands reflecting the diversity of subjective viewpoints from which a shimmering impression of objective truth gradually emerges. It is hardly surprising that critics have drawn parallels with the principles of musical composition.[55] Each successive point of view, endowed with its own distinctive tonality, adds a new dimension to the events recalled and casts a new shaft of light on the estate's last masters, and as the emotions stirred by memory oscillate between horror and exultation, sorrow and anger, love and hatred, the crippling malaise of Sukhodol is slowly exposed.

Although the narrator's attention is chiefly focused on the masters, the introduction of Natal'ya and the prominence of her personal perspective on the past reflect Bunin's habitual refusal to make any significant distinction between masters and serfs. Like the brothers Krasov in *The Village*, Natal'ya performs more than one role in the work. On the one hand, her story in chapters III and IV and her scattered replies to the narrator's questions are the main source of purely factual information about the last spasms of life on the moribund estate; on the other, they convey a specific attitude to Sukhodol that substantially assists the narrator in his task of diagnosis. Her recollected experiences and reactions to events reveal to him a cast of mind and mode of thought that shed abundant light on the reasons for the rapidity of

Sukhodol's decline. Thus, even though Natal'ya is a former serf, his judgments on her are relevant to the entire Sukhodol community. She emerges, in fact, as the very "soul" of its mysterious existence. There is much in her, as in Sukhodol itself, that delights the narrator and wins his admiration— her unaffected simplicity, her gentleness, her capacity for love. But in her unquestioning acceptance of brutality, her emotional instability, her superstitious dread of the primitive forces of nature, and her craving to play a part, even if it be the part of a martyr, that impelled her after her release from Soshki to devote her life to the service of the demented aunt Tonya[56]—in all these aspects of her conduct and character, he perceives the symptoms of the cancer that destroyed the Khrushchovs. The uncontrollable caprices, impracticality, and idiocy of the masters, he concludes, simply mirrored the similar deficiencies of their serfs. Natal'ya's fear of her masters was paralleled by her masters' fear of Gervas'ka, while her timorous attitude to nature was magnified in the madness of aunt Tonya. "The character of the masters," remarks the narrator, "contained the same compulsion as that of the serfs —either to dominate or to fear" (3:160).

It should not be thought, however, that the narrator's indictment of the meekness and passivity of Natal'ya reflects a reassessment by Bunin of the virtues he had ascribed a decade before to such characters as Meliton and Mitrofan. His fundamental convictions were totally unaffected by the extended scope of his inquiry, and as if to reaffirm this fact he pointedly contrasts with the life of the *sukhodol'tsy* that of the Ukrainian peasant Sharyy and his wife, the tenants of Soshki, through whom the same old virtues are loudly acclaimed. The submissiveness of Mitrofan has its source in an intuitive understanding of life and of man's place in it; it does not paralyze his creative vitality or condemn him to a life of fruitless indolence. The mentality of Natal'ya, conversely, and of all the last inhabitants of Sukhodol is a product of ignorance and illusions, of the rarefied, "arid" atmosphere of "Dry Valley" with its small windows and dark, oppressive floorboards, of the unreal life fed solely by legends, fantasies, and groundless fears they have created for themselves in the isolation of the steppe on the crumbling foundations of a once strong and vital past. The headless figure of St. Merkuriy of Smolensk that adorns the Khrushchovs' family icon is an awesome symbol of their detachment from the natural processes of life. And it is precisely the unreality and "unnaturalness" of their dreamlike existence, their alienation from nature epitomized in the terrified reactions of Natal'ya and aunt Tonya to the nocturnal cries of the eagle-owl (3:142), that condemns them, like the inhabitants of Durnovka, to chaos and self-destruction. The manifestations of chaos are identical to those depicted in *The Village*—impracticality, aimless violence, and disintegration of the family. In the first redaction of the work, the narrator remarked on the passing of the "ancient family feeling" and of the "old blood relationship with the remoteness of the steppe."[57] In the final version he laments: "At Sukhodol they were incapable of rational love or rational hatred, of rational affection or healthy family feeling, of work or of communal life" (3:425). In all these respects the *sukhodol'tsy* are at one with the masters and peasants of Durnovka. The recurrent conflicts of the Khrushchovs merely echo the feud of the Krasovs and likewise signal the imminence of their extinction.

Bunin's verdict, therefore, on the Khrushchovs has much in common with the one he pronounces on the peasantry of the postreform era. The only significant difference is the difference of period. His conclusion, quite simply, is that even before 1861 the breakdown of the old productive relationships was already in evidence, and characteristically the ultimate cause is sought not in class divisions or economic factors but again in the psychological effects of alienation from the soil. But now this alienation is attributed to a progressively intensifying process of decay which he traces to the peculiar conditions of life on the typical Russian estate—to its isolation and to the inertness, stagnation, and sense of unreality it tended to breed. The emancipation of the serfs, he now implies, served merely to hasten the "Slavonic soul" on the self-destructive course to which it was already committed.

Although the Petropolis edition of 1935 toned down somewhat the severity of his comments on the suicidal inclinations of the national psyche—possibly, as Krutikova has suggested, in response to the racial theories of German National Socialism[58]—this contention remained central to his thinking on the decline of the old order. For final clarification, however, of his views on this question it is necessary to turn to the works written before *Sukhodol* in which his interest is less obviously engaged by the problems of Russia and, in particular, to those in which he makes it clear that he saw the decline of Russia not only in a Russian context.

4. Citizenship of the Universe

Describing in his "travel poem" "The Shadow of the Bird" his journey to Turkey in 1903, Bunin recalls his thoughts as the ship bore him on his way: "You dress yourself by an open porthole through which the April freshness of the sea is wafted and you remember with joy that Russia is three hundred miles away" (3:314). The first version of the work continued:

I have never felt any love for her, and I suppose I will never understand the meaning of that love for one's native land which is apparently characteristic of every human heart. I know well that one can love this or that style of life and that one can devote all one's energies to its creation. . . . But what does "native land" have to do with it? If the Russian revolution disturbs me more than the Persian, I can only regret it. Truly blessed is every moment when we feel ourselves to be citizens of the universe, and thrice blessed is the sea in which one senses only a single power—the power of Neptune! [3:428]

The reader's initial reaction to these words is to relate them to the sentiments Bunin had expressed earlier in "The New Road" and to regard them—as V. N. Afanas'yev does, for example[1]—simply as additional evidence of his intensely hostile response to the disappearance of the style of life that had inspired his elegiac epitaphs. But Bunin's announcement of his "citizenship of the universe" was not only a confession of displeasure with his citizenship of Russia, even though his discomfort in the latter capacity clearly enhanced the appeal of distant horizons. Above all, it disclosed the standpoint from which he conducted his critique of Russia and alluded to the universal implications of his censure. Bunin's lifelong passion for travel was a dimension of the universality of his thought, and his statement in "The Shadow of the Bird" was essentially a defense of his "universal" view of man and of his right to represent it. Restored personal contact with the universe and infinity was the goal that impelled him so often "to baptize his naked soul in the font of the sky and the seas."[2]

More generally, Bunin was intent in his travel poem on defending the right of the artist to elevate his subjective responses to universal forms of experience above the concern with political and social issues that was traditionally demanded of Russian writers. To this extent, his statement is a continuation of the reply he addressed in 1901 to V. S. Mirolyubov, editor of the popular journal *Zhurnal dlya vsekh* [A journal for all], who had criticized his "excessive dedication" to nature. He wrote: "I do not write about nature, you know, in a dry, factual manner. Either I write about beauty, i.e., regardless of where it might be found, or to the best of my ability I give the reader together with nature a part of my soul. Everyone writes in his own way, so let Mamin write about this, Gorky about that, and me about my own concerns. Is a part of my soul really any worse than some Ivan Petrovich whom I might depict?"[3] The belief that Bunin expresses here in the aesthetic validity and self-sufficiency of overtly subjective responses to life is reflected in almost every prose work he wrote before *The Village*. It explains his predilection for the genre of the lyrical monologue and his distaste, reminiscent of the early Tolstoy, for the "outmoded" artifice of plot. "Whatever you might say," he wrote to Teleshov in November 1899, "you have the wish to say it, and what you say will be a part of your soul. That is enough!"[4] In his peasant fiction, the prominence of the lyrical element varies considerably from one work to another, for at times he felt obliged to make certain concessions to the "old tastes." He remarked to his nephew N. A. Pusheshnikov in 1911: "I never write what I would like to write or in the manner that I would like. I do not dare. I would like to write without any form, disregarding literary devices completely. . . . As a matter of fact, all literary devices should be sent to blazes."[5] But even when a narrative element, in the most general sense of the term, is present in his early works on social themes, the fiction is still dominated by the meditative, lyrical digressions in which the author enlarges on his wide-ranging impressions of the scene. Events are submerged in the responses to them of the narrator, whose personality is continually in the foreground.

The lyrical monologue, however, in its purest form is encountered in the succession of early works that are completely devoid of topical references and in which the author's overriding preoccupation with universal issues is quite explicit. These works reveal most clearly the wholly egocentric character of Bunin's aesthetic thought and read most obviously like an extension of his poetry. With few exceptions, they are among his least impressive achievements. Only a few of them will be examined here, but it will become increasingly apparent that no study of the author of "The Gentleman from San Francisco" [Gospodin iz San-Frantsisko] (1915) and *Mitya's Love* would be complete without some consideration of them. The position of the narrator in these works is usually one of contemplative solitude. Having severed every social connection, he confronts the mysteries of existence in total isolation. He is a man "without kith or kin," the title [Bez rodu-plemeni] Bunin appropriately gave to a story of 1897 in which he declares through the lips of his alter ego, the student Vetvitsky: "I laughed at both the Marxists and the Populists and said that I could become a social man only in exceptional circumstances—for example, if a time of genuine social enthusiasm arrived or if I myself enjoyed just a little happiness in my personal life. . . . I love life, I love it hopelessly! I have been given only one life and that for some fifty years of which fifteen have gone on childhood and a quarter will go on sleep" (2:169 and 174). This egotistic commitment to the pursuit of exclusively personal aims in life was not only congenial to Bunin the man; it also commended itself to the artist as a means of achieving a distinctive literary identity among the prose writers of the period. His search for this identity explains, in part, his decision to place as an epigraph to his collected works his short "poem in prose" "The Pass" [Pereval] (1892–98) in which both the search and the literary posture in which it culminated are represented in the form of an allegory.[6] The work was well chosen, however, for another reason, for the contrast between mountain height and luring valley, which is an extension of the principal contrast in the allegory between night and day, may be seen as duly symbolizing the conflicting emotional impulses that underlie the entire development of his art—the conflicting tendencies toward self-detachment from life in all its futility and horror and self-abandonment to its sensual delights.[7]

In Bunin's works on rural themes, nature is generally represented from only one point of view—as the source of human creativity and psychological well-being. Self-detachment from nature is equated with sterility of the mind and self-destruction. But neither the "character" or "spirit" of nature nor the full implications for the individual of his absolute dependence on nature are explored in any detail. These are precisely the subjects that concern Bunin in those of his early works not devoted specifically to the problems of Russia. The recurrent dilemma of the "lyrical hero" of these works is perhaps most graphically expressed in an allegory entitled "The Fog" [Tuman], which he completed in 1901. Like "The Pines," it was written in the peaceful atmosphere of Chekhov's dacha in the Crimea.[8] The title, which echoes one of the central images of "The Pass," is obviously symbolic, alluding both to the hero's state of mind—to the perplexity with which he reacts to the mysteries of existence—and to his solitude—to the impenetrable barriers that separate man from man. In a poem of 1889, Bunin had announced: "My whole youth consisted of wanderings and the joy of lonely thoughts" (1:69), but the thoughts of the hero of "The Fog," at least initially, inspire very different emotions. Not the least important aspect of the work is the allegorical situation in which the hero is placed, for he is the first of the numerous characters in Bunin's fiction whose dramas are set on board ship, and the inherent symbolism of the situation, which becomes fully explicit in "The Dreams of Chang," is already apparent. Perceiving in the ocean a symbol of the forces of nature, the hero suddenly becomes aware in its presence of the terrifying fragility and insignificance of his individual identity. Detached by the night and the fog from every human contact and confronted solely with this awesome spectacle of omnipotent nature, he is compelled to acknowledge the folly of aspirations to personal happiness and to recognize in death a meaningful release from the ludicrous charade of life. "I do not understand," he states, "the silent mysteries of this night, and in general I understand nothing in life. I am completely alone, and I do not know why I exist. . . . I need no one now, and no one needs me. We are all foreign to one another" (2:233–34). But with the passing of night and the dispersal of the fog, the face of nature is abruptly transformed. As the lunar symbol of death surrenders the stage to the solar symbol of life, the hero's "lonely thoughts" suddenly yield to the spontaneous responses of his reanimated senses, and, "filled again with the unconscious joy of life," he declares: "It seemed to me that the night and the fog had existed only to make me love the morning all the more" (2:235).[9]

The allegory ends, therefore, by posing a question. Despite the inescapable evidence, the hero seems to be asking, of the essential absurdity of life, does not man's inborn capacity to derive a joyous sense of affinity with nature from contemplation of its beauty and mystery itself invest his life with a meaning in which he can find contentment and self-fulfillment? The question is implicit in almost everything that Bunin wrote, and negative and affirmative answers frequently alternate in his works with bewildering rapidity. Certainly the impression is often conveyed that in the instinctive delight of man in the activity of his senses Bunin perceived a source of reconciliation with the ephemerality of existence and the horror of death, but his tendency to relapse into the "nocturnal" state of mind of the hero of "The Fog" was ineradicable.

Many themes served him in the course of his career as pretexts for the development of his thoughts on this question, but undoubtedly the main one was the theme of love, and it is clear from such works as "Late at Night" [Pozdney noch'yu] (1899) and "In Autumn" [Osen'yu] (1901) that by the turn of the century he had already evolved the conception of love that was to inspire some of his greatest stories. Love is most typically represented by Bunin as an experience of evanescent beauty illuminating the gray monotony of life and doomed to swift extinction. While expressing man's delight in his physical existence and his pursuit of personal happiness, it also seems to confirm by the brevity of that happiness the transience of life itself and man's slavery to death. Love also expresses, however, the contradictory aspiration of man to find fulfillment beyond himself and thus to transcend the limits of his own personality. In this connection, we should consider the emphasis placed by Bunin on the capacity of love, as illustrated by the experience of the hero of "In Autumn," to instill in man a maximally sharpened sensitivity to his affinity with nature. Again the hero's monologue is delivered against a backdrop of night and sea, but his reactions are quite different from those of the hero of "The Fog." "Only the sustained triumphant roar of the sea was audible," he states, "and conscious of its might it seemed constantly to gain in majesty. The damp wind threw us down on the precipice, and we were long unable to sate ourselves with its soft freshness which penetrated to the depths of our souls" (2:251–52). Here the activity of nature is clearly more than a symbolic accompaniment to the lovers' surge of emotion. Refracted through the experience of love, the awesome power of nature not only intensifies the ecstasy of individual, sensual experience; it also inspires an exhilarating, instinctive awareness of personal communion with and participation in the elemental life of the universe. The bounds of individuality are momentarily breached, and the present dissolves into infinity. Hence the hero's reference to the face of his beloved as "the face of an immortal" (2:253). Presumably it was this heightened sense of affinity with eternal nature awakened by moments of intense emotional experience that Bunin had in mind when he wrote in a poem of the same year: "There is no death for the man who loves life" (1:159).

But, like love itself in Bunin's depiction, the awareness and exhilaration are inevitably short-lived. Their eclipse is predicted in the heroine's words: "When I was a girl I constantly dreamed of happiness, but everything turned out to

be so tedious and commonplace that this night—perhaps the
only happy night in my life—seems to me unlike reality and
criminal. Tomorrow I shall recall this night with terror, but
now I do not care" (2:252). The term "criminal" in this context is clearly double-edged. Her love is illicit (and a source of
terror) not only in the literal sense of constituting a betrayal
of her husband, but also in the metaphorical sense of sig-
nifying a moment of rapture and revelation that conflicts so
sharply with normal experience that it seems to transgress the
limits of the permissible. For a fleeting instant, her life is
illuminated with meaning, but rarely, the author implies, are
such insights given to man. His normal fate is the gloom and
anguish of ignorance and the frustration of his innermost
desires—the frustration vividly portrayed in Bunin's short al-
legories of 1906 "Numbers" [Tsifry] and "The Well of Days"
[U istoka dney].

The penetration of this gloom is the central endeavor of
all Bunin's early reflective heroes, and love is merely one of
the means by which they strive to attain to the intensity of
experience and depth of insight that will momentarily satisfy
their desire to perceive beyond the bounds of their isolated
individuality a meaningful universal unity of which the individual personality is intrinsically a part. Few of them are capable of devoting their lives to love of a single woman. As
for their successors in Bunin's later works, love for them
is a preeminently sensual experience sought for purely egotistic ends that preclude a profound and lasting attachment.
Thus even before the hero of "A Little Romance" [Malen'kiy
roman] (1909)[10] hears of the death of the woman he loves,
a journey on a bright spring morning is enough to prompt
his remark: "Nothing is necessary in life except this spring
and thoughts of happiness" (2:339). The memory of love has
evaporated, and, like the hero of "The Fog," he discovers in
the simple beauty of nature a comparable stimulus to the
activity of his senses from which he derives a no less potent
sense of seemingly meaningful vitality. But as "The Fog" confirms, this beauty is merely one of nature's aspects. It is the
other face of remorseless power, chaos, and horror, and in his

story "The White Horse" [Belaya loshad'], one of his most
ambitious undertakings before *The Village*, Bunin sought to
express the contradiction in a single graphic symbol.

In its present form, established in the late twenties, the
story is shorter by three chapters than the first redaction,
entitled "Asthma" [Astma], which appeared in 1908 in the
third of the *Shipovnik* almanacs, but neither the central idea
nor the biblical symbolism of the original was significantly
affected by the abridgment.[11] The story still provides the
most explicit statement in Bunin's prerevolutionary fiction of
his general conception of life. Although it differs from most
of his early prose works in that it is a third-person narrative,
the hero, a surveyor, is again an obvious mask of the author-
narrator whose purpose it is to present the reader with yet
another "part of his soul."

As he returns home on his horse from some unknown
destination, the hero is portrayed succumbing to an onset of
his congenital asthma, but this physical affliction is patently
symbolic of the spiritual unrest with which he contemplates
the world about him. From the beginning he is prey to an
inexplicable apprehension. He is conscious of something
vaguely threatening in the beauty of the surrounding woods
and fields, and his anxiety is suddenly intensified by the spectacle of a white horse with an unusually large head drawing a
cart that contains the body of a seemingly dead peasant. The
transition from this symbol of death to the actuality of death
is effected rapidly with the appearance of a young girl at a
railway crossing who with a singular lack of emotion informs
him, while her mother is warming water to wash the dead
body of her youngest child, of the death shortly before of
another of her brothers beneath the wheels of a passing train.
This meeting with death, however, is sensed by the hero as
merely the prelude to a more significant encounter. "Becoming increasingly agitated," the narrator remarks, "at the
thought of the powerful, merciless, and mysterious force that
surrounded him on all sides and seemed to be challenging
him to a contest, he waited for something with growing anxiety" (2:318), and he is duly rewarded with the vision of a

second white horse that seems to be pursuing him. A figment of his feverish imagination, this biblical symbol[12] of power and beauty, reminiscent in its magnificence and ferocious energy of the beasts of Delacroix, combines within itself all the strident contrasts that excite his contradictory reactions to his environment—"terrifying rapture" (2:315), "sensual terror" (2:316), "sensual trepidation" (2:318). The horse is an emanation of the spirit of nature itself, a mirror of the Creator, and thus, like the sea in "The Fog" and "In Autumn," an embodiment of the force that controls the life of man. Restored to the sanctuary of his home, the hero turns to the Book of Job which inspired the vision, and as he reads he imagines the kind of confrontation with God that every man is ultimately fated to experience: "He will remind the madman of his insignificance. He will remind him that the paths of the Creator are inscrutable, menacing, and joyous, and He will reveal to him the unlimited extent of his greatness. He will merely say: 'I am Strength and Mercilessness,' and He will terrify him with the beautiful manifestations of this strength on earth which from time immemorial has been the scene of a gory contest for every mouthful of air and where the most helpless and unfortunate of all is man" (2:329).

Such is the Creator who dominates the fictional world of Bunin—the Schopenhauerian *perpetuum mobile* that reveals itself in the life of man and nature. Never before had he identified man so explicitly with the entire world of nature or expressed so unequivocally man's total dependence on its inflexible laws, and his "un-Schopenhauerian" conclusion, though still implicit, remains the same: man must yield, he must recognize his subservience and mold his life accordingly. He must become a "companion" of nature and make no attempt to replace the way of nature with the way of man. He must strive to know his own nature, to nourish it, and to adapt it to the natural process. Thereby he may partake of the universal. Only humble submission, Bunin implies, releases the creative force of nature that dwells within man; the price of self-delusion is pain and self-destruction. In harmony with nature, man suffers the cruelty of its blind justice, but he is also the recipient of its rewards and the beneficiary of its beauty, and from the sense of identity with nature that is born of his self-knowledge he may ultimately derive a consciousness of participation in some meaningful universal design. Many are the times in Bunin's works, especially in *The Life of Arsen'yev*, when this level of consciousness seems almost to have been achieved. His fictional and nonfictional writings are scattered with paeans to the Creator who has blessed man with the gift of life on earth. But equally numerous are the cries of anguish and incomprehension. The foundations of his faith in a meaningful universe were constantly threatened by the fact and reality of death and the manifestations of nature's savagery, and in the years ahead the despair of incomprehension was occasionally to impel him to reflect with approval even on Schopenhauer's antidote to suffering—the renunciation of the will to live, nirvana. But in his early works, despair is less conspicuous than the search for meaning, for escape from the solitude of individuality, for "the combination in this world," as he put it in his poem of 1901 "Night" [Noch'], "of beauty and eternity" (1:149). In this connection we need to consider his concept of the "sensual" or "pre-existential memory" to which he refers repeatedly in his travel poems and first introduced in his lyrical account "Holy Mountains" [Svyatyye gory] (1895) of a visit that he made in the spring of 1895 to the Svyatogorsky monastery in the Ukraine.

Strictly speaking, the term "travel poems" (*putevyye poemy*) was reserved by Bunin for the accounts of his visits to Turkey in 1903 and to Egypt, Syria, Palestine, and Lebanon in 1907, which he entitled initially *The Shrine of the Sun* [Khram solntsa][13] and later, in 1931, *The Shadow of the Bird*, taking the latter title from the first poem in the cycle.[14] Since "Holy Mountains," however, displays many of the most characteristic features of the genre, the designation may legitimately be extended to it. Like all Bunin's travel poems, it is as much an account of a journey through time as a description of a specific geographical location. It illustrates his usual practice in these works of concentrating his attention on places of particular historical interest and thus on specific moments in

time or episodes from the past with which he feels a curious
subconscious affinity that intensifies his sense of the continuity of life. The result is a kind of psychological conquest
of time which in 1925, in his short philosophical work "Night"
[Noch'], he was to attribute to the ability of a certain "category" of people "to feel with particular intensity not only
their own time but also other times, the past, not only their
own country and nation but also those of others, not only
themselves but also other people—the ability, as it is usually
described, 'to be reincarnated'" (5:302). The travel poems are
essentially a record of Bunin's own "reincarnations."

Thus, as the narrator of "Holy Mountains" looks down
from the commanding height on which the monastery is situated and sees below the winding stream of the river Donets,[15]
the barriers of time momentarily collapse. The centuries separating him from the fleeing Prince Igor', to whom the river,
according to Russia's greatest heroic epic, had offered shelter
from his Polovtsian pursuers, seem suddenly to telescope, and
past and present briefly converge. The identity of setting becomes a bridge across time, a common point of reference for
temporally unrelated events, and thus an analogue of the universal, extratemporal unity of life.[16] The effect of this experience is to induce a kind of universalization of the self,
a pantheistic expansion of consciousness that transcends the
limits of both time and space. As F. D. Batyushkov wrote in
1915, "In animation of the past and spiritual reunion with it
Bunin sees, as it were, an extension or . . . 'multiplication' of
our own life."[17] The awareness born of this experience of the
indissoluble bond between the individual and the whole of
creation throughout time is the source of the repeated references in Bunin's later works to the evolutionary nature of individual consciousness, to its dependence on and progressive
enrichment through the experience of past generations which
sociological criticism has been inclined to relate simply to his
pride in his lineage and nostalgia for Russia's past.[18] In reality,
they are further reflections of the battle against time and death
that is fought on the pages of most of his lyrical monologues, of
his obsessive aspiration to partake of "the joy of an existence in

which death is merely a step to perfection, of the joy of filial closeness to one's father and fraternal closeness to everything living, and to partake of the beauty and harmony of the radiant cosmos" (3:444). This summary that he offers in the first redaction of his travelogue "The Delta" [Del'ta] (1907) of the spiritual rewards of ancient Egyptian pantheism admirably defines the level of consciousness he sought in his "spiritual reunions" with the past.

But the past, like the present, also revealed to him the other face of nature—the "strength" and "mercilessness" of the implacable Creator. His "reunions" not only reinforced his impersonalistic conception of the individual as a passing heir to the immense biological legacy bequeathed to him by evolution; they also inspired his distinctive philosophy of history. The travelogues that comprise *The Shadow of the Bird* were written between 1907 and 1911—at the time when Bunin was chiefly preoccupied with the preparation and composition of *The Village* and *Sukhodol*—and although explicit references to Russia are rare, it is clear that as he made his way through the countries of the Middle East, the state of his own country was seldom far from his thoughts. The result is an implicitly comparative approach from which emerged the conception of history as the repetitive enactment of immutable universal laws that is reflected in his judgments on the Russian peasantry and landed gentry. As a means of enhancing the cogency of his generalizations, Bunin consistently adopts the procedure of representing the history of the Middle Eastern countries as a fulfillment of biblical prophecies. Few pages are without some quotation from or allusion to the Bible, and the predictions of the prophets are elevated to the status of an unimpeachable authority. The primitivism of these countries is seen as testimony to the veracity of the Bible's eschatological pronouncements, as a predicted restoration of the savage world in which Christ lived and suffered. "Life," he declares in the "poem" "Judaea" [Iudeya] (1908), "has completed an enormous circle. On this land it created great kingdoms, and having destroyed and annihilated them, it has returned to a primitive poverty and simplicity (*k pervobytnoy nishchete i prostote*)" (3:366). And the once resplendent center of Baal-worship in Lebanon evokes the comment: "This land, one of the most fertile in the world, is now desolate and wild (*zapushchena, odichala*)" (3:400). The vocabulary is identical to that Bunin employs in "The Pines," "The New Road," "The Gold Mine," and *The Village* in his descriptions of the new Russia, and there can be little doubt that between the wildernesses of the Holy Land and the wasteland of rural Russia he was intent on drawing a direct parallel.[19] The decline of Russia is viewed against the background of the circular movement of history predicted by the prophets, and no essential distinction is recognized between the reversal of evolution in Durnovka and the historical fate of Judaea. If any further evidence were required of Bunin's insistence on subordinating the will of man to the all-embracing power of universal laws of life, the historical philosophy of his travel poems manifestly provides it.

Bunin does not restrict himself, however, in his travel poems to judgments on the past and present. His visit to Turkey in 1903, which Muromtseva has described as one of the most important experiences in his life,[20] also presented him with a vision of the future. In his account of this journey, "The Shadow of the Bird," the implicit parallels of the later travelogues are preceded by an implicit contrast—a contrast between contemporary Russia and "the great cosmopolitan realm of the future," which he sees prefigured in the life of Constantinople. Few parts of the "eternal city" are unscarred, in Bunin's portrayal, by the ravages of time and man's barbarity, but amid the ruins and squalor he perceives the beginnings of a new creative phase in the historical cycle, and the suburb of Galata prompted him to exclaim in the first redaction of the sketch:

Life does not tolerate repose. Time is destroying walls, mosques, and cemeteries. Poverty is destroying areas of Skutari, Istanbul, Galata, and Fanara and is transforming them into slums and dens of thieves. But life creates incessantly, and there are too few places on earth like the Golden Horn and the Bosphorus. Galata, the heart of the laboratory, is often called the cesspit of Europe and compared to Sodom.

But Galata will not perish. The rabble that inhabits it is working relentlessly. They are poor and they frantically thirst for life. Though unaware of it themselves, they are creating a new tower of Babel, and they have no fear of the mixture of tongues. In Galata a new language is already being born—the language of work. An unprecedented tolerance of all languages, customs, and faiths is being born. . . . One can be a monarchist, an anarchist, or a republican—in Galata it concerns no one. . . . One can be a pagan, a Christian, a worshiper of the devil or of the Prophet, and this also is no one's concern. [3:431–32]

It has been argued that Bunin's excision of this passage in emigration might be interpreted as evidence of his eventual loss of faith in the prophesied "new world" of which Galata represents a nascent microcosm,[21] but as the same conception, albeit less succinctly expressed, is still perceptible in the final version of the sketch, the deletion is most plausibly attributable simply to a desire to avoid repetition. There is, in fact, no evidence at all that Bunin ever departed from the historical theories reflected in his travel poems, and since his views on the evolution of states were essentially nothing more than an extension of his invariably "biological" view of man, this is not unduly surprising. States, he believed, no less than individual human beings, are organic phenomena subject to immutable laws of growth and decay, and with his interpretation of history as a cyclic process that stemmed from this belief, he both anticipated the fundamental thesis of Blok's *The Collapse of Humanism* [Krusheniye gumanizma] (1919), and Oswald Spengler's *Der Untergang des Abendlandes* (1918)[22] and echoed certain aspects of the theory of organic cultures formulated by Konstantin Leont'yev in his *Byzantinism and the Slavonic Peoples* [Vizantizm i slavyanstvo] (1875), a work with which he is not known to have been familiar.

The passage on Galata is important for three reasons. In the first place, it expresses indirectly an outright rejection of the belief that significant change can issue from purposeful action, such as revolution, and thus prefigures Bunin's treatment of the revolution of 1905 in *The Village* as merely a symptom of Russia's relapse into chaos. Changes of genuine historical importance, he implies, result not from violence or social pressures but from the responsiveness of man to the self-regenerative forces of life working through him. Second, the passage offers some indication of a future that may be regarded as a blueprint of Bunin's ideal society, and in the process it confirms our observations on his attitude to the concept of nationality. It is above all the cosmopolitanism of Galata that attracts him and the emphatically un-Russian virtues of political and religious tolerance that he associates with it. The self-liberation of the Galatean from all social, political, and nationalistic prejudices has endowed him with the spiritual freedom of a "citizen of the universe" which Bunin implicitly contrasts with the empty freedom proclaimed by the real-life counterparts of Deniska Seryy. Finally, however, the passage paradoxically discloses a tragic awareness of the futility of all idealism based on the achievements of man, for like the great societies of the past, the cosmopolitan society of the future must itself ultimately collapse with the next turn of the historical wheel. Societies, like men, are condemned to death from the moment of their birth. They are simply links in an evolutionary chain of unknown purpose. "Why has nature so primitively encroached upon this divine house of prayer?" Bunin asks as he surveys one of Jerusalem's mosques (3:376), and his paean to Galata provides the answer: Life tolerates no repose. Nature is beautiful and incessantly creative, but in order to create it must first destroy, and it destroys when man has so far detached himself from nature that its creative force no longer evokes his responses. This phase of detachment and stagnation, Bunin argues, is an inevitable stage in the evolution of all societies, and it is precisely this phase in the evolution of Russian society that he depicts in his works on the peasantry and landed gentry.

Although, therefore, the works discussed in this chapter, with the exception of the travel poems, would not merit serious consideration on aesthetic grounds, there are clearly good reasons for dwelling on them at some length. Not only do they add a new dimension to Bunin's portrayal of the last years of imperial Russia; they also provide a preliminary insight into the major philosophical preoccupations of the mature writer and anticipate virtually everything he had to say subsequently about the relationship between man and nature. In addition, they show that the tendency of contemporary critics to associate him, at least initially, with the early symbolists was not based solely on the fact that in 1901 "Late at Night" and *The Fall of the Leaves* were published by *Skorpion*. The overtly egocentric character of his aesthetic views, the indications of a metaphysical level of thought, and the recurrent posture of a lonely wanderer searching for beauty and meaning—these aspects of his early works understandably prompted comparisons. After the appearance, however, of *The Village* and *Sukhodol*, reviewers duly acknowledged their error of judgment, and by 1912 his complete independence of literary "schools" had ceased to be seriously questioned.

5. From Lyrical Monologue to Impersonal Narrative

The most conspicuous aesthetic feature of the prose works written by Bunin before *The Village* is clearly the dominating presence of the author himself in the person either of the narrator or of the central character. In all these works the intrinsic interest of events, characters, and situations is less important than the author-narrator's responses to them, while the landscapes are either projections of his thoughts, feelings, and moods or pretexts for his speculations on the mysteries of life. The conventional discipline of a narrative continuum is replaced by the authoritarian discipline of the author's personal sensibility and preoccupations. The result is a fragmentary composition in which the sequential logic of the traditional narrative is usually forsaken for the structural principles of parallelism and juxtaposition. Successive compositional elements—landscapes, reflective soliloquies, character portraits, snatches of dialogue—are linked less commonly by a momentum generated from within than by the thought processes and emotional reactions of the apprehending subject. Hence the abruptness of changes of scene and of switches to different points in time that explain the relatively large number of chapters into which even very short works are frequently divided.[1]

Bunin's consistent adoption of this compositional principle in his early works immediately identifies his prose as the prose of a poet. The principle may be equated with the technique of "association by similarity (or contrast)" which R. Jakobson has contrasted, as the distinctive "impulse" of verse, with the principle of "association by proximity" that he perceives in the structure of prose.[2] But in applying this principle to the "alien" medium of prose, Bunin evidently failed to foresee the problems that inevitably ensued. Apparently believing that simple transposition was aesthetically admissible, he seems to have been unaware of the need to compensate in the prose medium for the absence of the feature that makes the procedure fully acceptable, and indeed natural, in verse —the rhythmic similarity of its constituent segments, which provides the basis and precondition for association by similarity (or contrast) on every other level. In the absence of a comparable basis within the medium itself, the accumulated parallelisms and juxtapositions, even when recognized as such, and also the conclusions of these works, often appear arbitrary and inadequately motivated.[3] More commonly, their significance is simply overlooked because there is no visible integrating force to direct the reader's attention inward and to prompt him to establish the necessary connections. Some works are obviously exceptional in this regard. Thus in "Antonov Apples" and "The Epitaph" the central images and the thematic contrast between past and present are sufficiently strong in themselves to support and integrate the finely wrought patterns of associations and digressions. But in general the author's poetic sensibility and the philosophical implications of the scenes described are rarely capable of imposing on the disparate compositional elements a system of relationships conducive to a cohesive unity, and the effect produced is frequently one of complete submission to what E. Auerbach has termed "the random contingency of real phenomena."[4]

It is not difficult, therefore, to understand the intolerant attitude of contemporary criticism to the early Bunin's extended portraits of nature. They drew the following comments, for example, from Yuliy Aykhenval'd:

The various characteristics of nature, even the subtle ones, and all these details of quintessential rural life are too lavish, and in the end they bore and weary us. Moreover, Bunin often speaks of nature when it is clear that it is only he, not his characters, who needs it—when their psychological situation is such as to make it impossible for them to notice all the scattered details on which the subtle landscape painter dwells with his searching eye. In this sense analysis prevails in the author's works over synthesis.[5]

Similar comments are encountered in most contemporary reviews of individual works. Bunin seems to have believed that, as in a lyric poem, an expressive synthesis could be achieved by simply maintaining the emotional key in which the prose was pitched. When speaking of his early prose, he frequently stressed the importance of its tone.[6] "For me," he informed Pusheshnikov, "the main thing is to find the sound. Once I have found it, everything else comes easily by itself."[7] But as the edifice of details relentlessly expands and image continues to spawn image, the burden frequently becomes excessive and the compositional inadequacy of the "tonal synthesis" is clearly exposed. Hence Chekhov's reaction to "The Pines": "It is very new, very fresh, and very good, but too compact, like thickened broth."[8]

For the first twenty-five years of his literary career Bunin consistently shunned the obvious means of providing his prose works with the "vertebrate quality"[9] in which they are conspicuously lacking—the reinforcement of the organizational role of the central fictional situation. Nevertheless, it is clear that even by 1901 adverse criticism had already had a strong effect on him. "It seems that I don't have a grain of real talent," he wrote to his brother Yuliy in January of that year,[10] and in 1902 he wrote only two prose works—"Dawn Throughout the Night" [Zarya vsyu noch'][11] and "Hope" [Nadezhda].[12] 1903 was almost equally unproductive, and apart from an inconsequential sketch entitled "From a Height" [S vysoty] (1904), which he later omitted from the final edition of his collected works, he avoided prose completely for the next two years. In fact, only five more stories were written before he began work on *The Village* in 1909. Thus the evidence would suggest that by 1901 doubts about the aesthetic validity of the lyrical monologue as a prose genre were firmly planted in Bunin's mind and that the problem of achieving variation was becoming increasingly intractable. Certainly the "lowering" of the lyrical tone in the first redaction of "The

White Horse" ("Asthma"), which resulted from a liberal injection of *byt*, that is, of details relating to the surveyor's domestic life, pointed the way to *The Village*, but in general the five stories written between 1906 and 1909 are devoid of significant innovations. The last of them in particular—the appropriately titled "The Same Old Story" [Staraya pesnya]—presents clear evidence that he was no longer capable of extracting novelty from the genre, for three of its chapters were virtually verbatim repetitions of works published earlier—"From a Height" (chapter II), "In the Alps" [V Al'pakh] (1902) and "The Nocturnal Bird" [Nochnaya ptitsa] (1902) (chapter III), and "Lodging for the Night" [Nochleg] (1903)[13] (chapter V). Nothing is more indicative of the impasse to which he had been brought by his studious avoidance of invention and literary devices than his readiness to publish this curious amalgam of scattered fragments.

Bunin was compelled, therefore, by the natural evolution of his early art to recognize that the procedures of lyric poetry and the poetic mode of thought and perception could not be transferred to prose without the compensatory integrating force of at least a well-defined fictional situation. The continued exclusion of artificial structures, of rationalistically coordinated sequences of compositional elements with a planned beginning and planned conclusion, had not only resulted in monotony and sterile repetition; as in the early fiction of Tolstoy,[14] it had also deprived his works of the generalizing power he sought to impart to them. In vain he had tried to convince Mirolyubov of the existence in "Late at Night" of a "universal mood" (*nastroyeniye obshchechelovecheskoye*); the editor persisted in regarding it as a tale about his "personal domestic life."[15] Responses such as this eventually taught him the paradox that universal truth is effectively communicable only by untruth, that without the "distancing" power of invention the reader remains impervious to the implications of art for himself.

Despite, however, Bunin's newly born respect for the artifice of plot, it should not be thought that it significantly affected his distinctively poetic approach to the art of prose fiction. Both the nature and the extent of the transformation have often been misinterpreted. In 1912 he was still intent on pointing out to a correspondent of *Moskovskaya gazeta* [Moscow Newspaper]: "The poetic element is naturally inherent in works of literature, regardless of whether they are written in verse or prose,"[16] and it may be assumed that he was referring here as much to questions of composition as to those of style. From 1912 onward, his only major deviation from the compositional principles of his early prose was to replace the author-narrator's personal responses to given situations with events or situations experienced by invented or "distanced" characters. The discipline changed, and the consequences for his style were of the greatest importance, but his compositional methods remained essentially the same. The "cinematographic"[17] or "mosaic" technique of the early Bunin was more than mere literary contrivance; it was a projection of his *manière de voir*, of the imaginative process by which he was naturally disposed to recreate reality, and it was perhaps the evidence he perceived of Chekhov's evolution toward a similar "bloc technique"[18] that caused him to greet his last stories, particularly "The Bishop" [Arkhiyerey] (1902),[19] with such fervent enthusiasm.[20] Thus even after 1912 a tendency toward simple juxtaposition, as distinct from overt logical connection, remains the most characteristic structural feature of his works, extending from the general compositional level even to the "microcosmic" level of sentence structure, where it reveals itself in his disinclination to subordinate. On virtually every page of his oeuvre it is possible to find sentences that confirm the observation of the Soviet scholar R. Spivak that "basically the complex sentence of Bunin differs only externally or formally from a number of simple sentences."[21] On both levels, the compositional and the syntactic, it is precisely this general looseness of the connections between the parts comprising the whole that differentiates his prose most markedly from that of his predecessors and contemporaries.

The main difference after 1912 is that the compositional elements are no longer combined in a manner that seems arbitrary. The reader is conscious of a more dynamic relationship between them, of a powerful centripetal force generated by the strong central situations that usually hinge on a single climactic event or experience. From this time forth it becomes increasingly difficult to discuss parts of Bunin's works without relating them to the whole from which they have been extracted. He still continues, in Stepun's phrase, "to think with his eyes,"[22] but now their sweep is controlled by a firm situational criterion and the selected details are usually striking for the subtlety of their relevance and suggestiveness. The result is not the simplification of reality, but a more economic and expressive evocation of its complexity. He once remarked in reference to the style of Gustave Flaubert that "not only every individual word, but even every sound and letter has a meaning."[23] The attempt to achieve a similar refinement of his own style is clearly visible in the stories that follow *The Village* and *Sukhodol*. These stories show that by 1912–13 style and structure had evolved in his art into functions of plot, into a means of subjecting the meaning inherent in the plot to a process, in David Daiches's phrase, of "continuous symbolic expansion."[24]

The Village marks the beginning of the transition. Its aesthetic deficiencies, of course, are many and obvious and are chiefly attributable, despite the clarity of its basic structural design, to the defect that it shares with his earlier fiction—the coordinative weakness of the main center of dramatic interest (the story of the brothers Krasov). Despite its unprecedented size and much greater complexity, *The Village*, like *Sukhodol*, was a natural outgrowth in structural terms of everything he had written before, and this general structural kinship most probably prompted him in 1921 to give the common genre-designation *poema* to these otherwise dissimilar works. Perhaps an additional reason for the structural weakness of *The Village* was its interrupted composition—the eight-month interval separating the two short sessions in which it was written.[25] However that may be, neither the symmetrical scheme of the triptych nor the uniform severity of the descriptive tone is adequate to the task of integrating the enormous diversity of material that Bunin squeezes into it, and Gorky was fully justified, when commenting on the work, in echoing Chekhov's criticism of "The Pines:" "If it is necessary to speak of a defect of the story—a defect, for I see only one—it is its richness. It is not the colors which are rich, no—there is too much material. . . . Three or four objects are crammed into every sentence. Every page is a museum."[26] Bunin accepted the criticism without demur[27] and even reiterated it himself some years later on learning that André Gide considered *The Village* his masterpiece.[28] Nor was it invalidated by his third revision of the work in the last years of his life.[29] In the final redaction the lengthy descriptive passages and the throng of episodic characters still enjoy a prominence and autonomy that detract seriously from the sharpness of the main portraits and from the inherent drama of the events, particularly in the third section where the brothers are almost driven from the stage. It might perhaps be argued in the author's defense that he declared it his purpose in the work to place the emphasis "not so much on the characters, even Tikhon Krasov himself, as on the whole character of everyday Russian life,"[30] but the task was aesthetically impossible in a work of such size without the substitution for the main characters of a focal point for the various aspects of "everyday Russian life" that would reduce them to the necessary coherence. The only focal point, however, apart from the story of the Krasovs, lies outside the work in the author's head. In terms of the author's idea, everything in the work is undeniably important and intelligible, but in aesthetic terms, that is, in relation to the drama of the Krasovs, much of it is clearly superfluous. The story of the brothers reads in the total context of the work as merely one, albeit the most extensive, of its numerous constituent episodes—as merely the most substantial of the diverse pieces of evidence the author amasses in support of his thesis. Its links with the rest are sufficiently tenuous to justify its complete detachment.

The paradox of *The Village*, however, is that the feature of the work that is primarily responsible for disrupting its aesthetic coherence—the inordinate attention paid to details

of *byt*—is simultaneously indicative of Bunin's emergence
from the impasse he had reached with the lyrical monologue,
for although he abides by his usual practice of endowing the
poema with a sustained narrative and descriptive tone, it has
nothing in common with his earlier lyricism. "In *The Village*,"
he declared, "there is not a trace of lyricism or sadness. It
seems to me that my tale is written very simply, very objec-
tively and very realistically."[31] Quite apart from the fact that a
lyrical response to life in Durnovka was precluded by the
material itself, the significant development in this regard
was the complex role he devised for his two principal characters. They present themselves in three distinct capacities—
as judges, *dramatis personae*, and objective observers—and in
the latter two of these guises they are independent of the
author. The effect of this innovation is that the life of the
village is seen mainly through their eyes, and their convergent
points of view chiefly determine the descriptive tone of the
author-narrator. No longer, therefore, is it possible to regard
the descriptive passages merely as objective correlatives of the
narrator's moods and emotions. Indeed, the criticism most
commonly leveled against them is that they are even excessively independent of the author-narrator, that the details
comprising them are "insufficiently dematerialized or spiri-
tualized."[32] In other words, it is alleged that Bunin went too
far in renouncing his former lyricism.

Again, however, the problem is basically one of structure.
As the contemporary critic L. Gurevich observed, "many
pages slip from one's memory immediately after reading them
because there is no artistic need for them."[33] The wretchedness of life in Durnovka is meaningful in the fiction only as an
extension of the wretched lives of the Krasovs, but that which
is essentially an extension repeatedly becomes an end in itself
controlled by criteria that lie outside the fiction. Hence the
second paradox of the work that resides in the objective representation of material that cannot be justified in terms of
the fiction itself and owes its inclusion solely to the author's
inability to contemplate his subject dispassionately. Having
effected his withdrawal from the fiction as principal observer,

he continually reveals his presence in the excesses of descriptive detail and, in addition, in the superabundance of dialogues in which judgment is passed explicitly, for as judges both Tikhon and Kuz'ma, like Balashkin, are clearly the mouthpiece of their creator.

Thus, despite the considerable power of its impact, *The Village*, like most transitional works, is flawed by intriguing inconsistencies and discords. With the aid of the two "reflectors" the subjective element is suppressed on one level only to assume correspondingly greater prominence on another, and the effect is the replacement of lyricism by tendentiousness. Bunin's awareness of this defect is confirmed not only by the reservations about the work that he expressed subsequently, but also by the steps he immediately took to rectify it in *Sukhodol*. His answer to the problem was the more complex interweaving of differing points of view that resulted in the unusually elaborate structure of this work. The evidence suggests that he had two main objectives in mind: not only to reintroduce the lyrical element, but also to use it as a means of ensuring that the descriptive detail would be directly relevant to the experience of the characters—to the physical experience of Natal'ya and to the psychological or imaginative experience of the narrator. Thus it may be deduced that like the narrative tone of *The Village* this lyricism, which makes the designation *poema* seem more appropriate in this case, is quite different from that of his earlier works, for neither the author himself nor his fictional mask is its source. Of the three distinct angles of vision from which the repeated sequence of events is examined, only one can be unequivocally identified with the author—that of the narrator as adult, whose function is comparable to that of the Krasovs as judges. The lyrical element is introduced mainly by the other two, which are independent of the author—that of Natal'ya, whose role corresponds, in part, to that of the Krasovs as participants in the events, and that of the unenlightened narrator of the past (before his visit to Sukhodol), who has no counterpart in *The Village*. Thus the lyrical responses to Sukhodol are

associated almost exclusively with points of view that are often
at variance with that of the author.

In *Sukhodol* the problems bequeathed by *The Village* were
resolved with complete success, but like the defects of the
earlier *poema*, the success cannot be adequately explained
without reference to thematic factors. Bunin's retreat from
the recent past to the distant epoch of serfdom was important
not only because it motivated his revival of the lyrical element;
above all, it enabled him to construct the work around a mystery that justifies both the lyrical attitude and the other points
of view. Everything in the work is directly related to the contrasting aspects of Sukhodol from which the narrator endeavors to extract the truth. Every landscape, dialogue, and
descriptive detail is essentially an amplification of one of the
contrasting viewpoints and is thus meaningful both to the
observer or speaker in question and in relation to the central
theme of the work. Sustained by the continually alternating
angles of vision, the tension produced by the mystery is the
primary integrating force in the fiction and the key to its
remarkable unity and compression. *The Village*, of course,
had also contained a mystery, but it was not the kind of mystery that could generate a comparable tension. The reality of
Durnovka existed in the present. It was beyond debate. The
mystery was the cause of the village's condition, not the condition itself. The same problem of cause, as we have seen, is
equally the concern of the narrator in *Sukhodol*, but the task
of analysis cannot begin until the reality of life on the estate
has been disentangled from the distortions of memory and
legend, and this can be achieved only by collating the differing viewpoints. The reversion to the past, therefore, posed
a different problem and required a different solution, and
the work vividly confirms the truth of the adage that was
rarely far from the tip of Bunin's tongue: "A writer's form is
inseparably related to his content and is itself born of the
content" (9:374).

But although *Sukhodol* is one of the outstanding prose
works of twentieth-century Russian literature, it was still a

transitional work in the context of Bunin's development. The
author's overt presence in the fiction had been greatly reduced, but not eliminated. The impersonalism of his thought
had not yet ousted completely the procedures of the lyrical monologue and inspired a correspondingly impersonal
mode of narration. The process of transition was to be completed in his stories of the next five years in which the emphasis is once more on the contrast between past and present
and, more particularly, on the present—on the death of the
past rather than on its dying.[34] All Bunin's works of these
years on rural themes are third-person narratives, and they
all reflect the enrichment of his technique that had resulted
from his experiments in *The Village*, *Sukhodol*, and also "A
Nocturnal Conversation" with differing points of view, for
life is repeatedly represented by the narrator as it is colored
by the sensibility and attitudes of the characters and by the
situations in which they find themselves. Certainly the author's presence continues to be sensed, but the reader can no
longer distinguish easily between his interventions and the
experience or outlook of the characters. No longer involved
in any overt emotional sense in the situations or predicaments
of his characters, the author reveals himself only in subtleties
of intonation and emphasis and in his general control over
the fiction—for example, in the effects obtained from various
kinds of contrast and juxtaposition and from changes of narrative tempo. Such are the elusive forms of subjectivity that
we encounter in "A Gay Farmhouse," where all elements of
the fiction are subordinated to the task of reinforcing and
amplifying the contrast between mother and son. His attitudes to Anis'ya and Yegor are revealed neither explicitly nor
in any obvious indirect manner. They emerge, as it were,
from the intonational unity of their portraits, from the general coloring of the descriptive passages, and from the variations of pace and rhythm. Thus, when speaking of Anis'ya, he
tends to slow down the narrative—most conspicuously in the
episode of her "death march"—as if harmonizing its tempo
with the graceful, unhurried tempo of her way of life, and the
rhythm of the prose seems to imply the narrator's approval.

Equally suggestive of his censure, by contrast, are the alternations between interludes of apparent immobility and bursts of convulsive activity that characterize the sections relating to Yegor. The portrait of Anis'ya provides a foretaste of the manner the lyrical element in Bunin's third-person narratives was henceforth to be woven inextricably into the experience of his characters and, in general, if it were possible to relate the inception of his mature manner to any single work, "A Gay Farmhouse" would perhaps be the most appropriate choice. The period of experimentation was by no means concluded, as chapter 6 will confirm, but the dramatic intensity of the work, the oblique representation of life through the eyes of the main characters, the restriction of their number to no more than two, the pivotal role of structural contrast, and the generally impersonal tone of the narrative all combine to identify the story as a typical creation of the mature writer.

"A Gay Farmhouse" was the second important work (the first being *The Village*) in which Bunin employed the simple thematic and structural scheme of a contrast between two individuals, and relatively simple plots were to remain a characteristic of his art. Although dramatic external action began to play an increasingly important role in his works, he still retained his former distaste for the notion of plot as intrigue. His continuing use of the scheme of contrasting portraits in several stories of the next three years—for example, in "A Prince among Princes," "A Spring Evening," and "I Never Say Anything" [Ya vsyo molchu] (1914)—was not only dictated by the recurrent thematic contrast between past and present; it is also explained by the opportunities it offered for indirect characterization, for the portrayal of each character from the standpoint of the other, which he clearly valued at this time when he was bent on rendering his narrative style increasingly impersonal and objective. Thus, in "A Prince among Princes," the social crudity of the prosperous octogenarian *kulak* Luk'yan Stepanov is conveyed by the reactions to his eating habits of the landowner's daughter Lulu Nikulina, while the Nikulins' impoverishment is simultaneously exposed by Luk'yan's unceremonious behavior in their presence. The actions and mannerisms of each are primarily significant for the light they cast on the other, and precisely the same technique is adopted in "A Spring Evening" in the description of the ill-fated encounter between the beggar and the peasant in the inn. In both stories the attitudes of the characters to one another determine the slant of the narrator's descriptions and his selection of details, and the result is not only a more cogent illusion of objectivity than would have been obtained by conventional description from the neutral standpoint of the narrator, but also a striking economy of expressive resources, for one and the same observation increases our knowledge of both the observer and the observed.

Together with the centralization of the fiction in a simple but well-defined and potentially dramatic situation, the development of an impersonal mode of narration had the effect of extending this brevity and compression to all spheres of Bunin's art. "A Prince among Princes," for example, consists of only ten pages, yet within this brief span Bunin contrives to encompass the economic and psychological decline of the gentry, the rise of the *kulak*, the primitivism of the *kulak* despite his material prosperity, the flight of the impecunious gentry to the capitals, and their attempts to find salvation in advantageous marriages. Devoid of chapter divisions, the story develops by means of a series of swift transitions— from the Nikulin estate to the homestead of Luk'yan and from there to Moscow—but each transition serves merely to deepen our insights into the contrasting situations and personalities of the principal characters. Counteracting the structural looseness is the mesh of eloquent details that continually rivet our attention to the central contrast, thus binding the three sections of the narrative into a coherent whole. The poverty of the Nikulins, for example, is further disclosed by the simple detail of the mourning attire they are obliged to wear for the journey to Moscow in the absence of suitable traveling clothes, while the soul-destroying thrift of Luk'yan is conveyed in a similarly oblique manner in the short opening paragraph of the tale: "Luk'yan Stepanov came to see the landowner Nikulina on a bright September day. His farm was fifteen versts away, and his horses were the apple of his eye. So he had come on important business" (4:60). Most of the details woven into the fabric of the work could likewise be adduced to illustrate Bunin's newly developed method of indirect psychological and social characterization that enabled him to combine the most widely divergent phenomena on the basis of the pivotal contrast. And since each detail is designed to extend and intensify the contrast, it plays its part in reinforcing the general unity of effect. The descriptive details, in short, play a vital synthesizing role in the story, and henceforth this compositional function of Bunin's details becomes an aspect of his technique that merits particular attention.

Certainly some mention should be made in this connection of the repeated lexical elements or leitmotivs employed in individual works of the period from 1909 to 1916 as a means of conveying a general unity of impression. Perhaps the most obvious example is the ubiquitous epithet "gray" (*seryy*) in *The Village*. Like Tolstoy, however, Bunin most commonly uses leitmotivs as a device of characterization.[35] Much more important on the compositional level is the unifying role of what might be termed allusive anticipatory details usually inserted into the early paragraphs of a story to provide in advance an oblique intimation of the dénouement. In the numerous tales in which Bunin uses this device, the climax of the action has the effect of triggering off in the reader's memory a kind of retrogressive chain reaction whereby the preparatory allusions and associations are fused into a single chord and the various sections of the narrative are drawn together to form a resonant synthesis. Such is the effect, for example, of the explosive dénouement of "A Spring Evening."

Whereas most of Bunin's works begin, like "A Prince among Princes," with a terse, factual statement, this story opens with a long descriptive sentence consisting of forty-nine words that fills the whole of the first paragraph. As in many of his later stories, description of the landscape is used here as a means of creating a slow, leisurely narrative tempo that gradually yields to a progressively quickening momentum as the finale approaches. The first five sentences record the beggar's arrival in the village where he is ultimately to meet his end, and they present a purely visual portrait of the scene. In the sixth, however, Bunin introduces an auditory detail that, since the beggar is almost blind, is the first detail of life in the village to stir his senses: "Somewhere on the far side which was warmly and caressingly illuminated at point-blank range by the low sun—somewhere, it seemed, very far away—a child was weeping, having lost his way behind some threshing barn or warehouse, and it was touching to hear at daybreak his plaintive, monotonous wail" (4:245). Between the terrified child at daybreak and the terrified beggar at sunset, who trembles before the threatening demands of the drunken peasant, there is an obvious correspondence. Like the child, the beggar, a graphic symbol in his meekness and humility of the rejected past, has lost his way in a hostile world, and two pages later, as he struggles to gain some impression of his surroundings, the child's lament again invades the silence.

Just as the misery of the child anticipates the beggar's predicament at the end, so the obstacles to the beggar's progress through the village foreshadow the appearance of the peasant: "He walked along holding his stick in readiness in his outstretched hand. Now a malicious, hoarse-voiced little dog would rush headlong beneath his feet, and having completed its dash it would suddenly fall silent; now a fluffy yellow hound would furiously tear up and fling the earth with its hind legs as it stood by a barn and with fiery eyes it would choke as it roared" (4:246). Almost every detail in the description of the dogs is echoed in the dénouement, where reference is made to the insane fury of the peasant,[36] to the hoarseness of his voice,[37] to his silence before committing the murder,[38] and to his attempts to tear a suitable weapon from the foundations of the inn.[39] All these details are examples of parallelism, but equally important is the anticipatory role of details contrasting with the dénouement that are inserted in the same unobtrusive manner—for example, the kindness of the little girl who, lacking any other gift, presents the beggar with her half-eaten roll (4:246), and the touching impression of friendship conveyed by the two doves that glide over the roofs and settle on the bank of the village pond (4:247). The catalog could be extended, but these examples will suffice to illustrate the particular procedure in question and, more generally, to highlight the significance even the most apparently digressive and unrelated details can acquire in Bunin's stories of this period. With its astute variations of narrative tempo and subtly allusive patterns of descriptive details, "A Spring Evening" demonstrates very clearly the exacting demands that Bunin now makes of his reader.

Since virtually everything in the story is teleologically oriented toward the climax, its structure gives an impression of much greater tautness than that of "A Prince among Princes." Highly characteristic of the mature Bunin, however, is the appendage of a brief final paragraph that reads almost like a rider to the story proper. The reader feels initially that the story should have ended with the peasant bent over the beggar's prostrate body and striking his throat with the stone, that is, at the end of the penultimate paragraph. But Bunin adds a postscript in which he depicts the peasant ten minutes after the murder. Now fully sober, he strides briskly across the steppe clutching in his hand the amulet that he has ripped from the beggar's cross, and suddenly he stops and hurls it toward the mounds of newly plowed soil. Three short descriptive sentences later, Bunin places the final full stop, having provided no hint whatsoever of the meaning we should attach to this unexpected gesture. Most critics seem to have accepted the interpretation of Batyushkov, who refers to the act as the sign of a reawakened conscience and thus as an indication of Bunin's "Tolstoyan" discovery of a human personality behind the peasant's brutal exterior.[40] But any semblance of remorse would be so totally at variance with the general character of the peasant's portrait that this notion cannot be seriously entertained. It is surely far more plausible to regard the gesture as a further indication of the psychological determinism that dictates the actions of all Bunin's "alienated" peasants. Without the final paragraph, the reader might be inclined to ascribe the murder to greed or to drunkenness, but the postscript, with its revelations that even ten minutes after committing it the peasant was sober and that in reality he cared nothing for his trophy, eliminates the possibility of either explanation. His desire to relieve the beggar of his meager possessions is exposed as merely a pretext for murder; its cause, like the cause of Yegor's suicidal inclinations in "A Gay Farmhouse," lies deeply buried in his psyche —or, more precisely, in Bunin's deterministic conception of Russia's imminent collapse.

The points that concern us here, however, are the extra dimension Bunin adds to the story beyond the dénouement of the action and the impression of incompleteness with which the reader is left by the short sequence of stark, unelucidated statements. Precisely the same deceptive impression is conveyed, as we shall see, by the similar postscripts appended to a number of other stories written in this period, particularly "Ignat" (1912), "Ioann the Weeper" [Ioann Rydalets] (1913), and "Light Breathing" [Lyogkoye dykhaniye] (1916). Although the function of each can obviously be assessed only in relation to the work of which it forms a part, they are all examples of one of the most effective procedures devised by Bunin to invest his usually very short works with a remarkable capaciousness. The simple juxtaposition of dénouement and postscript and the classical, "Pushkinian" translation of the meaning and psychological implications of the latter into a wholly visual scene oblige the reader to introduce his own hypotheses, thereby often expanding the thematic range of the given work far beyond the text itself.

As "Ioann the Weeper" confirms, however, postscripts of this kind may also perform an important compositional role. The story is one of three written between 1913 and 1916 that continue the critical appraisal of Russian religious fanaticism and the phenomenon of the "God's fool" (*yurodivyy*) that Bunin had begun in *Sukhodol*, the other two being "I Never Say Anything," in which the indictment is linked with the social-psychological theme of self-destruction, and "Aglaya." The setting of the opening scene is the new railway station of the village of Greshnoye ("Sinful"). From the windows of a train that has stopped there, one of the passengers, a pipe-smoking

Englishman, gazes with incredulity at the figure of a peasant standing nearby—at his cap, his coat, and "the primitive thickness of his beard" (4:126), which mark him as a creature from another world, another age. Bunin's use of trains to effect abrupt confrontations of various kinds can be traced back to "Kastryuk" and to several other stories written before *The Village*, but "Ioann the Weeper" is the first of the numerous tales in which he reverses the customary situation of his early works by replacing the impact of the train on the external observer with the impact on the traveler of the scene visible from the train. The confrontation in this instance is once more between present and past, but the changed angle of vision betokens an entirely different attitude to the past on the part of the author-narrator. As in *Sukhodol*, the emphasis is on those features of Russia's past that explain her present, and the incomprehension of the Englishman sets the tone to be maintained throughout. With the introduction of this tone and attitude, his role is exhausted, and the train bears him away, leaving the reader to accompany the peasant on his journey home which takes him past the adjacent graves of the "God's fool" Ioann Ryabinin and a once powerful local prince.

The encounter with the graves motivates the transition to the story of the lifelong antagonism between Ioann and the prince that ended with the former's death and the latter's command that on his own death he should be buried alongside him in the grounds of the village church. The story is introduced by the statement: "This is the story which they tell about him [Ioann] in the village of Greshnoye" (4:127). In other words, the tale is told exclusively from the point of view, and in the dialectal medium, of the villagers, whose most salient characteristic, like that of the inhabitants of Sukhodol, is their ability, the narrator informs us, "quickly to forget the past and quickly to transform reality into legend" (4:129). Like Natal'ya's narrative of events at Sukhodol, the point of view of the villagers embodies the author's indictment of the Russian inclination to replace unpalatable fact with emotionally charged fiction—in this case the obvious fact of Ioann's idiocy with the myth of his holiness. The command of the prince is a sign not so much of recognition that in death all men are equal as of his own eventual submission to the same delusion. But Bunin does not end his narrative at this point. Again he appends a seemingly superfluous paragraph, which on this occasion introduces an entirely new character, and reverts the scene to the point of departure—to the village station, where every autumn, we learn, an aristocratic lady arrives dressed in mourning to pay her respects and shed tears at the grave of the legendary "God's fool." The effect of the paragraph is to create at once a parallel and a contrast with the opening scene. The basic situation is the same in both cases—the arrival of a train bringing to the village a character from the world without—and the repetition produces an "annular" structure that reinforces the links between the four somewhat rigidly compartmentalized sections of the tale (the prelude, the walk with the peasant, the story of Ioann and the prince, and the postscript). But while the Englishman is alienated from the village by his nationality and European cast of mind and regards the peasant as a quaint object of curiosity, the old lady is severed from it solely by birth; she is still Russian, and she responds to the legend in the age-old Russian manner. In spirit, she is at one with the peasant, and her graveside posture at the end is identical to that of the peasant earlier as he pauses in the churchyard on his journey from the station. The postscript, therefore, is employed both as a compositional device and as a means of equating once more the two main classes of the Russian nation.

An additional important feature of "Ioann the Weeper" is the presentation of the main narrative (the story of Ioann and the prince) in the form of a recapitulation. It begins, as it were, from the end—from the graveside of the principal characters. This procedure of more or less directly preannouncing the dénouement at the beginning, which may clearly be compared, in part, to the anticipatory devices noted in "A Spring Evening," was used by Bunin from 1912 onward in a number of his most successful stories. Restricting the narrative to a clearly defined perimeter, but otherwise imposing the mildest constraints, the device was ideally suited to the free, subtly constructed type of composition that Bunin always favored. With few exceptions, the stories concerned are dominated by a single character, whose name is often indicated in the title, and their conclusions, not unexpectedly, are usually tragic. Such is the case, for example, in "Zakhar Vorob'yov" (1912), which begins with a bare statement of the protagonist's recent death and then records the events that led up to it. Thus the first sentence, in effect, introduces the principal unifying element of the fiction, and, as if to reinforce it, Bunin inserts a slightly varied statement on the second page of the tale before launching into the fatal sequence of events: "He died unexpectedly" (4:36). Thereafter everything in the narrative is colored by the known dénouement, and the scope for vague allusions and associations is virtually unlimited. Of particular interest in this connection is the association Bunin establishes between the hero and a detail of the setting.

Zakhar is a younger version of Ivanushka in *The Village*. He is another survivor of a breed nearing extinction. "He felt," we read, "that he belonged to a different breed from other people. . . . It is said that in olden times there were many like him, but the breed is coming to an end" (4:35). He is a kind of peasant *bogatyr'* endowed with immense strength and vitality that find no application in the stagnant life of rural Russia and, like Ivanushka, he is hounded to his death by his own frustration and the hostility of the lesser men about him. In the absence of a more worthy challenge to his powers, he accepts the bet of three villagers that he cannot drink a quarter (about three liters) of vodka in an hour, and despite his rivals' success in diverting his attention and abbreviating the hour to thirty-five minutes while he alternately drinks and expatiates in colorful language on the hardships of the impoverished peasantry, he emerges triumphant. But the victory merely stimulates his desire for greater accomplishments, and, having defeated the challenge of man, he pits himself against the forces of nature. From the beginning the story is punctuated, like many of Bunin's works, with inconspicuous references to the heat of the sun, and the slow, predetermined movement of the sun across the sky is like a distant reflection of the hero's equally predetermined progress toward the dénouement. But now, after the successful outcome of the wager, the implicit parallel becomes fully explicit as Zakhar resolves to cover before sunset the distance to the neighboring village of Zhiloye. From a detail of the backdrop, the sun is elevated to the role of the hero's antagonist, and like the villagers it is duly vanquished. In the final pages the *bogatyr'* and the heavenly body seem to be linked by invisible threads, the latter sinking before the onset of the deathly moon and the former slowly collapsing beneath the weight of his inhuman exertions. The death of the sun, a symbol of life, mirrors the death of Zakhar, a symbol of Russia's lost vitality.

In this story, therefore, an individual detail is gradually filtered from the setting and related directly to the drama of the protagonist, simultaneously amplifying its symbolism and projecting it onto a screen of cosmic proportions. Like the references in *The Shadow of the Bird* to the "circular" history of Judaea, the parallel with the sun links the decline of Russia with the natural, organic processes of growth and decay. In addition, as one of the main elements of continuity in the tale, the descent of the sun to the horizon contributes significantly to its structural coherence, linking together the various strands of the narrative and reinforcing the sense of inevitability that is initially introduced by the preannouncement of the dénouement. The story offers a clear indication of the extent to which setting and landscape in Bunin's fiction were henceforth to be subordinated to plot. Even in his early works, as we have seen, nature is never a completely autonomous element of the fiction, but its function in most cases is simply to evoke the narrator's responses or to instill a certain attitude to life in the minds of the characters. The situation after 1911 is markedly different. Man's relationship with nature remains Bunin's central concern, but it is no longer expressed directly. The life of man and the activity of nature are now conducted on quite separate planes, and the reader may well be induced by the separation to regard the landscapes as mere background and perhaps to conclude that Bunin had still not eradicated his old tendency toward descriptive excess. The separation, however, is merely an aspect of his new impersonal mode of narration, for in reality the two planes are never dissociated. They invariably exist in a relationship of meaningful parallelism or divergence, and failure to recognize the associations precludes a proper understanding of Bunin's purpose.

Another work in which the movements of the sun run parallel to the development of the action is "The Last Day," perhaps the most chilling of all Bunin's tales about the impoverished gentry. The "last day" in question is that of the landowner Voyeykov whom need has compelled to sell his ancestral estate to the merchant Grigoriy Rostovtsev. The story records his preparations for departure and his parting gesture to the new master—the hanging of his celebrated pack of borzois. Again the progress of the day (from 3 P.M. onward) is signaled by gradations of sunlight and the lengthening of shadows. Once more a cosmic dimension is added to the ebbing life of old Russia. But the role of nature in this work is rather more complex than in "Zakhar Vorob'yov," for while the sun attends the death of the past, the rest of nature exists in a relationship of contrast with the hero's predicament. Although the story begins, for example, with the statement: "Everything was finished" (4:104), we note that the winter of Voyeykov's discontent coincides with the month of April. The disintegration of the estate and the execution of the hounds are consistently offset by the signs of nature's rebirth. As the peasant Sashka digs the first grave, we read: "In the distance the rooks were making a din in the lower part of the garden. All around the starlings were singing, a magpie was chattering, and the sun was drying the compressed leaves at the roots of the bushes" (4:106). And just before Rostovtsev discovers the swinging corpses with their bulging eyes and tongues, Bunin inserts the brief digression: "In the profound silence the chinking voice of a nightingale trying out its low notes reverberated clearly and warily through the garden.

The night was mild, light, moonlit, and slightly misty" (4:110). By means of these short interpolations, Bunin creates an eloquent counterpoint to the ugliness of death and desolation. Set in a context of resurgent nature, the social change is allotted its place in the natural order of things and a record of destruction is subtly transformed into a paean to the creative force of life.

"The Last Day" is by no means the only one of Bunin's stories in which details of nature are invested with this contrastive role. And, in general, the emphasis in my analyses of the stories discussed in the last few pages has deliberately been placed on features of his new impersonal type of narrative that remained permanently characteristic of his technique. The simple juxtaposition, as distinct from the explicit causal connection, of compositional elements within the confines of a clearly defined plot situation, the coordinative function of unobtrusive details, the compositional role of anticipatory procedures, the expansion of meaning achieved by various kinds of postscript, and the structural and symbolic importance of settings and landscapes are perhaps the most distinctive features of the narrative technique that Bunin evolved in his stories on rural themes after completing his two *poemy*. Among his best-known stories, however, of the period from 1912 to 1916 are several that reflect the extension of his inquiry into the relationship between man and nature to different character types, both Russian and foreign, who, superficially at least, bear little resemblance to the peasant and landowner. In these works, both the universal implications of his thought and the lingering vestiges of the lyrical monologue are much more clearly apparent, and the eradication of overt subjectivity seems to have posed somewhat greater difficulties that require separate examination.

6. Urban and Western Degeneracy

The tendency of critical works on Bunin to convey the impression that the tales with urban and foreign settings that he wrote between 1912 and 1916 are thematically quite distinct from his works on the Russian peasantry and landed gentry is seriously misleading. In reality, "The Cup of Life" [Chasha zhizni] (1913), "The Brothers" [Brat'ya] (1914), "The Gentleman from San Francisco," and "Gnarled Ears" [Petlistyye ushi] (1916) are related almost as closely to *The Village* and *Sukhodol* as "A Gay Farmhouse," "Zakhar Vorob'yov," and "A Spring Evening." In each of these stories it remains Bunin's purpose to represent the psychological effects of modern man's alienation from nature. The only major difference is the succession of new guises in which modern man now presents himself. In *The Village* the destructiveness of the alienated Russian peasant had been contrasted with the respect for order and general well-being that were allegedly characteristic of other nations and of the Russian Germans and Jews.[1] After 1912, Bunin ceased to make such distinctions.

When he wrote in a poem of 1917: "It is given to me to be the witness of a contemptible, savage age" (1:448), he was not referring solely to Russia. Even before the outbreak of the Great War, he had detected in Western civilization as a whole evidence of the same cancer that he had diagnosed in his native land, and it was already clear to him that the cyclic catastrophe he had predicted in *The Village* was not to be the historical fate of Russia alone. Looking back in the thirties to the years preceding the beginning of hostilities, he remarked: " 'Woe, woe, the great city, Babylon, the strong city!'[2]—these terrible words kept ringing in my soul several months before the Great War when I was writing 'The Gentleman from San Francisco,'[3] for I sensed in advance the unprecedented horrors and abysses that lay concealed in our culture."[4] The

American protagonist of this famous story, no less than the
English colonel in "The Brothers," the triad of leading characters in "The Cup of Life," and Sokolovich in "Gnarled Ears,"
is a victim of the same degeneracy that predetermines the fate
of the peasants of Durnovka and the masters of Sukhodol.

From 1911 onward, the terms "degeneracy" and "degeneration," together with related nouns, verbs, and adjectives and with both Latin and Slavonic roots (*degeneratsiya*
and *vyrozhdeniye*), recur in Bunin's works and conversations
with intriguing persistence. We have already observed, for
example, that the narrator of *Sukhodol* refers to the "degenerating (*vyrozhdayushchegosya*) *sukhodolets*" (3:426). Similarly,
the Englishman in "The Brothers" comments that among
Europeans the power of instinct "has degenerated (*vyrodilsya*)
and is still degenerating (*vyrozhdayetsya*)" (6:275). "I am a so-
called degenerate (*vyrodok*)," declares Sokolovich in "Gnarled
Ears" (4:389), and the hero of *The Cornet Yelagin Affair* [Delo
korneta Yelagina] (1925) is attributed with "strongly expressed
degenerate (*degenerativnymi*) features" (5:272). Again, in conversation with Galina Kuznetsova in February 1931, Bunin
referred to the "long arms" of the iconlike Aglaya in the
eponymous story of 1916 as a mark of "degeneration" (*vyrozhdeniye*).[5] By analogy, we may legitimately regard the unusual physical features or gross deformities of numerous
other characters in his works—perhaps most obviously, the
"gnarled" ears of Sokolovich—as emblems of the same psychological affliction. A typical example is the portrait in *The
Village* of Yegorka, an assistant in Tikhon Krasov's shop: "The
crown of his head was wedge-shaped. His hair was wiry and
thick. . . . His forehead was concave. His face was like an egg
placed at an angle. His eyes were fishlike, protuberant, and
the lids with their white, calflike lashes seemed to be stretched
over them. It seemed as if there was not enough skin, that if
the lad were to close them, he would have to open his mouth,
and that if he closed his mouth, he would have to open wide
his eyelids" (3:26).

Despite the rarity of comic effects, it is perhaps in his
treatment of the degenerate that Bunin most clearly reveals

his debt to Nikolay Gogol'. At the same time, his portraits equally reflect his profound interest in criminal anthropology that prompted him to observe in 1919 in an indictment of the Bolsheviks: "Modern criminal anthropology has established that the vast majority of natural criminals have pale faces, large cheekbones, a crude lower jaw, and deeply set eyes. How can one not recall after this Lenin and thousands of others?"[6] The body in Bunin's fiction is almost invariably a mirror of the mind. It is the visual expression of a character's sensitivity to nature, and since degeneracy is rarely unaccompanied by conspicuous physical defects or peculiarities, we may deduce that the term is used to denote the loss or weakening of precisely this sensitivity. Its normal meaning— the loss of qualities proper to the kind—is qualified to signify the loss of the one particular quality that for Bunin eclipsed all others in importance. The effects of the loss are spelled out by Sokolovich: "In every degenerate certain perceptions and capabilities are sharpened or heightened, while others, conversely, are diminished" (4:389). In "Gnarled Ears," as in "A Nocturnal Conversation" and "A Spring Evening," Bunin concentrates on the former phenomenon, in particular, on the "sharpening" of the destructive "capability"; in "The Brothers," "The Cup of Life," and "The Gentleman from San Francisco," as in most of his works on the peasantry, the emphasis is rather on the results of "diminution." In combination, the two types of work constitute a powerful exposé of a diseased and moribund civilization.

The action of "The Brothers" is set in Ceylon, which Bunin and Muromtseva had visited in March 1910, and the inspiration behind the work is revealed by its epigraph from the *Sutta-nipāta*[7] and the quotations from Buddhist writ that punctuate the narrative. Bunin recalled in 1921: "When I was in Colombo, I was struck equally by the light of the sun, which is dazzling and impossible to convey, and by the teaching of Buddha in which there is much of this sun that dazzles the eyes and the soul."[8] "The Brothers" is the first of several works reflecting the interest in Buddhism that Bunin shared with Tolstoy,[9] and it may be noted that when writing *The*

Emancipation of Tolstoy more than twenty years later, he was particularly attentive to the recurring Buddhist elements in the novelist's thought. In the Buddhist conception of personality and the human condition the two writers found much that harmonized with their own thinking.

The first of the two parts that comprise "The Brothers" —the story of a nameless Ceylonese rickshaw boy and an English traveler who enlists his services—is essentially a parable on the second and third of the "noble truths" of Buddha: the truth of the cause of pain and that of the cessation of pain. To define it as such is not to reject the customary view of the work as a powerful indictment of colonialism,[10] but rather to argue the superficiality of this view, for the phenomenon of colonialism is interpreted by Bunin as the corollary of an attitude to life that is no less characteristic of the Ceylonese than of their English overlords. Hence the title of the work and the disclosure of the nature of this attitude in the parable through the experience not of the Englishman, but of the rickshaw boy and his father. The role of the colonel here is entirely passive. In Bunin's depiction, the misery of the lives of both father and son is consequent on their thralldom not to the English, but to desire—to the "craving for existence" that nature implants in every living creature as the source of perpetual self-renewal and perpetual self-destruction. In the setting of Ceylon, Bunin recreates the beautiful and savage world of the "white horse," and the two parts of the work illustrate the operation of the laws of this world respectively on the level of individual existence and on that of historical evolution, thereby confirming the validity of the connection established earlier between Bunin's biological view of man and his cyclic view of history.

The inherent cruelty of natural law is dramatized in the brief story of the rickshaw boy's father. Here craving, the *perpetuum mobile* of nature, assumes two contrasting forms, rewarding man, in the form of the procreative instinct, with the ecstasy of love and condemning him, in the form of the ruthless struggle for existence, to hardship and pain. Link by link Bunin traces the chain of cause and effect that extends from the desire for "earthly love" to premature death, projecting it against the background of the beauty and horror that coexist in the lush Ceylonese landscape. "Everything in the forest," we read, "sang the praises of Mara, the god of life and death, the god of 'the craving for existence.' All creatures were engaged in pursuing one another and in gaining a short-lived joy from their mutual destruction" (4:258). After the "destruction" of his father, the rickshaw boy inherits not only his rickshaw but also his subjection to Mara of which the rickshaw, like the constant, oppressive heat of the sun, is an obvious symbol. The narrator comments: "Then he himself began to transport people and to earn money, preparing for his family and for his love, the desire for which is a desire for sons, just as the desire for sons is a desire for property, and the desire for property is a desire for well-being" (4:260). But his father's life is not reenacted. The spell of desire is suddenly broken by the betrayal of the girl he loves, and it is consistent with the equation established in this section of the work between desire and existence itself that with the cessation of the former he should seek immediate release from the latter. His discovery of the betrayal is represented as a liberation of his will. Casting off the shackles of the rickshaw, "to which life had harnessed him from an early age, but not for long" (4:271), he turns to death, in accordance with Buddhist precept, for the restoration of his being to the "Indivisible Whole."

The highly contrived manner of his death—suicide by snakebite—is a symbolic expression of the parable's didactic purpose. The snake is clearly no real snake; it is a climactic symbol of Mara, a direct counterpart of the "white horse": "It was fabulously beautiful with black rings along its entire length edged in green, a light blue head, an emerald stripe on the back of its head, and a funereal tail. At the same time, despite its small size, it was unusually strong and spiteful, especially now after having been coiled in a strong-smelling wooden box" (4:271). The symbolism extends from the snake itself to the effects of its bite, which reflect the Buddhist conception of death as a reintegration of the elements or "aggregates" that comprise the personality with the unity of creation: "There is always a deep faint after the bite. . . . There are several of these faints, and each of them racks a man with pain and interrupts his breathing as it bears away a part of human life and some human faculty: thought, memory, sight, hearing, pain, sorrow, joy, hatred, and the final all-embracing element that is called love" (4:272). With this symbolic portrayal of liberation Bunin concludes his dramatic parable on the vanity and conquest of the desire that activates the natural process.

The second part of the story transfers the scene to the high seas and consists in the main of conversations between the Englishman and the Russian captain of the ship that is taking him home. The point of view of the "omniscient" narrator, which determines the form of the parable with its accompanying quotations from the Buddhist canon, is replaced by that of a participant in the action presented through the medium of dialogue. Characteristically, the two parts are simply juxtaposed; the task of connection is left entirely to the reader, and criticism has thus far offered little assistance. Thus R. Poggioli confines his discussion of the point to the observation that the two parts "are related only by chance and by a common, but negative trait: the mutual indifference of the two sufferers."[11] The indifference, of course, undeniably exists. It is a natural concomitant of the egocentricity that is inseparable from craving. But although the colonel never refers to the events of Part I, there can surely be no doubt that the issues on which he reflects, if not actually inspired by them, are at least directly related to them.[12] More precisely, they are related to the import of these events—to the idea of the reabsorption of the individual into the universal unity of life that is allegorized in the description of the rickshaw boy's death. The monologues of the colonel in Part II highlight the relevance of this idea to European civilization of the twentieth century.

In Part II the life and death of the individual, as portrayed in the story of the rickshaw boy's father, are paralleled by the rise and fall of civilizations, as analyzed by the author's alter ego,[13] while the import of the rickshaw boy's death has its counterpart in the colonel's explicit judgments on history. Like the life of the old Ceylonese, colonialism, in Bunin's submission, is itself a reflection of the natural process, a manifestation of the craving for existence. It is simply a collective form of obedience to Mara that breeds the same undeviating preoccupation with the demands of the self as the submission of the individual. On both levels, the result is a progressively widening breach between the egocentric self and the creative forces of life to which Bunin now points as the source of the crisis not only in Russia but in Western civilization as a whole. In the deification of reason by Western man and in his waning capacity for a nonrational, sentient response to the mysteries of the universe, the colonel perceives conclusive evidence of the decay that is a warning of disaster. He declares: "God and religion have long ceased to exist in Europe. Despite all our efficiency and greed, we are as cold as ice in our attitude to both life and death. If we fear death, we do so only with our reason and with the remnants of our animal instinct" (4:276). With the disappearance of these last "remnants," he implies, the might of Europe will collapse, and history will witness a repetition of "that which the Judaic prophets predicted for Sidon . . . , which the Apocalypse predicted for Rome, and which the Buddha predicted for India and the Aryan tribes that enslaved it" (4:278). By reference, therefore, to the phenomenon of colonialism, the Englishman, like the parable, argues the vanity of the self-sufficiency with which nature deludes nations no less than individuals. His conclusion is inspired by the philosophical impersonalism of the Buddha:

The Buddha came to understand what the life of the individual Personality means in this "world of being," in this universe which we do not understand, and experienced a sacred horror. But we raise our Personality to the skies; we wish to concentrate the whole world in it, whatever may be said about the universal brotherhood and equality of the future. Only on the ocean, beneath stars that are new and alien to us and amid the grandeur of tropical storms, or in India and Ceylon, where in the feverish darkness of black, hot nights one experiences the sensation of man melting and dissolving in this blackness, in the sounds and scents, in this awesome Indivisible Whole—only there do we weakly comprehend what this Personality of ours really means. [4:278]

With this renewed invocation of Buddhist thought, which clearly alludes to the rickshaw boy's death, the circle is closed and the link between the two parts of the work is securely established.

It is evident from this survey of the story that its structure is no less contrived than its symbolism. Bunin employs here a form of bloc technique that involves, as we have seen, a contrast between two distinct modes of narration hinging on the contrast between the two central characters, one of whom is active, the other predominantly passive. The medium adopted in the story of the active character, the rickshaw boy, is that of a third-person narrative, through which the basic idea of the work is initially dramatized in the form of a self-contained didactic allegory. The passive participant in the allegory is then detached from it in order to voice and interpret its significance for himself and for the European civilization he represents. The result is another example of the procedure of combining "telling" with "showing" (to borrow the terminology of Wayne Booth[14]) which Bunin had by this time abandoned in his studies of degeneracy in the setting of rural Russia. Thus not only is the colonel in Part II the author's obvious *porte-parole*; the allegory is itself repeatedly interrupted by overt references to the subtext it is designed to illustrate. Although this procedure has not saved the work from the misinterpretations it was presumably designed to forestall, it clearly diminishes its impact on the reader. The plausibility of the allegory is constantly undermined by the discordant quotations that mark the author's interventions, and one can only conclude from "The Brothers" that the more prominent the element of philosophic and didactic generalization in his fiction, the less inclined Bunin was to allow the bloc technique to function autonomously. He appears to have felt it necessary to compensate for the omission

of the link between the two sections of the work by excessive
clarification of the idea the allegory embodies.

Even so, comparison between "The Brothers" and "The
Cup of Life," written the previous year, indicates that a measure of progress toward the integration of objective and
subjective elements in this type of story had already been
achieved. As in "The Brothers," Bunin again endeavors in
this work to effect the integration by embodying the subjective element (the subtext) in the words and actions of one of
the characters, the eccentric Gorizontov. Like that of the Englishman, however, Gorizontov's participation in the drama
of the active characters is entirely marginal. He is merely a
personified indictment, hovering on the periphery of the
alien world of the three principal characters—Aleksandra
Diyesperova, the civil servant Selikhov, and the priest Kir
Iordansky—whose lives are irretrievably locked in a vicious
circle of mutual recrimination born of the two men's rivalry
for Aleksandra's hand and her decision, despite her love for
the handsome Iordansky,[15] to marry Selikhov.

The most striking compositional feature of this twenty-
page story, set in the Russian provincial town of Streletsk,
is its division into twelve short chapters involving constant
switches of attention from one character to another. The
procedure has its raison d'être in the temporal span embraced
by the events. The frequently large temporal intervals between successive chapters are indicative of the second contrast
Bunin is intent on drawing, parallel to that which exists between Gorizontov and the characters involved in the love
triangle—namely, the contrast between the static positions of
the latter and the relentless passage of time. The entire lives
of Aleksandra, Selikhov, and Iordansky are poisoned by the
outcome of their youthful relationship. To the end they remain, respectively, nostalgic, jealous, and resentful, prisoners
of their petty passions and frustrated desires, ever alert to
one another's actions but hopelessly isolated from one another by walls of accumulated hostility. The symbols of their
self-insulation are their enormous houses that shield them

from the life of vitality without, symbolized by the sun and the rhythmic rotation of the seasons. "Selikhov," we read, "never went out onto the street" (4:203); "Father Kir's gates were always locked and the boundaries of his grounds were marked by heavy boards" (4:205). Occasionally, the life stifled within them finds an outlet in dreams and bursts of frenetic activity—for example, in Selikhov's violent dancing to the accompaniment of his gramophone and in Aleksandra's dream of her violation by two young monks—but these moments are rare. Consumed with bitterness and regret in the gloom of their private domains, they close their eyes to the evanescent present, and by chapter III they are already approaching old age. The degeneration of Aleksandra's youthful vision of ecstatic romance into her mundane and obsessive aspiration to inherit her husband's house[16] is consistent with the general symbolism of the work, and it is fitting that death should eventually come to her on one of the rare occasions when she exposes herself to the alien sun and bustle of life. In the end, the motif of self-insulation is extended to embrace the entire community of this squalid little town. Just as they expel, at the behest of Iordansky, the pathetic Serb, who seeks merely to entertain them with his performing bear, so they bar their windows against the sun's incessant assault.

Alone among them stands the towering figure of the genial Gorizontov, whose name with its connotations of balance and equanimity is itself suggestive of the philosophy of life that sharply distinguishes him from his fellow townsmen. In effect, this philosophy differs negligibly from that which is implicitly attributed to Bunin's early peasant heroes, and, despite superficial appearances to the contrary, it is entirely consistent with the subtext of "The Brothers." Having established that in the latter work death denotes the rejection not of life, but of life controlled and distorted by craving, we should not be surprised to find Bunin defending through Gorizontov the proposition that the prolongation and enjoyment of a life free from craving are the most worthy goals of man's endeavor. Gorizontov's entire approach to life is based on the avoidance of every stimulus to desire that would constitute a distraction from or impediment to the realization of these objectives. Hence his refusal to entertain the idea of relations with women. But every appetite that does not seem to him to conflict with the body's interests is indulged to the maximum. The simple, "zoological"[17] pattern of his life is wholly geared to the achievement of peace of mind and physical well-being, and there can be little doubt that this primitive hedonism, founded on due appreciation of the fact that between man and beast there is no essential biological distinction, was the philosophy of life that commended itself to Bunin's reason.

Just as the story of the three active characters exactly parallels the story of the rickshaw boy's father in "The Brothers," so the role of Gorizontov effectively combines the functions of the Englishman in Part II and the quotations in Part I. While the positioning of the main exposition of his philosophy in the very heart of the story, in chapter VII, may be compared with the insertion of the quotations into the parable, the restatement of this philosophy in chapter XII bears the same resemblance to an interpretative epilogue as the colonel's meditations. The difference lies in the fact that the dynamic action of "The Cup of Life," which resides in the conflicts between the characters and in the swiftness of the transitions that propel them from youthful vitality to withering and death, has no counterpart on the level of thought. The principal characters are frozen in their initially established attitudes, and herein, of course, lies the entire point of the story as far as Aleksandra, Selikhov, and Iordansky are concerned. The frozen stance of Gorizontov, however, is in no sense connected with the main sequence of events. In "The Brothers," the epilogue is delivered by a character who emerges from the narrative to pronounce and enlarge on its import and whose participation in the narrative, though passive, has significantly affected his attitude to life. The epilogue expressing this attitude is thus an integral part of the work. This is not the case in "The Cup of Life," where chapters VII and XII are merely appendages, as distinct from responses, to the action, and the story would have benefited considerably from their exclusion, not only because of Bunin's failure to achieve more than a caricature in the portrait of Gorizontov but, more pertinently, because the essence of Gorizontov's philosophy is both deducible from the action and almost explicitly conveyed by the symbolic motifs that pervade it. In addition, the retardation of the narrative that results from the insertion of these chapters manifestly conflicts with the purpose to which the structure of the tale is otherwise effectively adapted—that of evoking the swift and inexorable passage of time. Comparison of the two stories, therefore, highlights the closer fusion achieved in "The Brothers," despite its indicated defects, of "showing" and "telling."

In the following two years, Bunin's experimentation with the fusion of narrative and interpretative elements in the more overtly philosophical kind of tale continued unabated, and complete success, not unexpectedly, continued to elude him. Among his attempts to solve the problem, two are worthy of special note. The first may best be illustrated by his well-known tale of 1916 "The Dreams of Chang." The major structural innovation in this story is the extended role he gives to the interpreter of the action, the nameless sea captain's Chinese dog Chang. Not only is Chang present throughout the narrative; he actually assumes the leading role from the start, for although Bunin retains his position of "omniscient narrator," the action—the changing fortunes of the captain—is seen through the eyes of the dog. The allocation of this central role to an anthropomorphized dog would seem to have been determined precisely by the author's need for an interpreter, who, while playing no direct part in the main action or influencing the course of events, is perpetually at the side of the principal active figure, the captain. A much closer relationship is thus established between interpreter and actor (that is, the subjective and objective or dramatized elements) than in either of the two earlier stories. Separation of the two elements is now replaced by their constant alternation.

Presenting the action through the prism of a single mind endowed with the faculty of memory, Bunin is able to switch

the narrative abruptly to different points in time and to effect
a maximally sharpened contrast between past and present.
The dreams of Chang resurrect the happy past of the captain,
while his waking introduces the painful present, and the recurrent temporal contrast achieved by this abandonment of
the chronological exposition that Bunin had adopted in the
early redactions of the tale[18] provides the basis for dramatization of the contrast between the "two truths" he inserts into
the captain's thoughts at the beginning: the first, "that life
is indescribably beautiful," and the second, "that life is conceivable only for madmen" (4:371). For the captain, the first
truth has died with the past, with the betrayal of his wife
and the loss of his beloved daughter. Even at the height of
his happiness, which is recaptured in the second dream of
Chang, the intensity of his love had vied with thoughts on the
ephemerality of experience fed by the oriental philosophies
with which his travels had brought him into contact. "It is
very frightening to live in the world, Chang," he had once
remarked; "it is very good, but it is frightening" (4:377), and
his fears are ultimately realized. In the present, vodka alone
saves him from insanity or suicide. Like Chang, he strives to
maintain himself in the world of dream in which the first
truth prevails, but, as in Tyutchev's poem "A Dream at Sea"
[Son na more], the illusion is constantly threatened by the
pain and grayness of the irrupting present, and only in death
does the captain, like the rickshaw boy in "The Brothers,"
discover the release he craves.

Between the death of the captain, however, and that of
the rickshaw boy there is the important difference that the
former does not mark the end of the narrative section of the
tale. The story of Chang is still incomplete, for his role, unlike
that of the Englishman, is by no means exclusively interpretative. Chang is raised from the depths of despair by the
impressive and moving funeral service, which fills him with
a sense of the immense power of the love he feels for his
old master, and this love now leads him to a new master
in the person of an artist friend of the captain, whom he
meets at the funeral. A relationship of instinctive mutual love,

founded on their common love for the captain, is immediately
established between them, and in the light of this experience
Chang comes to realize that "there is on earth another truth,
a third truth which is unknown to me." The author intervenes
to comment: "If Chang loves and senses the captain, if he sees
him with the eyes of his memory, that divine attribute which
no one understands, it means that the captain is still with him
in that world without beginning or end which is inaccessible
to Death" (4:385). Thus not only is the captain not dead; his
invisible presence remains as an active force in the world
capable of influencing the lives of others. Here we encounter
the theme that was to acquire increasing prominence in Bunin's works of the twenties—the theme of the immortalizing
memory.

The conclusion of "The Dreams of Chang," therefore,
while inseparably related to everything that precedes it, is
certainly not a contrasting appendage, like chapter XII of
"The Cup of Life"; nor is it an interpretative epilogue, like
Part II of "The Brothers," for unlike the latter it advances the
action as well as the thought of the work beyond the point
reached at the time of the death of the principal active character and signifies rather an intellectual victory over that
death than a mere interpretation of its import. For the first
time in the cycle of philosophical tales based on a combination
of narrative and interpretative elements, the customary passive role of the interpreter is complemented by a significant active role, and the transition is clearly motivated. The
dreams of the passive Chang not only dramatize the conflicting truths reflected in the experience of the captain; they
also prepare the way for the enlightenment of the "active"
Chang. There is no longer, therefore, the same dichotomy of
action and thought that characterizes the structure of "The
Brothers." The bloc technique is now employed to represent,
by means of abrupt juxtapositions of past and present, dream
and reality, the conflict in the mind of Chang between the two
truths about life from which he is ultimately delivered by the
sequel to the captain's death. In other words, it is adapted to
the externalization or dramatization of Chang's psychic con-

flict, of the thesis and antithesis from which is born his culminating insight, and the result is the closest integration of
narrative and interpretative elements that Bunin had thus far
achieved.

This result, however, left much to be desired, and not
only because of the general implausibility that stems from the
choice of a canine interpreter. The representation of the main
dramatic action, the experience of the captain, through the
eyes of the interpreter inevitably means that it is witnessed at
a distance. Together with the repeated disruptions of chronology, the procedure precludes a direct emotional response
by the reader to the tragedy of the captain's life. The in-
corporation of the drama of events, in short, into the personal story of the interpreter has the effect of imparting to
the former both an excessively fragmentary quality and a
distinct philosophical chill that is wholly inappropriate to
the subject. Bunin's dissatisfaction with the result may be deduced from his attempt in his next story, "Gnarled Ears," to
solve the problem of integration by a diametrically opposed
means.

There seems to be little doubt that "Gnarled Ears" was
intended by Bunin to be the most comprehensive study of
degeneracy he had thus far undertaken, for the tale as it
exists today was initially conceived as merely the beginning of
a much longer work, parts of which have survived in regrettably inaccessible manuscripts.[19] Even in its present, entirely
self-sufficient form, however, the story still contains his most
explicit statements on the subject. Moreover, with its sporadic
allusions to the battlefields of Europe, it stresses perhaps
more emphatically than any other work the topical relevance
of the theme. But this does not mean, as critics have tended to
argue, that the protagonist, Sokolovich, is simply an emanation of the atmosphere generated by the war.[20] Quite apart
from the fact that the story is based on a crime that was committed in St. Petersburg in 1909,[21] the philosophy of crime
that impels Sokolovich to murder the prostitute Korol'kova is
clearly yet another manifestation of the sickness Bunin had
diagnosed long before the outbreak of war and of which the

war itself, in his conception, like the revolutions to which it subsequently contributed, was merely a symptom. The real-life crime of 1909 is employed in "Gnarled Ears" as a means of dramatizing the contention that lies at the basis of most of Bunin's prerevolutionary fiction.

It seems hardly coincidental that Sokolovich, like the captain in "The Dreams of Chang," is cast in the role of a sailor who has abandoned the sea, Bunin's perennial symbol of the life force. *Pace* Afanas'yev,[22] we should not allow the difference of setting or Sokolovich's distinctive ability to articulate his conception of crime and human nature to obscure his psychological affinity with the peasant in "A Spring Evening" or the symbolic affinity of his crime with that of Yegor in "A Gay Farmhouse." The manner of the crime is very different, but its meaning is identical. Superficially, of course, there is nothing in common between Anis'ya and Korol'kova save their sex and their helplessness, but the differences are indicative merely of the extended range of Bunin's inquiry in the later story and of the tendency toward philosophic abstraction and maximum generalization, first revealed in "The Cup of Life" and "The Brothers," which this extension brought in its wake. It is precisely because of this tendency that in "Gnarled Ears" the single, fundamental attribute of the victim's sex is the sole focus of his attention. As a woman and thus as a giver of life, Korol'kova, like the sea Sokolovich has forsaken, is a symbol of the natural, elemental life from which modern man has become fatally estranged, while her profession, her ill-fitting clothes, and her ultimate fate are symbolic of the perversion of life that has resulted from this estrangement. It is in terms of this symbolism that we should understand Sokolovich's comments: "In general, people are much more inclined to kill a woman than a man. Our sensual perceptions are never so attentive to the body of a man as they are to the body of a woman, an inferior creature of the sex that gives birth to us all" (4:391). From the very beginning of his conversation in the early part of the story with two sailors in a restaurant, woman is the object of his venom and the torment of women the source of his fondest memories.

Recalling the time when he served as a chauffeur, he remarks: "It gives one, you know, a very keen pleasure to see the street bearing down on one and some fine lady rushing about ahead, not knowing to what side she should hurl herself" (4:388). When, six pages later, the "fine lady" assumes the form of Korol'kova and obstructs his menacing advance along the Nevsky Prospect, he loses no time in hastening her to her doom: "Suddenly she barred the way of Sokolovich as he strode along with his stooping gait. Looking her over with his piercing eyes, he immediately shouted in a deep voice to the night cab on the corner" (4:394).

The symbol of the sea, the generalizations of Sokolovich, and the symbolic role of Korol'kova leave little doubt that in this story Bunin is no more concerned specifically with the problems of Russia than in any of the other stories considered in this chapter. Why, then, it might be asked, does he revert to a Russian setting? The first point to be made is that the setting is urban and that whenever Bunin wished to limit the implications of the fiction specifically to Russia, he almost invariably selected a rural setting. Moreover, on the few occasions when he deviated from this practice (for example, in "The First Monday in Lent") his choice usually fell on Moscow. In "Gnarled Ears," by contrast, the setting is the least Russian of Russia's cities—Petrograd. In addition, despite the richly detailed descriptive passages and the numerous references to specific landmarks, Petrograd is portrayed by Bunin more as a projection of the protagonist, his "philosophy," and his crime than as a setting of intrinsic geographical or national importance. It is primarily a symbolic representation of the dark and menacing world of the degenerate.

There is also another reason, however, for the selection of Petrograd, which equally explains the otherwise inconsequential fact that the hero and his victim are also Russian. It emerges from Sokolovich's tirade in the restaurant against the obsession of writers with the criminal's conscience. Here he expresses the view that man is so constituted that he is capable of killing not only without remorse, but even with pleasure and a sense of relief, and after cataloging in support of his claim some of the more celebrated murderers of history, he concludes: "It turns out that Raskol'nikov was the only one to suffer torment, and the only reasons for it were his own weakness and the will of his spiteful creator who had the habit of thrusting Christ into all his cheap novels" (4:391). Given the fact that the subsequent cold-blooded execution of his own crime is partly conceived as a vindication of his view of human nature, it follows that it is also an implicit challenge to Dostoyevsky's portrayal of the criminal mentality.[23] It was clearly appropriate, therefore, both that the challenge should be issued in the city that had been the scene of Raskol'nikov's interminable agony and that his victim should share the profession of Raskol'nikov's savior, Sonya.[24]

The crucial point, however, is that the challenge is issued by Sokolovich, not by Bunin. Afanas'yev, who regards the attack on Dostoyevsky as simply a reflection of Bunin's personal dislike of the novelist,[25] is merely one of several critics who have failed to make this important distinction.[26] In reality, Bunin was far from wishing to dissociate himself from the view that a crisis of conscience is the normal human reaction to the shedding of blood. The confirmation is provided by the colonel in "The Brothers," for whom the European's increasing insensitivity to bloodshed, which he himself shares in full measure, is the most conspicuous mark of his degeneracy. He exclaims: "We do not even fear death as we should. We fear neither life nor the mysteries and chasms that surround us nor death—our own or someone else's. I fought in the Boer War. I ordered cannons to be fired and killed men by the hundred. Yet not only do I not suffer or go mad because of the deaths I have caused; I never even think of them" (4:276). In these few words, the colonel assigns to the psychology of the degenerate the feature Sokolovich equates with normality. Although the hero of "Gnarled Ears" refers to himself as "the son of man" (4:388), he is merely the "son of man" as he conceives him, for his conception of human nature is simply a generalization of his own professed degeneracy. Bunin made this point in a letter of 11 February 1917 to the critic A. B. Derman, who had charged him with intervening too blatantly in Sokolovich's conversation with the sailors. He replied to him quite simply: "Is there really much of the author in the arguments of Sokolovich? In my opinion, the words of Sokolovich are fully harmonized with his character."[27]

Between the monologues of Sokolovich, therefore, and those of the colonel, Gorizontov, and Chang there is the basic difference that they are not simply a fictional exposition of the author's personal views, and this difference is directly consequent on the structural innovation that Bunin devised for the work. Having experimented in "The Dreams of Chang" with extending the role of the interpreter, he now extends in a similar manner the role of the principal actor. The actor, Sokolovich, becomes the interpreter of his own actions as related by the omniscient and totally dispassionate narrator. He provides the rationale of his crime before it is actually committed. And since in the previous works of the cycle the relationship between action and interpretation is either wholly or partly one of contrast, it is entirely consistent that the interpreter's views should now diverge radically from those of his creator, just as they would have done, for example, in "The Cup of Life," had the interpreter been Aleksandra, Selikhov, or Iordansky.

Once more, however, the result is far from satisfactory. Stripping the veil from the abstractions, which are otherwise translated into a powerful fictional reality, Sokolovich's rationale is as superfluous as the declarations of Gorizontov. With its almost palpable atmosphere, its expressive variations of narrative rhythm and phrasing, and its intricate patterns of subtly allusive and obliquely related details that punctuate the narrative, in Valentin Katayev's phrase, "like somber chords played by a great organist,"[28] the dramatization of Sokolovich's argument displays many of the most characteristic features of Bunin's mature art. After the hero's exit from the restaurant, the narrative swiftly assumes a distinct momentum, and theory is converted into practice with a chilling sense of inevitability. Particularly striking is the concentration of details that point the way to the dénouement —the transportation of the bright yellow coffin in the opening paragraph, the voice in the nocturnal fog announcing the death of a famous writer under the wheels of a passing carriage, Sokolovich's reminiscence, already cited, of the pleasures of driving, and the carriage that hurtles past him bearing a young officer and his mistress in close embrace. The effects are by no means as obvious as this inventory would suggest, for each detail is deeply submerged in its immediate context, and due recognition of Bunin's skill, as usual, requires a sustained effort of concentration. Yet, despite this skill, the effect of the whole is vitiated by the protagonist's "confession," which injects an element stridently at variance with the predominant character of the work.

The same mixture of contrasting elements, as we have seen, is encountered in each of the works that have so far been discussed. Each presents a different variation of a pattern that involves the combination of a dramatized idea with a direct statement of that idea or of the issues it raises either by a character whose participation in the main dramatic action is minimal or, in the case of "Gnarled Ears," by the protagonist himself. Since Bunin's other works of this period are quite free from direct statements of this kind, his repeated adoption of this pattern, as already suggested, can only be related to the marked intensification of the philosophical element that is the most distinctive common feature of the stories concerned. In only one of his more generalized studies of degeneracy did he depart from his normal practice and allow the narrative and descriptive elements of the fiction to convey the idea without gloss—in the best known of all his stories, "The Gentleman from San Francisco," in which explicit interpretation is wholly replaced by symbol and allusion—and even in this work the voice of the author was silenced only in the last of its four redactions.[29]

The relation of "The Gentleman from San Francisco" to Bunin's studies of the degeneracy of twentieth-century Western man is comparable to that of *The Village* and "A Gay Farmhouse" to his studies of the alienated Russian peasantry. It is the work in which he brings together and integrates all the principal motifs that characterize his treatment of the theme. Basically, the story is a sadly ironic dramatization of the conclusions reached by the colonel in Part II of "The Brothers"—of his contention that the ills of modern civilization are explained primarily by the divorce between man and nature that has ensued from slavery to craving and from a paramount concern with the demands of the self. Here Bunin is no more intent than in the earlier tale on satirizing a specific national type. The figure of the American capitalist interests him solely as a particularly vivid illustration of the extent of this divorce and of its consequences. He is merely a magnified symbol of the fatal insensitivity the colonel imputes to Western civilization in its entirety—of modern man's insensitivity "to life, to the mysteries and chasms that surround us, and to death" (4:276).

The story differs, of course, from *The Village* in many obvious respects—not only in its settings and character types, but more notably in the greater structural cohesion that results from the focus of attention on the drama of a single person and from the centralization of the action in a single climactic event, the hero's death.[30] Even so, the work has a basic affinity with the *poema* in that it is likewise a detailed catalog of the symptoms of psychological disease. Despite the simplicity of its plot and the generalized portrayal of the protagonist, it displays a similar compactness and solidity that have elicited a similar critical response. Yuriy Olesha, for example, reacted with the remark that it "simply oppresses one with its colors," and he continues: "When reading this story, one has the impression that one is present at a performance in which an exceptional skill is being demonstrated—in this case, the skill of defining objects. In addition to the development of the theme and the expression of thoughts, something else takes place in the story which has no direct relation to it—precisely this performance of naming colors. This reduces the merit of the tale."[31] Although, however, it is true that Bunin's manner in *The Village* is reflected in the tendency to accumulate objects in often bewildering abundance and in the length and syntactic complexity of numerous sentences, a proper understanding of his purpose in the work deprives the criticism of much of its force and prompts one to question whether, in fact, any individual detail—with the conspicuous exception of the discordant vignette of the devil toward the end of the story—could be omitted without disturbing the intricate balance and harmony that he achieves between the complex, interlocking patterns of contrasting motifs.[32] And it may be noted in this connection that whereas *The Village* and most of Bunin's other works were progressively abbreviated in the course of their composition, the second redaction of "The Gentleman from San Francisco" was actually longer by a third than the first and was not significantly shortened in the third and fourth.[33]

Describing the journey of the rich American and his family to Europe on board a liner named the *Atlantis*, his death on Capri, and the return of his corpse to the New World, the story is constructed on the basis of a contrast between two distinct modes of existence—that of the hero and that of nature or "natural man"—that are related to one another as parody to reality. Each element of the contrast has its own superstructure of symbols and motifs that are constantly colliding and interacting with those of the other, and the effect of their collisions is the progressive exposure and indictment of the parody. The principal emblems of reality are the sights, sounds, smells, and mysteries of nature—above all, the ocean—and the Christian pantheism of the two mountain dwellers from Abruzzi; those of the parody are the eloquently named *Atlantis*, the simulation of life on its decks, and the various "motifs of restriction" that are woven into the portrait of the protagonist. In addition, the parody is amplified by the brief digression on the emperor Tiberius and the vignette of the vain, indolent Neapolitan fisherman Lorenzo.

As the American critic Seymour Gross has indicated, the entire work hinges to a significant degree on the portrait of the two mountain folk which is pointedly juxtaposed with the passages on Tiberius and Lorenzo after the description of the departure from Capri of the "gentleman's" family and corpse.[34] This short section of the tale is a fully dramatized equivalent of the interpretative sections of the other stories that have been examined, for the two pilgrims are the sole living embodiments in the work of the qualities that distinguish reality from the parody. Above all, they embody that special sensitivity to the visible and invisible realities of existence that is Bunin's invariable index of psychological and physical health, and it is one of the story's many ironies that these two humble peasants are the true heirs, as well as the fellow countrymen, of the saint whose name is borne by the city that has spawned the degenerate hero. Their senses are joyously alive to the full complexity of life—to its beauty and horror, its "good" and "evil"—and in humble acknowledgment of their own insignificance they devoutly chant their paeans to the Virgin and the elements. Here, of course, the terminological trappings of Christianity are no more important than the biblical source of the story's original epigraph. They merely constitute an appropriate formal expression, given the Italian nationality of the two worshipers, of an attitude to life which Bunin consistently refrained from identifying with any individual religion. The parody of life portrayed in the greater part of the tale is explained not by defection from God, but by an atrophy of the sensual awareness that gives man an insight into the true nature of life in general and of his own individual existence.

The gentleman and the inhabitants of the *Atlantis* have irrevocably lost this awareness. They have created for themselves a pagan, artificial reality severed by the steel of the ship's hull and the walls of their hotels from every aspect of life that is not amenable to human or rational control. Insulated from the nonrational kinds of experience that form the basis of moral and aesthetic criteria, they have created a world in which men are distinguished solely by power and wealth and objects by their material value. Everything that cannot be placed in the hierarchies erected on the foundation of these rationally comprehensible criteria is either dismissed or replaced by intelligible substitutes. Thus the concepts, symbols, and myths of Christianity are replaced by man himself and the products of his technical ingenuity. God is superseded by a captain who resembles a huge, pagan idol; hell by the

"submerged womb" of the *Atlantis* with its "infernal," gaping
furnaces; and the serpent by a "gigantic shaft" that is likened
to a "stretching beast" as it revolves with remorseless persistence and exactitude in its "oily bed" (4:328). And the ecstatic
paeans of the two worshipers have their parodic counterpart
in the cacophony of gongs, bells, and "screeching sirens" that
provide the euphonic accompaniment to the gentleman's last
days on earth. Behind the protective dikes of steel and stone
every action and emotion is transformed into an empty or
venal gesture, into a distorted, lifeless travesty of normality.
The emotion of love degenerates into a dance of death per-
formed by a hired pair of lovers or into the morbid infatuation of the gentleman's daughter with a corpselike oriental
prince, and the term "family" becomes a disembodied abstraction connoting neither warmth of feeling nor even co-
habitation. The gentleman and his wife live in separate rooms
and regard their daughter as an objet d'art. Each is the victim
of an oppressive solitude—a solitude so total that after the
gentleman's death no one can remember his name.

The fatal heart attack is merely the last of reality's destructive incursions into the world of the parody. From the
beginning, the dikes are under constant assault. Just as the
Atlantis is lashed by the ocean, so the gentleman is continually
assailed by the seen and unseen emanations of the world beyond the confines of his prison—by his dream, for example,
that presents him with a vision of the Neapolitan hotelier
before he actually meets him and, above all, by nature's irrupting sounds and smells. His first act on entering any room
is to ensure their immediate exclusion. Thus, on arriving
in his hotel room in Naples, he "closed the window which . . .
had let in the smell of the distant kitchen and of the wet
flowers in the garden" (4:318). And just before his death, as
though signaling its imminence, the window again admits
visible and audible evidence of the menace without: "The
gentle air blew on him from out of the darkness; he fancied
that he saw the top of an old palm stretching its seemingly
enormous branches to the stars, and the distant, unchanging
roar of the sea reached his ears" (4:321).

Just as his senses are stifled by his "outer shell" of steel, brick, and glass, so his body is stifled by the "inner shell" of his suffocating attire—by the choking collar that he struggles with on his last night, by the stud that pinches his flabby skin, by his starched underwear, and by the dancing shoes that encase his flat feet. And when death finally comes, it is described primarily as a release from these self-inflicted agonies. First the "inner shell" is cast off: "Many people saw the servants and lackeys tearing off the gentleman's tie and waistcoat, his creased dinner jacket, and even for some reason his dancing shoes" (4:322). Then, as his body lies alone in a secluded room of the hotel, the "outer shell" begins to crumble: "A window was opened in room forty-three. . . . The dead man remained alone in the darkness. Blue stars looked down on him from the sky, and a cricket on the wall began a melancholy, carefree song" (4:323–24). The death of the gentleman, like that of the rickshaw boy in "The Brothers," is a symbolic act of reintegration with the unity of cosmic life. The refinement and luminosity of his lifeless features (4:323) are the mark of his restoration to a state of grace. But for the other travelers, as for the gentleman himself in his last moments of consciousness, his death is an insidious, offensive intrusion of the irrational unknown. Death, like the marks of aging that wring the cry "Horrible!" from the gentleman's lips after his battle with the recalcitrant stud, has no meaning in the context of a purely physical mode of existence. It can only represent a senseless and vicious threat. Panic-stricken, the guests recoil before the evidence of their vulnerability, and although the breach in their shell is swiftly repaired and the illusion restored on the decks of the *Atlantis*, to the ever-present menace of the furious ocean is added that of the corpse beneath their dancing feet. Like the island after which it is named, the ship is doomed to share the fate of its lifeless passenger. With this warning, Bunin concludes his most celebrated study of Western degeneracy.

The charge that has most commonly been leveled against the tale—usually in the context of invidious comparisons with Tolstoy's *The Death of Ivan Il'ich* [Smert' Ivana Il'icha] (1886)—

is that of excessive generalization and abstraction.[35] Critics have lamented Bunin's failure to provide intimate revelations of his hero's thoughts and feelings comparable to those that form such a vital part of Tolstoy's character study. Without due consideration, however, of the salient thematic differences between the two works, it is plainly ludicrous to bewail his different methods of portraiture. A tendency toward generalization, of course, is also detectable in Tolstoy's narrative, but the theme of an individual's gradual enlightenment in the face of unavoidable death obviously required a degree of intimate psychological analysis that would have been completely out of place in Bunin's study of an unrepentant materialist. In life the gentleman undergoes no change whatsoever. He is the same in his violent struggle against death as he is at the beginning—a creature devoid of any significant inner life, whose sole claims to attention are a yellowish, Mongoloid complexion, a clipped silver moustache, an imposing set of large teeth with gold fillings, and a bald head that resembles old ivory. What, we may ask, could convey his insignificance more effectively than the restriction of his portrait to these expressive details of his external appearance? The silence that shrouds the rest of his personality and his inability to articulate anything save monosyllabic directions to waiters and servants are more eloquent than any paragraph of explicit information. Like the coldly objective mode of narration, the silence is itself an important element of characterization that is less indicative of the author's striving for maximum generalization than of the protagonist's yawning inner void.

The portrait of the gentleman offers further evidence of the high degree of expressive economy that Bunin was now capable of achieving in a fully dramatized narrative composition. Yet only in this one instance did the theme of Western degeneracy inspire him to write a work of this kind in which the subtext is wholly submerged in the narrative and descriptive elements of the fiction. Here there is no intermediary between author and reader, no self-revelation of the protagonist or explicit exposition of a philosophy contrasting with that dramatized in the events. The representation of the criteria for indictment in the form of descriptive symbol and in the lyrical vignette of the two pilgrims from Abruzzi endows the tale with a unity or consistency of aesthetic effect that cannot be found in any of the other works to which it is thematically related. In this sense the story is exceptional. But it is already apparent that in the general context of Bunin's art of the period from 1912 to 1916, the complete elimination of "telling" from the tale is by no means untypical. The same feature is encountered consistently not only in contemporaneous stories on the Russian peasantry and landed gentry, but also in those devoted to his third major theme of the period—the theme of love.

7. The Degeneracy of Everyman

In October 1912, Bunin remarked to a correspondent of *Moskovskaya gazeta*: "Hitherto the problem of love has not been developed in my works and I feel a pressing need to write about it."[1] In one sense the statement is misleading, for his development of the theme had not only been fore-shadowed in such works as "In Autumn" and "A Little Romance"; it had already begun in the story "Ignat" that had been serialized in July 1912 in the newspaper *Russkoye slovo* [The Russian Word]. But the interesting point is the compulsion he evidently felt to express himself on the subject at a time when the impression conveyed by the overwhelming majority of his works is that his thoughts were dominated by issues that bore little relation to it. It is true, of course, that the theme is touched on in "The Cup of Life" and "The Brothers" and even in "The Gentleman from San Francisco," but in none of his stories thus far had he really disclosed what he meant by the *problem* of love.

The "pressing need" that impelled him to write his love stories of the period from 1912 to 1916 was essentially the same as that which had given birth, in the decade before the appearance of *The Village*, to the succession of lyrical mono-logues on explicitly universal themes that had culminated in *The Shadow of the Bird*. The two groups of works are basically complementary to his studies of Russian and Western degeneracy in the sense that they transfer the emphasis from the condition of the degenerate to the condition of Everyman. But this does not mean that the theme of degeneracy plays no part in his love stories. On the contrary, it remains Bunin's central theme. But in this context he is concerned with degeneracy of a notably different kind. Hitherto the theme had inevitably imposed limits on his depiction both of man and of nature. We have seen that in the stories devoted to this theme they are simply the negative and positive poles respectively of a recurrent contrast—a contrast between a specific type of human being and a specific image of nature. In the love stories, conversely, there is no delimitation, and even though the contrast, when present, expresses the same human predicament, its implications are quite different and immeasurably broader.

Presenting in these tales his fundamental conception of the human condition and of nature in all its aspects, Bunin portrays the experience of love exclusively as an expression of man's dependence on nature's laws. As before, therefore, the emphasis is predominantly on the sensual character of the experience. His concern as an artist extends only to the kind of love that exposes the subliminal realm of human instinct. Like birth and death, it is represented as an elemental, biological phenomenon that illuminates man's kinship with bird and beast, and as such it is never tainted by the suggestions of profanity and moral guilt that color the portrayals of carnal passion by Turgenev and Tolstoy. For Bunin that which is natural can never be an object of moral censure, particularly when its meed of pleasure and insight is so inestimable. But the rewards of sensual love are much less in evidence than the sufferings it inflicts, and this emphasis is indicative of the contrast between man and nature that lies at the basis of almost all Bunin's love stories and casts the most revealing light on the intrinsically tragic nature of his view of life. The contrast hinges on the tension in man between his instinctive demands as a child of nature and his conscious demands as an individual personality—a tension that, insofar as it distinguishes man from nature, is ipso facto unnatural and thus a mark of degeneracy and a source of pain. In other words, man's reactions to the experience of "natural" love—to the torment of desire, to the brevity or anticlimax of consummation, to the agony of betrayal or loss, and so forth—are represented by Bunin as tragic illustrations of the degeneracy or unnaturalness that is the unalterable fate of man simply by virtue of the qualities that make him an individual human being. While portraying in his other works the fatal consequences of forms of degeneracy that man has the ability to control, in his love stories he dramatizes the degeneracy inherent in the human condition. We may now distinguish, therefore, between two distinct kinds of human degeneracy in his fiction that might be termed for convenience "inherent" and "social" or "cultural."

Since the theme of love enabled Bunin to express more dramatically and comprehensively than any other theme his principal conclusions on life, it is not surprising that it ultimately became almost his only theme. Never before had the theme of love passion played such an extensive or central role in the works of a Russian writer. The settings of his first important love stories, like those of his early works on other themes, are, not unexpectedly, Russian and rural, and although he was later to transpose the theme, even before 1920, to foreign soil (for example, in "The Son" [Syn] [1916]), he was generally less inclined in his love stories to forsake the Russian backdrop than in his other works. There are two obvious reasons for this. In the first place, the theme did not require the support of a foreign setting to highlight its relevance to the world beyond Russia's frontiers. And second, given the importance that he manifestly attached to nature in his love stories not only as a thematic element, but as the primary source of color, tone, and atmosphere, it is natural that he should have retained a preference for the landscapes with which he was most familiar. Even in the love stories, therefore, that he wrote in emigration, non-Russian settings are rare. At the same time, the character of the Russian settings is by no means uniform. Though almost invariably rural, they change considerably from one story to another, and the determining factor here, of course, is the social position of the protagonist. Thus, succumbing to the "pressing need" to write about love in the year 1912, at a time when his attention was still mainly focused on the peasantry, he naturally selected peasants as the central characters of his first two major love stories, "Ignat" and "By the Road," projecting their dramas against the primitive background that runs through all his peasant fiction. In "The Grammar of Love" [Grammatika lyubvi] (1915), by contrast, the main character is a landowner and the setting is consequently a country manor, while the tragedy of Olya Meshcherskaya, a schoolgirl of middle-class parentage, in "Light Breathing" is set in an indeterminate, average country town. Although, therefore, these stories essentially present four variations of a single theme, the first two differ sharply in their atmosphere from the latter two.

In "Ignat" and "By the Road," however, Bunin's choice of characters and setting was determined less by his concern with the peasantry as such than by his wish to expose yet again the peasantry's "social degeneracy." The two stories provide a clear indication of the close connection between the themes of love and social degeneracy that existed in his mind at this time, and thus lend support to our contention that the former was basically complementary to the latter. In "Ignat" the two themes are developed conjointly through the two main characters—the shepherd who gives his name to the work and the servant girl Lyubka—and there is some evidence that Bunin was at first undecided as to which of the themes should take precedence. Such, at least, is the impression conveyed by the changes of title in the early drafts. His first title, "Grushka," taken from the name of Lyubka's predecessor, would suggest that the emphasis was on the theme of the corruption or degeneration of love that is developed through Lyubka in the final version. The second title, "Love" [Lyubov'], however, suggests that the accent had already been transferred to the universal theme, and Bunin finally removed all ambiguity with a title that indicates the character whose drama embodies this theme. While synthesizing, therefore, the two dominant themes of Bunin's prerevolutionary art, the story of Ignat's craving for Lyubka, their marriage, and its catastrophic outcome owes its special position among his works to the fact that here his conception of the "problem" of love is dramatized for the first time. In addition, it is an outstanding example of the distinctive type of narrative that he evolved in the years following the completion of *Sukhodol*.

Although it consists of only six chapters, the tale is con-

siderably longer than most of Bunin's works of this or any
other period, but its length in no sense diminishes its impact.
From the opening portraits of the two main characters and
the descriptions of the Panin estate, Izvaly, where they work,
he demonstrates once more his unique ability to generate a
sense of tension simply from the structural rhythms of the
narrative—from the alternations of action and descriptive
digressions. In "A Spring Evening" and "Gnarled Ears," the
effect is mainly achieved by the gathering momentum of the
crescendo that resolves itself in the violence of the climax and
by the sprinkling of allusive details that knit the descriptive
passages into the narrative of events. In the much longer
"Ignat," Bunin duplicates this procedure, constructing the
work on the basis of two climaxes, the first leading directly
to the second. The first—the gratification of Ignat's desire
for Lyubka and their marriage—coincides with the end of
chapter II, while the second—his discovery of Lyubka in a
compromising situation with a visiting merchant whom he
ultimately murders—marks the culmination of the events related in chapters III, IV, and V. Chapter VI is the first example in Bunin's works of the kind of postscript he was to
adapt to a wide variety of purposes in his stories of the next
three years. The result is basically a two-part narrative that
involves successive transitions from tranquillity to contrasting
forms of emotional derangement, the one expressing itself in
ecstasy and the other leading to death, while the coda denotes
the reverse transition to the gentle rhythms of normal experience. The contrast between the two climaxes prefigures
the illusion of an almost causal connection between love and
death that is created in most of Bunin's later love stories.

Although, however, the two transitions give contrasting
results, they resemble one another in the sense that they both
involve a progressive convergence of hero and heroine. For
all her physical activity, Lyubka is psychologically a completely
static character. The dynamic element is introduced by the
primitive urges of Ignat—by his lust and his craving for revenge that activate the two transitions. Each of the two sequences traces the gradual movement of Ignat toward the

object of his desire, in the first instance as a lover, in the second as a destroyer. In each case, the crescendo of tension reflects the surge of emotion within the hero that transforms him from a sluggish, dull-witted shepherd into an irresistible automaton. And just as the leisurely coda restores a general sense of normality, so it depicts Ignat, in the last words of the tale, applying handfuls of snow to his temples in a desperate endeavor to recover the innocuous personality that collapsed under the assault of his intoxicated senses.

The process of Ignat's "depersonalization" is vividly recorded in the first section of the work that embraces the first two chapters. The impression is one of diffuseness, yet every scene and every detail seems to contribute in some measure to Ignat's sensual awakening against the bleak background of the snow-covered fields. The fleeting proximity of Lyubka in the servants' hall instantly ignites his sense of smell: "There was a smell of the kitchen, of premature spring freshness, of the dogs whose eyes burned like pairs of reddish emeralds and moved about before him, but he noticed only the sweet, intoxicating smell of perfume and the even more intoxicating smell of hair, pomade of cloves, and a woolen dress soaked in sweat under the arms" (4:8–9). In Lyubka's absence, his attention reverts to the dogs—above all, to the beauty of the black-eyed borzoi Strelka, and as though competing for her attentions with her handsome, red-haired mate, he strives to lure the bitch into a secluded barn. As the chill is leavened by the first breaths of spring, the same impersonal force of desire dictates the actions of both man and dog, and the bounds between the human and nonhuman are momentarily breached. With each passing day, Ignat's agony is intensified. He witnesses the mating of the cattle and the willing submission of Lyubka to her playful young masters, and finally relinquishing the last vestiges of self-control, he hurls himself at Lyubka's body only to halt at the last moment in perplexity, as though briefly waking from a hypnotic trance. The door is slammed in his face, and in despair he seeks refuge in vodka and in the arms of the demented beggar woman Fiona. But the setback is only temporary, for as if by design, fate soon presents him with an opportunity to redeem himself. While searching one day in the forest for Fiona, he suddenly meets Lyubka, and nature's will is finally done.

The encounter with Lyubka results in her pregnancy and a marriage that ensures the resumption of Ignat's suffering. Their life together continues, in fact, for only three months before he is obliged to embark on four years of military service, but the period is more than enough for him to bring about a miscarriage with the beatings that he inflicts on her for her past misdeeds with the young Panins. The episode foreshadows the ensuing sequence of events. For Ignat, the four-year interval is an agony of suspicion; for Lyubka, it is a heaven-sent opportunity to revert to her former ways. With its end, the process of convergence is renewed, and disaster is sensed from the outset. The return of Ignat to Izvaly, first by train and then by foot, is a subtly contrived arpeggio of tension and rising emotion that is again offset by the chill of the snow-covered fields and nocturnal frost. References to the landscape repeatedly interrupt the account of his advance, delaying the dénouement and evoking a sense of his mounting impatience, but the sight of his goal lends firmness to his step, and, like Sokolovich striding down the Nevsky Prospect, he rapidly assumes the guise of an implacable nemesis. The prose with its rhyming adverbs and isosyllabic adjectives reproduces the rhythm of his march: "Shagal on tvyordo, rovno i sporo. . . . V pole bylo pusto, myortvo i tikho" (4:20).[2] In a fever of expectation, he peers through the window, observes his wife and her latest admirer, and awaits his moment to intervene. The hours pass, and the frost numbs his flesh, but his body is now little more than an instrument of his raging passions. When the moment duly arrives, he bursts through the door only to find the merchant prostrate after a stroke and Lyubka applying a wet towel to his face. Taking a step toward her, he draws back the axe in his hand, but even in the face of death Lyubka outwits him: "At the last second she riveted him to the spot with a firm voice. 'The sin is mine,' she said rapidly. 'Kill him off quickly. We will be rich. We will say that the stroke felled him. Quickly!'" (4:31–32). Transfixed by the motionless stare of her piercing black eyes, he instantly yields, and the butt of the axe descends on the dripping white towel. The arpeggio breaks off abruptly.

Although it announces the discovery of the corpse, the coda adds nothing to the drama of events. Yet to minimize its importance in the manner of Aykhenval'd, who found the rallentando pointless and irritating,[3] is to display a complete misunderstanding of Bunin's purpose in the tale. Its function cannot be appreciated without considering once more the details of setting and landscape that abound in every chapter. Like "Zakhar Vorob'yov" and "The Last Day," the story is strewn with copious references to the movement of the heavenly bodies and the alternations of night and day, while the detailed chronicling of the rotation of the seasons is reminiscent of "The Epitaph." Every page presents evidence of an intriguing concern with time and with the reflections in nature of its passing. In chapters I and II, for example, we are successively informed that "it was the eve of the Day of Forgiveness" (4:9), that "it was the Day of Forgiveness" (4:11), and that "Holy Week had passed" (4:14). Ignat's arrival in the village after his nocturnal walk from the station coincides with "the crowing of the cocks" (4:21); his vigil outside the house is interrupted by "the second crowing of the cocks" (4:29); and the coda begins with the phrase: "At the third crowing of the cocks" (4:32). The changing positions of the moon on the fateful last night are similarly noted with punctilious exactitude. Thus the beginning of the vigil is marked by the detail: "The radiant night . . . was increasing its power and attaining to its maximum beauty and might" (4:24), while five pages later the author observes: "The power, light, and beauty of the night began to weaken. The moon was turning pale and inclining toward the west. Orion with its three diagonal stars standing low like silver buttons on the southwestern horizon was now closer and brighter. A shadow fell from the servants' hall over which the moon was inclining and embraced half the farmstead" (4:29).

The contribution these details make to the buildup of tension by retarding the onward rush of the narrative has already been mentioned, but this does not exhaust their role. The combined effect of these visual and auditory indicators of time's relentless flow is to create in the background to the narrative a pervasive sense of ceaseless, regular movement or rhythm against which Bunin projects the rhythm of the action itself. Occasionally, especially in the first two chapters, the two rhythms seem to coincide, but the point of the work lies in their more frequent divergences, in the discords between the calm, repetitive rhythms of nature and the crescendos that record the human experience of love. Representing sensual love as a manifestation of man's subjection to nature, Bunin highlights with every expressive device at his disposal man's "unnatural" experience of this subjection. Submission to the demands of the senses is portrayed as an act of self-surrender to a nightmare or delirium that fatally shatters the harmony between man and nature. Hence the reference to Ignat's insensitivity to time as he waits outside the house: "He did not notice time. He was wholly absorbed in his passionate desire for his suspicions to be confirmed" (4:29). The juxtaposition of this statement with the reference, which it directly precedes, to Orion and the waning beauty of the night succinctly conveys the conflict of rhythms that lies at the basis of the tale—the conflict between the invariable rhythms of nature and the feverish, disjointed rhythms of human ecstasy and suffering. The resolution of the conflict is recorded in the coda. The crescendo of the human drama has now passed. The discordant counterpoint is silenced, and nothing disturbs the rhythms of nature and normal experience. "In the west," we read, "the presence of night and its secret could still be felt" (4:32), but slowly the day dawns, and the merchant's servant, unaware of the night's happenings, prepares the horse for departure. The daily round on the estate begins once more, and against this background of life's normal rhythms Ignat reemerges from his nightmare. But the nightmare was reality, and the corpse remains to signal the tragedy.

In the course of the next forty years, Bunin was to write some fifty stories on the basis of the conception of love that he dramatizes in "Ignat," constantly surprising the reader with his different approaches to the theme, with the diversity of effects that he obtains by emphasizing different aspects or phases of the experience, and with his endless variations of atmosphere. His prerevolutionary love stories provide an illuminating foretaste of this virtuosity. Each tale creates a totally distinctive fictional reality that may well resemble that of another work in individual details but can never be confused with it. The points in common, for example, between "By the Road" and "Ignat" are by no means confined to Bunin's repeated concern, in his portrayal of the young girl Parashka, with the process of sexual awakening. Again the social milieu is that of the peasantry, and again the theme of social degeneracy occasionally intrudes, above all, in the characterization of Parashka's widowed father Ustin. In the opening paragraphs of the story, we are informed that Ustin had "long ceased to live like a peasant. He lived not by the land, but by lending money at interest" (4:176). As always in Bunin's peasant fiction, abandonment of the land is reflected in psychic abnormality, implicitly explaining Ustin's "unnatural" relationship with his daughter which in chapter VII almost culminates in incest. The fate of Parashka, however, is affected by her father's degeneracy in a more significant way, for the unnatural circumstances of life to which she is condemned by his abandonment of the land play an important part in determining the attitude to love that leads her to ruin. Not for nothing does Bunin hint at these circumstances in his title, which alludes as much to the psychological as to the physical effects of Ustin's "emancipation."

His home, we read, "was by the main Novosil'sk road.[4] The place that he chose for himself on leaving his masters was desolate and uninhabited" (4:176). On one level, the image of the road, which runs through the entire work, is symbolic of Ustin's renunciation of the stable, settled way of life of his ancestors, of his commitment to a nonpeasant way of life that involves constant travel and long absences from home. On another, it alludes to the predicament of Parashka, to the solitude in which he leaves her, and thus to the elevated, unrealistic notion of love that she conceives in this solitude. The road becomes a symbol of her dream of happiness through love. The travelers wending their way along it seem to her to be "making for some distant happy land" (4:180), and when it suddenly confronts her with the horse thief Nikanor, her dream dictates her reaction. But from Nikanor she learns the reality of love, and the discord between reality and dream predetermines the tragic dénouement—Parashka's murder of Nikanor, her flight, and her violent capture.

In "By the Road" there is no concluding rallentando. The story ends at the highest point of tension with the complete realization of the presentiments that Bunin arouses in chapter I with the aid of characteristic anticipatory details— the rumor that Ustin had killed his wife in jealousy, the old man's warning to Parashka of the dire consequences of involvement with Nikanor, the romanticized picture of such a fate to which her imagination promptly gives birth, and the brief portrait of Nikanor's horse. As portrayed in chapter I, the horse, a Kirgiz mare, directly prefigures the deranged Parashka who crushes Nikanor's skull in chapter VII. When the mare first appears with Nikanor on its back, Parashka's attention is drawn to the rebellious spirit it displays despite its obvious exhaustion and to the wounds it has inflicted on itself in its attempts to unseat its vicious master. By chapter VII, Nikanor has asserted his mastery over Parashka, and his new victim reacts with similar violence. After the murder, the parallelism between girl and horse becomes fully explicit. For both, the crime is an act of liberation—for Parashka from grotesque reality, for the mare from oppressive captivity— and together they flee into the steppe: "Parashka leapt up, sped like an arrow from the stall, and rushed to the gate. Nikanor's horse, which was standing by the gate, snorted and flew out onto the road together with her. Raising dust and thundering along with its cart it struck out in one direction, toward the town, into the shining, whitish distance beyond the pass, while Parashka went in the other, across the road, toward the fields of rye" (4:199–200).

Like *Sukhodol* and "Ignat," "By the Road" is one of the many works of Bunin that prompt comparisons with the techniques of musical composition. Recurrent details assume the resonance of motifs, contributing to the single crescendo that spans the whole work, and again the cyclic rhythms of nature provide a contrasting counterpoint to the violent rhythms of human experience. But now, the discord is unresolved. Parashka's rejection of the reality of love, even in the form of Nikanor, is a rejection of nature, and it is entirely consistent that nature at the end, in the form of the fields into which she flees, should prove equally oppressive. Shortly before her flight, the fields are described as follows: "It seemed as if the sea of ripe corn had converged. It formed a tighter circle round the road and farmstead, and the thick dust of the road shone with a dull light. And the sandy color of the corn as it bowed low its heavy ears and froze in the silence, in the thick, hot air, gave an impression of ghastly, oppressive heat" (4:198). For five days Parashka struggles to break out of the siege, but the fields, like Nikanor, hold her captive, and the grip of the new oppressor cannot be loosened. The story ends: "It took them five days to catch her. In her attempts to beat them off she showed a terrible strength and bit the three peasants who twisted her hands with a new length of twine" (4:200).

Thus the ending is quite different from that of "Ignat," and the difference, of course, reflects the difference of character between the two protagonists, one of whom, Ignat, remains throughout a slave to his passion, while the other seeks refuge in futile rebellion. More important, however, than the difference is the tragic irony that the effects of both submission and rebellion are the same—murder and self-destruction. In both instances the gratification of desire is the source of destructive human emotions, jealousy and revulsion, which are implicitly contrasted as unnatural with the even rhythms of the natural process. Exploring in his first two major love stories the consequences of contrasting responses to the experience of sensual love, Bunin expresses the bitter conclusion that for man the outcome of both is madness and pain.

"By the Road" was the last story in which Bunin at-

tempted to combine the theme of love with the theme that
had hitherto dominated his fiction. He evidently concluded
that extraneous thematic assistance was no longer required to
enable him to transmute his distinctive approach to the theme
of love into significant works of fiction. At the same time, he
was perhaps aware that the universal implications of the experience of his protagonists had been somewhat obscured by
the presence of the social-psychological theme. His next love
story, therefore, "The Grammar of Love," is not only free
from serious distractions from the central theme; as its title
suggests, it purports to be a kind of definitive work in the
sense that it distills and synthesizes those aspects of the experience of love that Bunin regarded as basic and quintessential. Having presented two variations on a given formula,
he now proceeds to the formula itself, and although the formula is fictionalized and by no means unadorned, incidental
elements are greatly reduced. The result is a very different
kind of work from the two that precede it. The dramatic
mode is now temporarily abandoned. The story records not
the evolution of a tragedy, but the hero's attempts to understand a tragedy that has already taken place. The emphasis,
accordingly, is on the past, and the role of the hero, the young
landowner Ivlev,[5] is entirely reflective.

The combination of these two factors inevitably imparts
to the story a narrative tone frequently reminiscent of that of
his early fiction. As always when Bunin contemplates the past,
even through the eyes of an intermediary and even when the
past is fictional, the lyrical element is notably enhanced. The
result is the tendency of critics to regard the tale as marking,
in the words of a recent Soviet commentator, "a transitional
stage between the lyrical tales of the early period . . . and the
objective narratives of his later novellas."[6] Since, however, the
complete abandonment of the objective or impersonal mode
makes the story unique in the context of Bunin's fiction of the
period from 1912 to 1916, it would be more appropriate to
relate the resurgence of the lyrical element to the specific
purpose he had in mind when writing it.

Like *Sukhodol*, the story hinges on the resolution of a

mystery—the mystery of the legendary romance between the landowner Khvoshchinsky and his maid Lushka, which Bunin seems to have based on a real-life episode[7]—and relates the stages by which the reflective hero gradually penetrates to its heart. The beginning is slow and descriptive. It depicts the country scene witnessed by Ivlev as he journeys by carriage to a distant part of his estate. Eventually, at the request of his driver, who is anxious to rest the horses, he decides to pay his respects to the count who owns the adjoining estate, and in the course of a conversation with the count's wife he learns of Khvoshchinsky's recent death. The news immediately stirs recollections of the deceased's renowned love for the humble girl who had died in early youth, and on taking his leave, Ivlev resolves to visit "the empty shrine of the mysterious Lushka." As the carriage plows its way along the crude tracks and across the neglected fields of Khvoshchinsky's estate, he continues his reflections on the landowner's life and character:

What kind of a man was this Khvoshchinsky? Was he a madman or simply a man whose soul was stunned and focused on a single object? According to the tales of old landowners, contemporaries of Khvoshchinsky, he was once reputed in the district to be a man of rare intelligence. And suddenly this love came down on him, this Lushka, followed by her sudden death, and everything went to rack and ruin. He shut himself up in the house, in the room in which Lushka lived and died, and for more than twenty years he sat on her bed. He wore a hole in the mattress on Lushka's bed and attributed to Lushka's influence literally everything that happened in the world. [4:300]

Khvoshchinsky's state of mind is the mystery to which his journey, he hopes, may provide the key. The descriptive manner is now resumed. The journey, the lands of Khvoshchinsky's estate, the external appearance of the house, its interior are all described in meticulous detail. Finally, Ivlev is led to the inner sanctum, the library, where he discovers, in the slender tome that gives the tale its title, a compilation of aphorisms on the nature of the tender passion that transformed Khvoshchinsky into a lifeless marionette.

The story is divisible, therefore, into four unequal sections comprising alternations of description and reflection that culminate in the discovery of the revealing volume. The function of the opening descriptive passage is primarily contrastive. The fine weather, the immaculate roads, and the vast expanses of corn and rye convey a sense of order and well-being that clearly contrasts with the later spectacle of misery and desolation. The conversation with the countess provides both the jolt that propels the narrative forward and the pretext for the initial reference to Khvoshchinsky's curious life, which is recounted in greater detail in the course of Ivlev's subsequent meditations. The extended descriptive passage that follows is a typical example of Bunin's mature technique of oblique psychological characterization. The house and estate of Khvoshchinsky are patently externalizations of their owner's state of mind. They are the outer façade of the inner man, the physical manifestations of his crippling disease. Like the bird cage and the bag containing a live quail that catch Ivlev's eye in the porch, the secluded house with its few small windows is a graphic symbol of love as a stifling obsession that severs man, even "a man of rare intelligence," from the normal processes of life, condemning him to an existence that is "neither sleep nor vigil; it lies between them, and in man it causes understanding to border on madness." With the aid of these words from Yevgeniy Boratynsky's poem "The Last Death" [Poslednyaya smert'], Bunin defines the "existence" not only of Khvoshchinsky, but of all the devotees and victims of Eros, whose agonies and ecstasies echo through his works of the next thirty years. All are imprisoned in this intermediate sphere of consciousness to which man is eternally prey by virtue of the truths enshrined in the "grammar of love":

Love is not a simple episode in our lives. . . . Our reason is in conflict with our heart and cannot prevail over it. Women are never so strong as when they are armed with weakness. We worship a woman because she holds sway over our dream of perfection. Vanity chooses; true love does not choose. The beautiful woman must take second place; the first belongs to the woman of charm. It is this woman who becomes the sovereign of our heart. Before we are fully aware of her ourselves, our heart becomes a prisoner of love forever. [4:306]

Since the narrative art of Bunin usually shuns the definitive statement, it was natural that, confronted here with the need to define, he should borrow his definitions from a poet whom he greatly admired and from an eighteenth-century treatise. His usual objective in the composition of a story, as we have seen, was to convey a sense of the mystery of life and human nature simply by the selection and arrangement of his fictional material and by the allusive description of external forms. The method may justly be compared, in part, to that of an advocate charged with the task of conveying an impression of elusive truth by means of suggestively combined fragments of circumstantial evidence, and it seems hardly coincidental that material for two of his best-known works —"Gnarled Ears" and *The Cornet Yelagin Affair*—was drawn from contemporary trials. This process of combining or piecing together often gives his stories their distinctive mosaiclike character, and the parallel with the procedures of advocacy acquires added cogency in the light of his habit of presenting illuminating insights into the minds and behavior of his heroes and heroines in the form of evidence submitted to courts of inquiry. This device was first used in 1912 in his story "Yermil," another penetrating study of the devious mind of the alienated Russian peasant. Four years later he employed it once more in the tale Konstantin Paustovsky has described as "one of the most lyrical stories in world literature,"[8] "Light Breathing."

Although this story was written, in Bunin's words, "with that delightful rapidity which came to me at certain happy moments of my writing" (9:369), he appears to have considered it inferior to "The Grammar of Love" and was surprised that criticism did not share his view.[9] Certainly it differs from the earlier tale in many obvious respects, for, dispensing with the services of an intermediary, he now returns to a more impersonal type of narrative. Events are no longer regarded solely from the fixed and distant standpoint of a fictional observer, but here are expanded into a sequence that embraces almost half the work. But again they are drawn from the past and lyrically apprehended from the vantage point of the present, for Bunin readopts in this story the procedure that had served him so well in "Zakhar Vorob'yov"—the preannouncement of the dénouement. Once more the reader is aware from the outset that the events will culminate in the death of the protagonist, and with the aid of this device Bunin achieves perhaps the most moving juxtaposition in all his fiction of life and death, immense vitality and the chill of the grave.

His point of departure, when writing the story, was his recollection of a visit to a small cemetery on Capri, where he had encountered the grave of a young girl adorned with her photograph.[10] The photograph inspired the conception of Olya Meshcherskaya, and the story begins with a succinct description of Olya's grave. Only two features are indicated in the opening sentence—the mound of clay and the new oak cross on the grave, which is described simply as "strong, heavy, smooth" (4:355). The positioning and simple juxtaposition of these three adjectives at the end of the sentence add notably to the impression of weight, immobility, and solemnity, and the same impression is conveyed by the rhythm of the sentence, the accumulation of words with stress on the initial syllable: "Na kladbishche, nad svezhey glinyanoy nasyp'yu stoit novyy krest iz duba, krepkiy, tyazholyy, gladkiy."[11] All four nouns and five of the six adjectives display the same accentological feature. In the next three lines, the initially established tone is reinforced by references to the gray April weather, the tombstones visible through the denuded trees, and the gusts of wind that extract a ringing sound from the porcelain medallion bearing Olya's photograph at the foot of the cross. This final detail may be seen as an allusion to her ringing laughter in life, just as the wind, to which in life she is compared (4:356), perhaps alludes to her former boundless energy. But the detail that receives particular emphasis is taken from the photograph—the expression of joy and vitality in the girl's eyes[12] that contrasts sharply with the oppressive lifelessness of the environment in which her body now lies. Thereafter, this leitmotiv of her characterization, which is used to motivate the transition to recollections of her life, is complemented by emphasis of three dominant features—her physical beauty, her carefree attitude to life (to which the title of the story seemingly refers[13]), and her speed and lightness of movement, which are effectively offset by the impression of weight and immobility conveyed by her grave.

The tragic irony of the story resides in the fact that Olya's beauty, vitality, and "light breathing" bring about her death. Indeed, the impression created by the succession of briefly sketched scenes and episodes from her life is that the closer she is to death, the greater becomes her joie de vivre. The first hint of imminent disaster is subtly inserted into this sequence of scenes by the passing reference to the effect of her beauty on the schoolboy Shenshin, to his despairing reaction to her fickleness, and to his attempted suicide. At first reading, these details appear merely to add another facet to Olya's portrait, but less than two pages later we realize that their primary function is to foreshadow the dénouement. Shenshin is driven by frustrated love to turn his hand against himself, but his feelings could have expressed themselves in a desire for revenge.

The episode involving Shenshin is recounted so concisely that it in no way arrests the tempo of the narrative or interrupts the characterization "through action" of the heroine. The same tempo is maintained for the whole of the next paragraph until, like Olya herself, who is described as "speeding like a whirlwind" in flight from her pursuing friends, it is brought to an abrupt halt by the announcement that the headmistress wishes to see her. The portrait of the headmistress, which is plainly intended to contrast with that of her vivacious pupil, is as condensed and expressive as the opening description of the cemetery and grave. Again the salient features are combined in a single sentence: "The headmistress, youthful but gray-haired, was sitting calmly at her desk under the czar's portrait with her knitting in her hands" (4:356). Like Olya herself, she is youthful, but her gray hair is the mark of the discipline she imposes on her youth, just as the portrait of the czar is symbolic of the authority she wields over others. The detail of her knitting perhaps alludes to the thread of life—to the threads of the lives she controls and, above all, to the thread that is about to be severed, that of the young girl who now stands before her. The conversation between them discloses the prelude to the tragedy. Criticized for the immodesty of her dress and behavior, Olya politely asserts her rights not as a girl, but as a woman, and names as her seducer the headmistress's fifty-six-year-old brother, Aleksey Mikhaylovich Malyutin, a friend of her father. To this grotesque illustration of the blindness of passion is now added a revelation of its destructiveness, for the next sentence reports Olya's death at the hands of an "ugly Cossack officer of plebeian appearance" (4:357) whom she had promised to marry and then rejected. Unlike Shenshin, the officer turns his hand against the cause of his despair.

The swift and dramatic transition from the presentiment of disaster to the disaster itself is followed by the officer's account under questioning of the events that impelled him to commit the crime and afterward by quotations from Olya's diary that fill in the details of the episode confessed to the headmistress. The circle is finally closed in the last section of the tale by the reversion of the scene to the cemetery. The length of this final section, which introduces a totally new character in the person of a former schoolmistress of the heroine, who is given to visiting her grave every Sunday, at first seems somewhat mystifying, like that of the coda of "Ignat." But this postscript is significant for two reasons. Not only does the schoolmistress add substantially to our mental image of Olya with her recollection of a conversation she once overheard; her reaction to the tragedy is an important element in the lyrical development of the theme. Though much more limited, her role is comparable to that of Natal'ya in *Sukhodol*, and with the aid of her reactions Bunin significantly reinforces the effect that he seeks mainly to capture in the tale by compositional means. She exclaims: "This wreath, this mound, this oak cross! Is it possible that beneath it lies the girl whose eyes shine so immortally from this convex porcelain medallion? How can one associate with this pure gaze the horror that is now linked with the name of Olya Meshcherskaya?" (4:359). The source of the horrifying discord, Bunin implies, is that "light breathing," that emotional fickleness or levity to which each part of the tale directs our attention from some new, unexpected angle. Like Parashka, Olya is portrayed as an innocent victim of subconscious forces that lead her irresistibly to destruction, and she could easily have shared Parashka's fate. The extract from her diary makes it clear that after her submission to Malyutin she was quite capable, like Parashka, of killing her seducer. "I feel such loathing for him," she writes, "that I cannot survive this" (4:359). But her "light breathing" not only ensures her survival; it also dictates the act of betrayal that brings her to her grave. To the end, she remains a pawn in thrall to this impersonal force that has taken possession of her body and mind, and her death, like the suicide of the rickshaw boy in "The Brothers," is represented as a release. The final sentence reads: "And now this light breathing has again dispersed in the world, in this cloudy sky and this cold spring wind" (4:360).

"The aim of literature," Bunin wrote in 1912, "is to make a direct emotional impact. It is precisely this emotional, organic element that is lacking in the works of contemporary writers, whereas the cerebral element is present in excess" (9:542). We have seen that the emotional impact of "Light Breathing" is mainly achieved by abrupt juxtapositions of events, scenes, and revelations produced by rapid transitions to different points in time. The opening scene in the cemetery is followed first of all by a selective, chronologically ordered account of the events that lead to Olya's death. But before the linkup with the present is completed, the temporal sequence is again reversed, first by the officer's description of the events that precede the dénouement, and then by Olya's account in her diary of her earlier encounter with Malyutin. The present then irrupts once more, in the form of the schoolmistress and

the second description of the cemetery and grave, only to
yield, in the schoolmistress's reminiscences, to yet another
excursion into the past before finally reestablishing itself in
the last sentence. The six-page story, therefore, contains six
abrupt changes of temporal perspective that not only maintain the reader in a state of continual surprise, but also convey
a volume of information that seems remarkably dispropor-
tionate to the size of the tale. Within the frame of the two
scenes in the cemetery, he recounts and illuminates from
a diversity of angles the mystery of an entire human life,
extracting from it a timeless beauty and alluding to the in-
herently tragic nature of life in general. Even more notable,
however, is the lyricism—a scarcely definable combination
of sadness and "poetic" exultation in the strangeness and
beauty of life—with which Bunin is able to imbue the story
while maintaining a pose of complete impassivity. The personal views and emotions of the author-narrator are never
explicitly disclosed. Restricting himself to the cataloging of
events and to the visual portrayal of characters and scenes, he
assumes no personal responsibility for the most revealing insights into Olya's mind and conduct, preferring to entrust
them to rumor (for example, the rumors about Shenshin),
to the heroine herself (her diary and recollected conversation), or to other characters in the fiction (the Cossack officer
and the schoolmistress). His personal "presence" is detectable
solely in the expressive pattern of the structural mosaic—in
the disruptions of chronology and abrupt transitions that give
the tale its most telling effects.

The other major love story written by Bunin in 1916,
"The Son," shares with "Light Breathing" a number of the
features that have been noted, in particular, its highly disciplined style and the tendency to bolster the illusion of objectivity by assigning revealing observations and part of the
responsibility for recounting the main events to characters in
the fiction. It is also another work in which the most dramatic
events are related in the form of evidence addressed to a
court of inquiry. The theme is essentially the same—once
more, the capitulation of reason to uncontrollable impulse

—but it is complicated in this tale not only by the more prominent role of the principal male character, but also by the introduction of a reaction to the experience of love that differentiates the work from all Bunin's other love stories. Certainly the most obvious source, however, of the story's distinctive coloring and atmosphere is its foreign setting— the Algerian city of Constantine, which Bunin had visited in 1910. In this setting, we are introduced to the central character, Mme Marot, who has lived there for fourteen years immersed in the chores and responsibilities of a typical middleclass housewife, and much of the work depicts her life as wife and mother and seems to confirm A. Tvardovsky's judgment that for Bunin married life was synonymous with tedium and vulgarity.[14] More precisely, he seems to have regarded the institution of marriage as merely another reflection of the human tragedy, as another form of degeneracy, and employing once more the symbolic contrast that recurs in "The Cup of Life," he sets out in "The Son" to demonstrate its ineffectuality in the face of the irrational urges of human nature.

"The Son" is another of Bunin's stories that are bathed in the searing heat and dazzling light of the merciless sun, and the important role he assigns to the sun no doubt explains, in part, his choice of setting. The life of Mme Marot, however, is conducted behind a barrier of walls and Venetian blinds. Throughout the fourteen years of her married life, we read, she "led the unsociable life to which the wives of all Europeans are condemned in the colonies. On Sundays she invariably went to church; on weekdays she went out rarely and kept to a small, select circle" (4:330). The reference to her weekly visits to church is one of those eloquent details that can easily be overlooked in a Bunin story. It alludes, of course, to the religious and moral beliefs that underlie her unquestioning devotion to the execution of her marital and parental responsibilities, beliefs that have been deeply instilled in her from childhood. "Mme Marot," the story begins, "was born and grew up in Lausanne in a strict and honorable family" (4:329). An obvious connection is thus forged between the heroine's Christian morality and the remorseless round of daily tasks that have hastened the passing of her youth and shielded her from the assaults of the sun.

The life of Mme Marot has been reduced to a repetitive sequence of lifeless conventions from which the needs of the body have been virtually eliminated,[15] and she offers no sign of discontent. The narrative continues: "The days passed monotonously, but no one observed any indication that Mme Marot was oppressed by the monotony of life. Her character showed no signs of heightened sensitivity or excessive irritability" (4:331). Clearly, however, these remarks would be pointless unless appearances were deceptive and Bunin immediately prepares the way for the collapse of the façade by recounting her husband's recollection of an episode from their early married life: "He was surprised by only one occurrence: once in Tunis an Arab conjuror hypnotized her so quickly and deeply that she recovered only with difficulty. But that was during the crossing from France. Since then she had not experienced such abrupt lapses of will or such abnormal susceptibility" (4:331). It emerges, therefore, that the respect for religious and moral law to which Mme Marot has been studiously conditioned by her upbringing rests on the foundation of an abnormal, congenital weakness of will of which she is totally unconscious, and by the third page of the story, when her "small, select circle" is suddenly invaded by the nineteen-year-old Emile du Buys, the son of an old friend, it is already apparent that the dutiful housewife is soon to be transformed.

Emile's role in the story, however, is not confined to that of merely reanimating the heroine's subconscious personality. The ensuing drama is as meaningful for him as it is for her, and his characterization is developed at some length. The exceptional feature of his portrait is the strong vein of satire that runs through it—a rare element in Bunin's fiction—and it was presumably the satirical purpose that caused him to choose the years 1889–90 as the time when the events of the story take place. The portrait is used as a means of lampooning the decadent fin de siècle poetry, inspired by the Parisian avant-garde, of which Emile considers himself a worthy exponent and which he is given to reciting "with a kind of somnambulistic expressiveness" (4:332), accompanying his recitations with plaintive entreaties to some nameless, ethereal female to join him in death. But these caustic allusions by Bunin to the poetry of his symbolist contemporaries should not be regarded as satire for its own sake. Their presence in the work is entirely justified and consistent with his purpose of confronting innocent, naive illusion with ecstatic and terrifying reality, for Emile's poetic entreaties to the lover of his imagination are finally answered by the real-life figure of Mme Marot. The dénouement signifies the simultaneous collapse of two distinct, but equally superficial, conceptions of life—the "poetic" conception of Emile and the moral-religious conception of the heroine.

The inner conflict between the conscious and subconscious levels of Mme Marot's personality is externalized with Bunin's customary subtlety. Consciously she has no doubt that her feelings for Emile are simply maternal, that they are explained by the yearning for a son of her own which she later confesses to her unresponsive husband after Emile's return to Paris to complete his studies (4:335). But a totally different impression is conveyed by the unusual concern for her appearance that she begins to display soon after Emile's arrival and by the generally rejuvenating effect on her of his presence; by the time of his departure, the illusion of maternal feeling is already crumbling. Her conflict is mirrored in the two telegrams she sends to Paris—the one confessing to Emile her distraction, the other imploring him to stay away and to think of her solely as a mother. At this point, Bunin contrives, in characteristically oblique fashion, to reemphasize once more the complete dependence of man at the most decisive moments in his life on the uncontrollable forces of his own nature and of the world about him.

As though sensing the imminence of the heroine's submission, the sun returns to Constantine as winter yields to the first days of spring, and its intervention is decisive. The episode in Tunis is swiftly reenacted. While she is sitting one morning in her garden and recalling that experience—the "delectable terror and blissful lack of will of those moments which seemed to presage death" (4:336)—her attention is suddenly drawn to the reflection of the sunlight in a spoon standing in a glass of water, and the effect of the light, like that of the conjuror's eyes, is to send her instantly into a deep hypnotic coma from which she eventually wakes to find Emile standing before her. This second collapse of Mme Marot's will is clearly intended to denote her release from self-deception, from the tension between reality and illusion.[16] Acting now with bewildering single-mindedness, she accompanies Emile to his villa and allows him to embrace her. But the surrender of her will signifies more than the triumph of subconscious desire over conscious belief or principle. Like the death of the gentleman from San Francisco, it implies the complete emancipation of her "natural," instinctive being from the "degeneracy" of her entire way of life with its "unnatural" standards and conventions. The thought of returning to this life is no longer tolerable to her. Yet it is not only this life that she rejects. Experiencing once more in the ecstasy of passion the sensation of total freedom that first came to her under the spell of hypnosis, she rejects life as a whole, not for reasons of shame—for her moral beliefs have now been irretrievably undermined—but because she realizes that in life the continuation of such freedom is inconceivable. She rejects, in effect, not only the "social" or "cultural degeneracy" of her former life, but also the "inherent degeneracy" of the human condition, the individual identity that detaches her "natural" being from the freedom of nature. Hence her demand, after submitting to Emile, that he shoot her and follow her death with his own. But only her first request is granted. After he has shot her, the mind of Emile disintegrates at the realization of what he has done. Confronted in reality with the situation for which he had begged in his poetry, the aspiring symbolist proves unworthy of his Beautiful Lady, and the story ends with him crying from the window and shooting wildly into the air.

The paradoxical implication, therefore, of "The Son,"

as of Part I of "The Brothers," is the contention that man becomes his "natural" self only by ceasing to exist as an individual. Strictly speaking, it is not a love story at all; it is a dramatization of the heroine's acquisition of self-awareness. Her changing attitudes to Emile merely reflect the stages of her evolving self-knowledge, and it is precisely her achievement of complete self-knowledge that makes her unique among Bunin's victims of Eros and the precursor in his works only of the Tolstoy, whose death and "emancipation" he was to describe twenty years later. For the idea of the rejection of inherent degeneracy was never again to be dramatized in Bunin's love stories, and the reason, of course, is obvious. It was a philosophical concept that simply could not be rendered in terms of plausible human experience. The many misconceptions to which the conclusion of "The Son" gave rise evidently persuaded Bunin that he had attempted the impossible, and henceforth he was to confine himself almost exclusively in his love stories to the theme that dominates all but the last page of the tale—to the representation of the experience of love simply as a reflection of man's absolute thralldom to nature and as a source of agonizing inner conflict. Only once was he to depart from this practice—in *The Cornet Yelagin Affair*—and the result was equally unfortunate.

Despite, however, the psychological obscurity and implausibility of its ending, "The Son" makes a powerful impression. The sense of classical restraint, the subtly instilled atmosphere of tragic inevitability, the allusive echoes that unite the most widely scattered details, the obliquely conveyed tension between mind and environment, and the sensitive appreciation of the weight and emotional register of every word are the features both of "The Son" and of the other four tales examined in this chapter in which his distinctive genius is most clearly to be perceived. The five major love stories that he wrote in Russia may be counted among his most brilliant achievements and would certainly have guaranteed him a place in the first rank of twentieth-century Russian writers even if 1917 had marked the end of his literary career.

Not only, however, did emigration fail to undermine his creative ability; in the opinion of many commentators, among whom, of course, the luminaries of émigré criticism figure prominently, it marked the beginning of his ascent to new heights.[17]

8. Postrevolutionary Meditations

The effect on Bunin's art of the October Revolution, the outbreak of civil war, and subsequent exile is in some ways comparable to that of the revolution of 1905–6. It seems hardly
coincidental, for example, that in the years immediately following both eruptions of national violence he wrote very few
genuine works of fiction. Just as in the three-year period from
1907 to 1909 he had turned mainly to the highly personal
genre of the travel poem, so in his first five years on French
soil his thoughts were chiefly expressed in a succession of
brief compositions that, though varying in character and
theme from the valedictory and topical to the philosophical
and speculative, are similarly distinguished by a generally
pervasive tone of subjective, private meditation. Indeed, the
reflective, as distinct from the descriptive, element and the
tendency to philosophize are considerably more marked in
these works, and this might well explain, in part, as K. Zaytsev
has suggested, the diminishing need he evidently felt at this
time to express himself in verse,[1] for in the past poetry had always been the principal vehicle of his explicit thoughts on the
problems that chiefly concerned him. The significant point is
that on both occasions his estrangement from the new Russia
was reflected in a conspicuous intensification of the intro-
verted or egocentric character of his art, and in the early
years of his life abroad he was no longer inclined to ascribe to
"invention" the importance he had attached to it since 1912.
His remarks on literature at this time, in fact, are highly reminiscent of those he had addressed more than twenty years
earlier to Teleshov.[2] Once more the role of the imagination
in literary art and the need for plots are forcefully decried.
"Why invent?" he asks in "The Book" [Kniga], a lyrical monologue of 1924: "Why should there be heroes and heroines?
Why should there be a novel or tale with a beginning and

end? It is the eternal fear of seeming insufficiently literary, too different from those who are glorified" (5:180). As he had acknowledged, he was by no means immune to this fear himself,[3] but for the expression of his thoughts and feelings in the five-year period that followed his departure from Russia he turned less to the resources of his imagination than to the faculty he prized above all others—the immortalizing faculty of memory.

The Revolution represented for Bunin, as we have seen, the fulfillment of prophecies that are implicit in his works almost from the beginning. It merely confirmed the validity, as he put it in his last letter to Gorky, of "my long-standing thoughts about holy Russia."[4] The sickness had been discerned and diagnosed, and death had followed amid the predicted chaos. There was little more to say about it, and apart from the explosion of resentment and indignation that resulted in the spring and early summer of 1919 in the compilation in Odessa of his pungent indictment of Bolshevism and the degenerate *narod* entitled *The Accursed Days*, his uncompromising hostility to the new regime rarely invades his postrevolutionary writings. His most direct statements on the subject are encountered in two works of quite different character—"The Eternal Spring" [Nesrochnaya vesna] (1923) and "The Goddess of Reason" [Boginya Razuma] (1924), and even the latter of these, though obviously written with the Bolshevik triumph in mind, was inspired by an episode from the French, rather than the Russian, Revolution. It is basically a historical reminiscence prompted by a visit in February 1924 to the grave in Montmartre of the singer and dancer Thérèse Angélique Aubry, who in November 1793 played the part of the Goddess of Reason in a celebratory performance in Notre Dame of a scene from François Gossec's opera *L'Offrande à la Liberté*. The event was intended to symbolize the liberation of reason from the power of the Catholic church. Fourteen years later her spectacular career was brought to an abrupt and tragic end by a serious accident on the stage that left her a cripple for the remaining twenty-two years of her life, subsisting on a meager state pension. The contrast between

her fame and subsequent anonymity not only parallels the
eclipse of revolutionary France; it is used by Bunin to reemphasize the transience of human endeavor in general and,
in particular, of revolutionary endeavor that purports to make
man, equipped with his pitiful reason, the master of his des-
tiny. Echoing the fate of the gentleman from San Francisco,
the story of Mlle Aubry predicts the doom of revolutionary
Russia.

In "The Eternal Spring"[5] the object of censure is completely unequivocal. Deriving its impetus from an act of imaginative self-projection into the wilderness of Bolshevik Russia,
the work takes the form of a letter received by the author
from a friend who has chosen to remain in the land of Lenin
—a letter amply larded with invective against prevailing conditions and with expressions of fastidious contempt for the
victorious working class. Like "The Goddess of Reason," the
work hinges on a contrast, a contrast in this instance between
town and country. Here Moscow with its "Asiatic multitudes,"
its squalor and disorder, and its hordes of peddlars, thieves,
and prostitutes is the present reality of Soviet Russia, from
which the narrator, to his immense relief, finds timely refuge
on receiving an invitation to visit an old friend in the country.
The village that he discovers on arrival bears little resemblance to the domain of the Krasovs. The countryside in this
context is exclusively the positive pole of a contrast with the
urban realm of the degenerate proletariat. Its natural, timeless beauty is an implicit indictment of the revolutionary uto-
pia. Together with the author, we are enjoined to picture a
scarcely credible scene of such prosperity, harmony, and tranquillity that the narrator is momentarily tempted to question
the reality both of the recent upheaval and of the emancipation of the serfs. We are also asked to imagine the derelict
eighteenth-century palace that he discovers in the forest adjoining his temporary rural abode. Describing the surrender
of this once resplendent house to the irresistible embrace
of nature, Bunin highlights once more the natural cycle of
growth and decay that is implicitly contrasted with the "unnatural" and purportedly sterile process of violent, revolu-

tionary change. And as the rural interlude nears its end and the specter of Moscow looms larger, the writer loudly proclaims his utter rejection of the present and spiritual withdrawal into the "eternal spring" of the Russia that lives in his memory: "I constantly have the feeling that the last link between myself and the world that surrounds me is crumbling and snapping. I feel myself renouncing it ever more and entering the world to which I have been tied not only throughout my life—from my childhood, my infancy, my birth—but even from the time before my birth. I am retiring into the Elysium of the past[6] as though into a kind of dream" (5:126).

Bunin's parting with Russia, therefore, in 1920, like his departure for the Middle East in 1907, may be viewed as the physical expression of his withdrawal into the past and as an oblique reaffirmation of his "citizenship of the universe." The only difference was that on this occasion he departed forever. In 1907, he had returned to the schizophrenic land that he both loved and hated, and the conflict between its irreconcilable personalities had become one of the mainsprings of his art. The past had become the criterion for his assessments of the present, a contrasting point of reference for the illumination of present ills. In his art of the twenties, however, the present of Russia was generally ignored with silent contempt, and Bunin seemed, in the words of a Soviet writer, "like a man who had fallen out of time."[7] Only one pole of the contrast now remained—the "Elysium of the past," that refined creation of his transfigurative memory. "From the life of mankind," he declared in the last paragraph of "The Goddess of Reason," "from the centuries and generations only the sublime, the good, and the beautiful remain on earth, only these. Everything evil, stupid, base, and ignoble ultimately leaves no trace. It does not exist. It is not visible."[8] Such is the conception of the past that inspired the lyrical compositions of the thinker and aesthete in the first decade of his life in emigration.

When Bunin speaks of Russia in his postrevolutionary art, it is almost always the Russia of this pure, distilled past, the Russia that Kastryuk, Meliton, and Mitrofan had known in their youth. His new peasant heroes are invariably cast in the mold of these venerable "children of nature." "It was a long time ago, an eternity ago, because the life that we lived at that time will never return" (5:68), reads the second sentence of "The Reapers" [Kostsy] (1921), a poetic farewell to the cherished peasant of his nostalgic dreams and one of his last and most evocative paeans to the beauty of the natural life. "They reaped and sang," the monologue continues, "and the whole birch forest, which had not yet lost its thickness and freshness and was still full of flowers and scents, loudly responded to them" (5:68). The exhilarating song of the reapers of Ryazan' is an expression of spontaneous delight in the mere fact of their existence, in their physical toil, and in their instinctive sense of oneness with their primitive, responsive environment. But like their predecessors in Bunin's fiction, they sing in the shadow of nature's vengeance, and the end records the idyll's passing: "Everything has its allotted span. For us also the fairytale has come to an end. Our ancient defenders have rejected us . . . and the end, the limit of God's forgiveness, has come" (5:72).

"The Reapers," however, was written two years before "The Eternal Spring," before the "Elysium of the past" had been finally cleansed of the present's destructive irruptions. By 1927, when Bunin wrote "The Tree of God" [Bozh'ye drevo], the natural life of the ideal peasant had evolved into an object of aesthetic and philosophical contemplation that was no longer overshadowed by the clouds of impending disaster, and in the "invented, generic figure"[9] of the smallholder (*odnodvorets*) Yakov Demidych Nechayev he presents his last fictional embodiment of its physical and psychological rewards. The title of the work, in which the term "God" is again little more than a synonym of "nature," expresses figuratively the simple philosophical principle on which Bunin's vision of the past had always rested. Nechayev declares: "I am, as they say, a tree of God that bends in the direction of the wind." His obedience to nature's rhythms is vividly conveyed by his succinct parallelism: "Day is darkened by night and man by sorrow" (5:354). He is at once a human counterpart of the birch in "The Epitaph" and a composite of the manifold unsophisticated virtues of Bunin's long line of peasant "fathers."[10] The portrait is less valedictory than prescriptive. The emphasis is less on the historical reality it allegedly reflects than on the timeless, universal relevance of the attitude to life that it enshrines.

The difference of emphasis between "The Reapers" and "The Tree of God" provides some indication of the problem to which Bunin's thought was almost exclusively devoted in the early years of his exile—the problem of time. Almost all his works, of course, of whatever period are related to this problem in one way or another, but never before had he dwelt on it so obsessively as in the aftermath of 1917, for it was precisely in terms of this problem that he viewed both the death of his country and the transformation that had taken place in his personal life. Now Russia had experienced in his eyes the fate of Judaea, and just as the ruins of the latter had inspired reflections on the whole nature of history, so the collapse of the former now focused his thoughts on the ephemeral character of life in general. Between the fall of the czar and the mournful exchanges of the two former rivals in "On the Nocturnal Sea" [V nochnom more] (1923) on the transience of passion, anguish, and hatred there is a direct, unmistakable connection. Emotions are no less subject to time's corrosive influence than the mightiest of states, and events that twenty years earlier, when the one nameless traveler had stolen the wife of the other, had almost ended in the latter's suicide are now recalled after her death with a chilling calm and indifference. "People talk about the past," declares the former cuckold. "It's all nonsense. Strictly speaking, people have no past. There is only a weak echo of everything that one once experienced in life" (5:105).[11] Similar thoughts, reinforced by Bunin's assiduous reading at this time of *Ecclesiastes*, underlie the contrast in "The City of the King of Kings" [Gorod tsarya tsarey] (1924) between the glorious past and the primitive present of Ceylon and form the unspoken leitmotiv of the song in "Temir-Aksak-Khan" (1921) about the once powerful Crimean khan who ended his days as a beggar. But in the latter work the emphasis changes once more. Here the accent shifts from visible fact to philosophical generalization, from the historically confirmed transience of human achievement to insistence on its utter futility. The khan's decline is the result not of defeat, but of an enlightened renunciation of all earthly possessions. In the form of this act of self-denial Bunin reiterates the deeply pessimistic implication of his entire philosophy of life that impelled him to proclaim, in a poem of 1922, his "contempt for the earth and alienation from all its meaningless beauty" (8:14).

As in the past, however, the conclusions he expresses in these works with a force and sense of resignation that can only be attributed to the effect of his recent experiences illustrate only one of his constantly alternating responses to the problem of time. In his thoughts on this question he was incapable of consistency. Even before 1917, he had provided abundant evidence in his art that man is not entirely defenseless in the face of time, and intervening events, despite the contradictory impression conveyed by some of his statements, had failed to undermine this belief. The very concept of an "Elysium of the past" denoted for him a kind of victory over time, and as though in reply to the demoralized protagonists of "On the Nocturnal Sea," the writer exclaims in "The Eternal Spring": "No, for me the former world to which I once belonged is not a world of the dead. For me it is returning ever more to life. It is becoming the only and ever more joyous abode of my soul to which I alone have access" (5:127). And as though in refutation of his remarks of 1924 on the transience of Ceylon's ancient glory, he writes in "Many Waters" [Vody mnogiye], a travel poem[12] of 1925–26: "We do not even suspect the immense power of the mysterious influence of this archaic past or its immutability and independence of transient earthly conditions. It destroys the barriers of time, place, and nationality" (5:316–17).

These reflections on the history of Ceylon make it clear that the past of Bunin's "Elysium" was by no means confined to the past of Russia. It comprised the cultural heritage of mankind, the achievements of the past that shape the minds of men in the present, the universal emblems of the past's own victory over time. Once more his cultural cosmopolitanism is vividly in evidence as he scans with the eye of memory the relics of the ancient civilizations with which his voyages had brought him into personal contact. From the ruins of Anuradhapura, Ceylon's ancient capital, his thoughts pass in "Many Waters" to the deserts of the Middle East that yielded the Codex Sinaiticus, and thence, in "Scarabs" [Skarabei] (1924), to the beetles of lapis lazuli and serpentine that for five thousand years of Egyptian history were placed on the breasts of the mummified pharaohs as symbols of the continuity of life. For Bunin the memory of these timeless monuments to the immortality of human achievement is enough to inspire once more the sensation that had overcome him nearly thirty years before on the height overlooking the river Donets —the sensation of direct personal communion with a living past and a deepened awareness of his personal participation in the unbroken continuum of life through the centuries.

In harmony with this attitude of Bunin to the culture of the past was the importance that he attached to his own literary activity as a means of self-immortalization. "The first thing that I must testify about my life," he wrote in 1921 in "The Book of My Life" [Kniga moyey zhizni], "is the need that I feel . . . to express myself and to prolong myself on earth."[13] His art was conceived, in a very real sense, as a gesture of defiance, as a challenge to oblivion, and this attitude no doubt partly explains some of the more conspicuous features of his fiction that have been stressed from the beginning—above all, his predominant concern as a writer with "certain immutable, organic things about which nothing can be done—death, sickness, love."[14] His confidence in his ability to elicit from the generations of the future a continuous, echoing response to the aesthetic record of his own experience and understanding of life was firmly grounded in his unwavering belief in the essential immutability of human nature and the human condition. "One man is not so very different from another" (5:175), remarks the old count in the miniature entitled "Inscriptions" [Nadpisi] (1924), and the same thought rings out in "The Blind Man"[15] and in the attack on racial prejudice that he titled "Third Class" [Tretiy klass] (1921). In the common membership of all men of the single fraternity of nature he perceived both the explanation of the survival and continuing appeal of the great art of the past and reason for hope that his own battle with time would not be in vain. His obsessive aspiration to immortality was more than a manifestation of conceit; it reflected the almost sensual pleasure he derived from the thought that with every work he wrote he was inflicting on time and death yet another defeat. He looked forward to a victory over time comparable to that which he had already achieved with his art over the dimension of space, over the barriers of race, creed, and nationality—the victory that forms the underlying theme of his fictional collection of letters entitled "An Unknown Friend" [Neizvestnyy drug] (1923). "Here is your new book," writes his unknown Irish reader, and she continues: "How strange it is! Someone's hand has written something somewhere, someone's soul has expressed in the smallest hint the smallest part of its intimate life . . . , and suddenly space, time, and the difference between our fortunes and positions disappear, and your thoughts and feelings become mine, common to us both. The world truly contains but a single soul" (5:91). Bunin contrasts the ideals of fraternity and equality trumpeted by the revolutionaries of France and Russia with this simple fraternity created by art and based on an awareness of shared experience between the men of all times and places.[16]

The metaphysical conception of man as part of the "single soul" of nature is reflected in most of the works of the early twenties that Bunin devoted to the theme of death. Man's death as an individual is repeatedly contrasted with his "natural" immortality. In the title and narrative, for example, of a story of 1920 he uses the term *iskhod* instead of *smert'* ("death"), restoring to it its old, etymological meaning (literally "the going out") which in the given context may perhaps best be rendered as "the passing on."[17] And as the wind ruffles the shroud that covers the body of the young Gavrilo's mother in "The Transfiguration" [Preobrazheniye] (1921), creating the illusion that she is breathing, he muses: "It does not matter. This wind is also my dead mother. She is the source of this unearthly, icy breathing which is as pure as death" (5:80). It is significant, however, that in both stories the conception of death as the reabsorption of the individual into the unity of nature is voiced only by peasants. The reaction of the young aristocrat Bestuzhev to the death of the old prince in "The Passing On" is quite different from that of the peasant women Yevgeniya and Natasha. "He tried persistently," we read, "to understand something, to gather his thoughts, to feel a sense of horror. But there was no horror. There was only surprise, the impossibility of comprehending or grasping what had happened" (5:14). This latter reaction, of course, no less than the former, belongs to Bunin himself, but to a very different Bunin—to the Bunin who saw death as merely the brutal end of man's capacity for sensual delight in the beauty of life. It is the reaction of the author of the love stories, for whom death is almost invariably a meaningless tragedy.

This "other face" of Bunin is by no means shielded from view in his lyrical compositions of the early twenties by his metaphysical speculations on the continuity of life and by his predominant concern with the present as merely a link between past and future. His retirement into the "Elysium of the past" implied no diminution of his capacity for relishing the simple fact of being alive, for exulting in the simplest, most primitive forms of experience, and it would have been wholly in character for him to have remarked at any time during these years, as he did in 1913: "If a man could be found who would guarantee me life for tens of thousands of years, I would unhesitatingly conclude a contract with him on any terms whatsoever."[18] This is the voice of the Bunin who found little consolation in the chilly stratosphere of metaphysical thought. It is the voice that we hear in "The Midnight Heat-Lightning" [Polunochnaya zarnitsa] (1921), where the young hero caresses the neck of his horse simply "in order to capture its coarse smell, to feel the earthly flesh, because without it, without this flesh, I find this world too frightening"

(5:76). And it is audible again in the exclamations of the hero of "The Hare" [Rusak] (1924) as he contemplates the cold, furry body brought back from the hunt: "There are no words to express the unintelligible delight with which I feel this smooth skin, this hardened carcass, myself, the cold window of the hall pasted over and covered with fresh, white snow, and this pale light of the blizzard that has flooded the house" (5:178). Here the presence of death serves merely to accentuate the sheer pleasure of being alive in the most primitive, biological sense of the term, and in "The Night of Renunciation" [Noch' otrecheniya], a short Buddhist parable of 1921, the author declares his total submission, even while glorifying the "Conqueror of Desire," to "the sweet illusion of this mortal life" (5:40).

In Bunin's reflections, therefore, on the problem of time in the aftermath of 1917 we encounter once more the vacillation between two irreconcilable attitudes to life that is characteristic of his thought in general. Although the death of imperial Russia had reawakened his sensitivity to the transience of all things mundane and directed his thoughts away from the present to man's eternal existence as part of the "single soul" that spans the ages, the specter of personal death inspired a contrasting exultation in the experiences of the mortal flesh. Even his impatience with the limitations of physical existence admits of two contrasting interpretations, and he himself could never be sure which was the correct one. He summarizes his position in the final words of "The Book of My Life":

The sadness of space, time, and form has pursued me all my life, and time and again throughout my life I have consciously and unconsciously overcome them. But with felicitous results? Yes—and no. I have an insatiable desire for life, and my life embraces my past as well as my present. It embraces thousands of other lives, the world of the present and the world of the past, the whole history of the whole of mankind and all its countries. I am filled with an incessant craving to acquire the experience of others and to convert it within me. But why? Is it in order to destroy myself thereby, to destroy my "I," my time and my space? Or is it my aim, conversely, to assert myself by enriching and strengthening myself with the experience of others?[19]

His metaphysical speculations, therefore, belonged no less to the slave of Mara than to the devotee of the Buddha. His remarkable, lifelong sensitivity to the evolutionary chain was dictated as much by his craving for self-assertion as by his aspiration to self-transcendence, and in his unusual susceptibility to these conflicting urges he seems to have recognized the special dilemma of the artistic temperament. He defined it most succinctly four years later in "Night": "The curse and happiness of such a man is an especially powerful Ego, a craving for the greater assertion of this Ego, and at the same time a greater awareness (by virtue of the immense experience acquired during the time spent in the immense chain of existences) of the vanity of this craving, a keen sensation of Universal Life" (5:302).

With "Night" Bunin brings to a conclusion the sequence of short, reflective, and occasionally semifictional works on themes related to the problem of time that he wrote in the seven years after the Revolution. In this brief philosophical "reverie,"[20] which till 1951 bore the title "The Cicadas" [Tsikady], he endeavors to knit together the various strands of thought that weave their way individually through these works and to translate his conflicting attitudes to life into a general statement on the essential nature of man's dual existence as an individual and as a link in the chain of natural evolution. As the revised title suggests, he makes use once more of the contrast, reminiscent of Tyutchev, between day and night, associating them respectively with his personalistic and impersonalistic approaches to life. Day is represented as the time of instinctive, unthinking action within the confines of space and time in which man is "a slave of earthly existence" and an individual entrusted by the biological heritage of which he is largely unaware with "a specific function, calling, and name" (5:300). With the coming of night, conversely, the dimensional constraints disappear; the sense of individuality is lost, and the personality is temporarily reintegrated

with the unity of nature that is symbolically conveyed in the
work by the ubiquitous drone of the cicadas. But night means
something different to the man whose reason obstructs the
natural course of the cycle; it means the temptation of aspiring to comprehend—an aspiration, it is claimed, that can only
culminate in his total incomprehension both of himself and of
the world about him. Such, by implication, is the position
here of the author himself.

At the basis of the work lies the contrast Bunin draws
between the overwhelming majority, who are normally men
of action, unconsciously obedient, like the cicadas (and like
the peasant in the guise of a "tree of God"), to the rhythms of
the repetitive cycle, and whose instinctive execution of their
allotted functions forges the true links in the chain of evolution, and this small category of "philosophizers" in which he
places himself. His remarks on this exclusive minority are an
extension, of course, of his self-analysis, though he attempts
to buttress the plausibility of his generalizations with references to the recorded experience of various historical figures,
including the Buddha and Tolstoy. The most obvious feature
common to them all, he argues, is the unusual richness and
complexity of their personalities, which he attributes to their
abnormal sensitivity to their biological heritage and to their
unique ability to reproduce in themselves the reactions to
experience of even their most distant and primitive ancestors.
This ability, he alleges, explains the extraordinary force and
freshness of their responses to life, their capacity for living
life with a degree of sensual intensity which the majority can
only contemplate with envy. Yet despite this capacity, the gates
of paradise are forever closed to them by the counterbal-
ancing power of their intellects, which irresistibly instill a
growing awareness of the vanity of sensual experience and
ultimately the realization that life can have no rationally justi-
fiable purpose save progressive self-extraction from the chain
and the conscious renunciation of individual identity. The
Solomons, Buddhas, and Tolstoys of this world, he observes,
"at first accept the world with immense greed, and then curse
its temptations with immense passion" (5:303). He attempted

subsequently to record the stages of this evolution in the spiritual biography of Russia's greatest novelist, in *The Emancipation of Tolstoy*, denoting by its title, as he put it in a letter to P. M. Bitsilli, "Tolstoy's fated 'withdrawal from the Chain,' his fated departure from life rather than from Yasnaya Polyana."[21] As he stresses, however, in "Night," the evolution does not eradicate the conflict. To the end the "philosophizers" are torn on the rack of an excruciating contradiction between "the agony of withdrawal from the chain, separation from it, consciousness of its futility, and the agony of an abnormal, terrible fascination with it" (5:306).

Such are the conflicting agonies that seem to have tormented Bunin throughout his life and with particular intensity in the wake of his emigration. Yet for all his reborn sensitivity after 1917 to the pitiful vanity of human endeavor, he ends by confessing in "Night" to his Maker: "I am still grieved by the thought of parting with the illusory and bitter sweetness of Being. I am still terrified by your eternity without beginning and end" (5:306), and the feeling of terror was to remain with him to the grave. Recalling a conversation with him on the day of his death, A. V. Bakhrakh writes: "He began to speak with visibly increasing agitation about the meaninglessness of death and about his inability to accept or comprehend how a man could exist one minute and not exist the next."[22] The "philosophical" attitude to death of Gavrilo in "The Transfiguration" is rarely reflected in his fiction of the years ahead. With his appeal to the Creator to leave him in peace he reaffirmed once more his exultation in the reality his reason rejected and prepared to embark on his greatest celebration of its glories, *The Life of Arsen'yev*.

Written, like "Night," at Grasse "under the sun of Provence,"[23] *The Life of Arsen'yev* is by far the longest of Bunin's works and, in the opinion of many commentators, his chef d'oeuvre and "one of the most remarkable phenomena in world literature."[24] Like most of his works, it has a protracted textological history. The first four of its five books were written between 1927 and 1929 and appeared as a separate volume in 1930 after individual sections had been published in various Parisian newspapers and journals. Book V, which covers the period of Arsen'yev's love affair with Lika, was completed in 1933 and published separately, under the title *Lika*, in 1939. Thirteen more years, however, were to elapse before the work appeared in its present form.[25] In all, therefore, it was the result of some twenty-five years of intermittent toil, and if we take the view of L. F. Zurov that "The Book of My Life" and other sketches written in 1921 should be counted as "the first drafts of the novel,"[26] we may conclude that its creation spanned his entire life in emigration.

Even though there seems to be little doubt that the novel proper was, in fact, begun in the summer of 1927,[27] there is still a certain justification for regarding almost all the short reflective works that he wrote during his first five years in France as a preparation for this major opus. Whereas these works are essentially a record of the sustained attempt to formulate his principal conclusions on life that he felt impelled to undertake on having reached, at the age of fifty, the end of his life in the country of his birth, *The Life of Arsen'yev*, at its most basic level, is an inquiry into the complex multiplicity of factors that gave birth to these conclusions and into the development of the sensibility that had transmuted them into art. It is the record of an attempt at self-definition, of the meditations of Bunin the artist and "philosophizer" on the experiences of his first twenty-four years on earth which, he believed, had decisively molded his personality. The result, as the author himself was at pains to emphasize, is clearly not autobiography in the normal sense of the term.[28] It is rather a teleologically orientated and chronologically ordered selection of disparate formative experiences, each of which is analyzed, poetically transfigured, or reappraised in the light of the major preoccupations of the mature artist. Distilled by the criteria of the elder Bunin and transfigured by his lyrical resurrection of the past, the actual experience of the young Bunin is converted into the formative experience of the young Arsen'yev. In the same way, the real personality of Varvara Pashchenko is remolded into the fictional personality of Lika.

It is evident, therefore, not only that the work differs significantly in character and purpose from the various "childhoods" and "family chronicles" of Bunin's Russian predecessors, but that the terms "novel" (*roman*) and "short novel" (*povest'*)[29] are equally inappropriate designations of its genre. Here there is no fictional reality independent of the narrator. His personality is totally dominant and omnipresent, and every detail in the work exists for the sole purpose of drawing from him a response that is relevant to the concerns and personality of his creator. In this respect, *The Life of Arsen'yev* differs negligibly from such incomparably shorter works as "Holy Mountains," "Scarabs," and "Many Waters," and it might, therefore, perhaps most accurately be characterized by the same term I have reserved for such works. It is basically an extended lyrical monologue in which the subjective, egocentric element in Bunin's art rises once more to the surface.

Like the sketches and reveries to which it is related, the monologue moves on two distinct, alternating levels—the descriptive level on which Arsen'yev's early life is recorded with due regard to time and chronology, and the speculative level on which time and place are no longer important. It proceeds, in effect, by means of constant transitions from the former to the latter, from the temporal to the timeless. Moreover, although the picture it presents of late nineteenth-century Russia is broad in its geographical and social range, its scope is severely curtailed by the constraints inherent in the author's purpose, which repeatedly dictates the exclusion of the historically significant and the magnification of the infinitesimal. Perhaps most striking on the descriptive level are the narrator's memorable character portraits of members of his family, his boyhood tutor, his early loves Annchen and Lika, and his fellow employees on the *Orlovskiy vestnik*; the vivid impression of contemporary Russian provincial life conveyed by the fragments that comprise his portraits of Yelets, Khar'kov, and Oryol; and the finely wrought landscapes that punctuate each section of the work. But description is usually ancillary to the responses evoked by the objects described and to the general subjects of speculation in which these responses repeatedly culminate. The recurrence of these general, abstract subjects contributes substantially to the compositional unity of the work, imparting even to this protracted monologue a structure that is basically musical in character. They provide, as it were, the six dominant chords from which the structure derives its cohesion—the intermingled chords of nature, death, love, art, the "soul" of Russia, and the biological heritage of the narrator himself. The work may be viewed as an elaborate pattern of variations on these six musical themes that form the prism through which Bunin regards the lost world of his childhood and youth.

Among the most resonant of the six chords is certainly that of death, which rings out at the very outset in Arsen'yev's question: "Are we not born with a sense of death?" (6:7) and again at the very end with his announcement of the death of Lika,[30] and it is repeatedly introduced into the intervening narrative even with the aid, if necessary, of a digression into the "present." Thus the account of a visit to Oryol in the late eighties by the Grand Duke Nikolay Nikolayevich is followed by a reference to his death in the twenties in the south of France. "People," remarks Arsen'yev, "are not completely alike in their sensitivity to death. There are some people who live their entire lives under its sign" (6:26), and it is this "sign" that Bunin places over his own formative years, expressing in the process the full range of reactions to death that he had recorded in his earlier works of the twenties and again voicing the view of art as a deliverance from its finality. In one of his preparatory sketches for the work he wrote: "Life is perhaps given to us solely in order that we may compete with death. Man fights it even from beyond the grave. It takes away his name, and so he writes it on a cross or stone. It seeks to cover his experiences in darkness, but he endeavors to bring them to life in the word" (6:311).

But *The Life of Arsen'yev* is a eulogy not so much of the power of art as of the wonder and beauty of life. Conceived as a challenge to time, it evolved into a devotional affirmation of the temporal. And as in "The Hare," the reverberating chord of death is paradoxically an integral element of the eulogy. The presence of death not only transforms life into a quest for personal immortality; it also increases man's awareness of the intrinsic value of life and instills a sensitivity to its beauty from which he may derive more than adequate compensation for his failure to perceive a meaning that may satisfy his reason. The irruptions of death, in consequence, are repeatedly juxtaposed with Arsen'yev's most uninhibited acclamations of life and with his most poetic evocations of the rapture of love. Thus the two chapters in Book I in which he recalls the death of his sister Nadya end with the reminiscence: "And again the earth which eternally deceives us drew me affectionately and insistently into its maternal embraces" (6:46), while the death of his relative Pisarev inspires the remark: "The world seemed to become younger, more free, expansive, and beautiful after someone had left it forever" (6:112).

In general, the reader learns little from *The Life of Arsen'yev* that is not deducible from or explicitly revealed in Bunin's earlier works. The monologue traces, in the Khar'kov interludes, the development of his hostility to radical theories of social reform.[31] It confirms his tendency to regard people either in abstract terms or simply as a means of his own self-fulfillment.[32] It offers abundant evidence of that "heightened impressionability" (6:30), of that instinctive curiosity and sense of wonder that enabled him to derive a feeling of almost "voluptuous delight" from the spectacle of a tree, a beetle, his father's dagger, or a tin of shoe polish at a local bazaar (6:11–12). And it expresses eloquently his ruthless commitment to the pursuit of experience for the sake of his art. These aspects of Bunin's personality are thoroughly familiar, and it is pointless for Soviet critics to argue that the views expressed in the work of which they understandably disapprove may be attributed to the animus of a frustrated émigré.[33] They merely echo the views expressed obliquely in his earliest writings. The novelty of the work lies not in distortions of the past, but precisely in the relentless vigor with which Bunin proclaims his attachment to life. Despite the pervasive aura of death, never before had he declared so unequivocally his acceptance of life in all its infinite variety. Yet this does not mean, of course, that *The Life of Arsen'yev* should be taken as a definitive statement of Bunin's attitude to life or as a legitimate basis for categorical generalizations on this subject. The scale of the work has induced numerous critics to regard it as a kind of testament enshrining his "final conclusions," but the inconsistencies of attitude to which his subsequent art continues to bear witness make this view untenable. For all its passion and vigor, *The Life of Arsen'yev*, in reality, marks simply a stage in the evolution of the inner conflict that ceased only in November 1953.

Nor is it possible to agree with the generally accepted view that the work ranks with Bunin's greatest achievements. For despite the proliferation of memorable scenes, portraits, and details, the pictorial excellence of its many landscapes, and the haunting lyricism that suffuses this entire "Elysium" of the author's personal past, the theme of the narrator's developing personality is inadequate to the task of instilling the dynamism and sense of continuity that are necessary to sustain the reader's interest. The resonance of the six "dominant chords" is only partly effective in counteracting the tendency of the work to break down into its constituent parts. Like all but the most diminutive of Bunin's lyrical monologues, the work highlights by contrast the vital importance to his art of the element of plot as a means of activating the elusive connections between the human and nonhuman that are perhaps the most distinctive feature of the typical Bunin story. In the nondramatic context of *The Life of Arsen'yev* these connections are replaced by the long and aesthetically dubious passages of "philosophization" that, like the interpretative sections of "The Brothers," "The Cup of Life," and "The Dreams of Chang," show him at his weakest. His art achieves its most telling effects, as we have seen, when the thought is permitted to arise naturally and without commentary from the concatenation of dispassionately observed characters, scenes, landscapes, and events within the perimeter superimposed by a clearly defined dramatic situation. And it is noteworthy that even in the period of his work on *The Life of Arsen'yev* he felt the need to impress on Galina Kuznetsova the importance of writing about "themes with a plot"[34] and to point out in a conversation with friends: "You should not 'bare your soul' to the reader or place yourself on his level. He will not respect you. You should beat him on the head. You should write sternly and calmly. Only thus will you make an impression."[35]

The statement is plainly irreconcilable with his own artistic practice of the time and can only be taken to imply his clear recognition of the inferiority of his lyrical compositions to his invented tales about invented people. The question obviously arises, therefore, of why he wrote them at all, and the simple answer, of course, is that they satisfied an instinctive demand of his profoundly egocentric personality and issued from his periodically unsuppressable urge to communicate his attitude to life directly and without equivocation. But again it is necessary to note the periods when they were chiefly written: at the very beginning of his career, in the aftermath of 1905, and again in the aftermath of 1917 and emigration. All three periods were times of uncertainty and stress for either the man or the artist or for both, and on each occasion the subjective, introspective element in his art assumed full control. In periods of relative calm, conversely, the dispassionate, objective manner tended to prevail. There would seem to be a correlation, and the validity of the hypothesis is supported by the appearance in 1924 of the first of the love stories that were his most notable works of the decade, for we know that by then he had at last settled into the peaceful and regular routine he evidently needed to write in this manner. But by the same token it seems clear that peace of mind was not so easily recaptured. The evidence is not only the resurgence of the subjective element in "Night" and *The Life of Arsen'yev*, but a change of emphasis in his second major group of love stories that distinguishes them perceptibly from his prerevolutionary tales.

9. Studies of Thralldom and Rebellion

In the course of his conversation with Bunin in January 1894, Tolstoy remarked: "There is no happiness in life; there are only flashes of it. Value them, live them to the full" (9:58). The point was taken up in one of Bunin's preparatory notes for *The Life of Arsen'yev*: "We are fully alive to everything that we experience only to the extent that we appreciate its value. Usually this value is very small. It rises only at moments of rapture—the rapture of happiness or unhappiness when we are clearly conscious of gain or loss" (9:366). The term "flash" aptly defines the type of experience the fictional situations of Bunin's love stories are normally designed to generate— sudden "flashes" of ecstasy and horror that briefly illuminate the splendor and tragedy of the human condition. Since the intervals between such experiences were of little interest to him, his works are usually constructed around a single "flash." To this extent they may be viewed as typical short stories. But Bunin's love stories are distinguished by the customary absence of any connection between the "flash" and the purposeful or premeditated action of those who experience it. Motivated almost invariably by the susceptibility of the characters to influences that elude their conscious or rational control, it is usually experienced by them either as a complete surprise or as an act of inexplicable surrender. Occasionally, as in "Light Breathing," the effects of these subconscious influences are examined without reference to any external source of stimulation, but more commonly, as we have seen, the victory of the irrational is the culmination of sustained interaction between the individual subconscious and the external forces of nature that are evoked in the descriptions of setting and landscape.

181

In none of Bunin's tales is interaction of this kind a more obviously significant element of the fiction than in the first two of the five major love stories that he wrote in the twenties —*Mitya's Love* and "Sunstroke" [Solnechnyy udar] (1925)— the latter of which seems to express the notion of the "flash" in its very title.[1] Indeed, one's first impression of this seven-page story is that few works of comparable size combine so many typical features of Bunin's mature art. There is the usual pair of principal characters, in this case a married woman and a lieutenant in the czarist army, who are fellow travelers on a Volga steamer. The plot, which has been compared, to no useful purpose, to that of Chekhov's "The Lady with the Little Dog" [Dama s sobachkoy] (1899),[2] is as skeletal as any he ever devised. It hinges on three events: the mutual infatuation of the characters, their decision to spend the night together at a stopping point on their journey, and their separation the following morning. Both are portrayed as completely average individuals, and "Everyman," as their anonymity suggests, is writ large on their brows.[3] But their failure to disclose their names—even to one another—is felt to be less a mark of generalization than an attribute of their brief relationship. It is indicative of their momentary transformation into willess marionettes, of the sudden capitulation to depersonalizing sensuality that represents for both of them a completely new experience. "In all their lives," we read, "neither the one nor the other had ever experienced anything like it" (5:239), and before her departure the woman declares: "I give you my word of honor that I am not at all the kind of woman you might think. I have never before experienced anything that even resembled what has happened, and it will not happen again. It was as though an eclipse came over me. . . . Or rather we both received a kind of sunstroke" (5:240).

For the characters, of course, the term "sunstroke" is simply a metaphor of the willess state of mind from which they have emerged, but ironically the heroine unwittingly identifies in her remark the real cause of the experience.

Again the sun enters Bunin's fiction as a potent influence on human behavior, as a force capable of usurping the authority of reason. Its dazzling light suffuses almost every scene, and even at night its presence is felt acutely. As the lieutenant, for example, kisses the woman's hand in the darkness before they disembark, he is struck by the smell of sunburn, and "in bliss and awe his heart sank at the thought of how strong and dark her whole body must be under the light gingham dress after lying for a whole month beneath the southern sun" (5:238). When they enter the dark hotel room, the sun's power again assaults their senses: "They entered a large but terribly stifling room which the sun had filled during the day with its searing heat" (5:239), and in this suffocating atmosphere the last vestiges of self-control are swiftly discarded.

No less typical than the plot of the work, the character types, and the motivation of the action are the expressive effects that Bunin obtains by varying the pace of the narrative. Disenchanted with his first two drafts, he noted in the margin of the final version the guiding principle: "Nothing superfluous" (5:525), and promptly deleted much of what he had written. As usual, however, his application of this principle did not prevent him from introducing detailed descriptive passages, not only to evoke scene and atmosphere, but also to arrest the flow of the narrative as a means of offsetting the tensions experienced by the characters. A typical example is the passage that relates the events following their disembarkation:

A minute later they passed through a small, sleepy office, stepped out onto the sand which was so deep that wheels sank into it up to their hubs, and silently sat down in a cab that was covered in dust. The uphill climb along a road that was soft from the dust and illuminated by a few crooked lamps seemed endless. But at last they reached the top and emerged onto the highway, and as they clattered along it they passed a square, some offices, and a watch tower and experienced the warmth and smells of a summer's night in a provincial town. . . . The cabby stopped at a brightly lit porch behind the open doors of which stretched an old, steep, wooden staircase. Resentfully an old, unshaven lackey in a pink blouse and frock coat took their baggage and walked ahead of them on misshapen feet that had often been trampled on. [5:239]

The slowing down of the narrative that results from the insertion of this highly detailed passage not only conveys a vivid impression of the arduousness of the journey with its initial climb from the jetty and the final climb up the steep staircase; it also forms an expressive counterpoint to the feelings of the hero, for whom every second is an excruciating eternity. His impatient desire for the contraction of time is offset by the expansion of narrative time, by the slowness of the journey mirrored in the fullness of its description.

At the same time, there is reason to assume that the meaning of some of the individual details included in this passage is as much symbolic as literal. Noteworthy in this connection is the imagined scene that, according to Galina Kuznetsova, served Bunin as his point of departure when writing the tale. She recalls: "The origins of 'Sunstroke' can be traced to a mental picture of coming out on deck after dinner—from the light into the darkness of a summer's night on the Volga."[4] The scene is recreated in the opening sentence of the tale: "After dinner they left the hot, brightly lit dining room, and stepping on to the deck they stopped by the handrail" (5:238). The setting on board a steamer is ideally suited, of course, to the theme of a "chance acquaintance," but the ensuing development of the story suggests that Bunin was equally attracted by the opportunities it offered for allusion. The transition from the light of the dining room to the darkness of the scene on deck introduces a contrast that is subsequently repeated on several occasions. Thus the third paragraph begins: "Ahead lay darkness and lights. A strong, mild wind blew from out of the dark and struck them in the face, while the lights sped by somewhere to the side" (5:238). Shortly afterward the motif reappears in the contrast between the "summer's night" and the sprinkling of lights that illuminate the road to the hotel, and it is repeated on the protagonists' arrival. From the darkness of the night they pass through the "brightly lit porch" and up the staircase only to meet darkness once more on entering the room with its "white lowered curtains" and its "two unlit candles on the pier-glass table" (5:239), and it is here, in this stifling darkness, that desire is finally gratified. The opening contrast, therefore, is echoed at each stage of the progression to the climax of the action, ultimately resolving itself in the triumph of darkness, and there can be little doubt that both the contrast and its resolution allude to the psychological experience of the characters. The alternations of light and darkness reflect the conflict between reason and the irrational that ends with the victory of the latter.

The externalization of psychological experience is yet another feature of Bunin's narrative technique in "Sunstroke" that is thoroughly familiar to us, but the same cannot be said of every aspect of the tale, for in one conspicuous respect it differs fundamentally from the love stories of the prerevolutionary period. The difference is immediately apparent in the much smaller proportion of the tale that is embraced by the external action, for by the end of the second page it is virtually complete. The remaining five pages are devoted entirely to the representation of the hero's reactions to the irreparable sense of loss that unexpectedly overwhelms him after the woman's departure. Once more Bunin portrays through the agonies of his hero the tragic implications of man's inherent degeneracy. The lieutenant, we note, now feels like an outcast from life. The sun no longer excites his senses. He is struck only by the "pointlessness" of its blinding light, by the vulgarity of the urban scenes that it illuminates, and by the incomprehensible contentment of the people performing in its heat their daily tasks. Like everything else, the light of the sun is eclipsed by the remembered "flash" of his own short-lived ecstasy and by the pain of its irrevocable passing, and his will to live is momentarily undermined. Whereas, however, in one of the early drafts of the story there is a reference to "the persistent thought of suicide" (5:525), the nightmare in the final redaction is eventually survived. As the lieutenant boards his boat the following night, the symbolic sequence of the opening scenes is reversed. From the darkness of the irrational he passes once more into the comforting light of reason. "Because of the throng," we read, "the steamer, which was already lit up everywhere and smelling of the galley, seemed unusually welcoming and attractive" (5:245). But although he is saved from self-destruction, it is clear that his life will never be quite the same again. The story ends with the simple statement: "The lieutenant sat under an awning on the deck feeling ten years older" (5:245).

The most striking feature, however, of this second and longer section of the tale is neither the theme nor even its extended development, but rather the change of technique that is mainly responsible for this extension, for the psychological experience of the lieutenant is no longer conveyed here exclusively by allusion or externalization. It is represented with the aid of techniques that in Bunin's prerevolutionary stories make only the most fleeting appearance—the interior monologue and free indirect speech. In no prerevolutionary tale had he attempted to convey so directly or extensively the feelings of a character who was not patently a mouthpiece of his personal judgments, and this development marks a stage of some importance in the evolution of his art, for it is by no means confined to "Sunstroke." All his love stories of the mid-twenties display a similar inclination toward more direct methods of psychological portrayal which he had previously tended to shun. At the basis of all five stories, two of which, "Ida" (1925) and "The Mordvinian Sarafan" [Mordovskiy sarafan] (1925), are first-person narratives, we perceive a common pattern that centers on the directly expressed reactions of the hero to the heroine and to the feelings that she provokes in him.

This does not mean, of course, that every aspect of the hero's psychological drama is elevated to the surface and exposed to the light of day. As in the first section of "Sunstroke," his subconscious receptivity to external influences continues to be represented by indirect methods. But his conscious reactions to the situations into which he is driven by these influences receive a totally unprecedented emphasis with the result that the tension between subconsciously or irrationally motivated action and conscious or rational response is significantly sharpened, and one of the most obvious effects of this development is the notably enhanced "presence" in the fiction of the heroes of these works compared with that of their predecessors. They enjoy a status that had previously been bestowed only on intermediaries like the colonel in "The Brothers," Chang, and the Krasovs in their "reflective" role, and this status seems to suggest a degree of compassion on the author's part that is strikingly at variance with the consistently dispassionate attitude reflected in the narrative style of his prerevolutionary love stories. Perhaps the source of this compassion and of the sensitivity to pain that it implies was the pain of the émigré confronted at the age of fifty with new, horrifying evidence of the intrinsic cruelty of life. Nevertheless, it should be stressed that the fictional reality of his heroes is never compromised. The voice we hear is not that of the author; it is the voice of the hero expressing himself in a manner that accords with his personality and with the situation in which he is placed.

Despite, therefore, the familiarity of its theme, the impression produced by "Sunstroke" is quite distinctive. It is the first *short* tale in which Bunin combines the new element of direct psychological portrayal with the allusive style that characterizes such stories as "By the Road," "The Grammar of Love," and "The Son." But the work that marks the transition to this synthesis is *Mitya's Love*, which had been written the previous year (1924). Not only is it the best known of all Bunin's love stories; it is also the longest, and its length is partly an indication of the unprecedented attention he devotes in it to the representation of mood and feeling. Never before had he subjected a mind other than his own to such intensive and sympathetic scrutiny.

In Bunin's prerevolutionary love stories the recurrent tension between conscious activity and subconscious, that is, "natural," impulse had only once expressed itself in conflicting notions of love—in "By the Road," in which Parashka perishes because of her inability to reconcile with her ideal

notion of love the initiation into the mystery of sexual love
that she experiences with Nikanor. Bunin returns to this conflict in *Mitya's Love*. Like "Sunstroke," the story is divisible
into two unequal sections. In the first, which comprises only
the first six of its twenty-nine short chapters, both hero and
heroine are present, and the scene is Moscow. In the second,
the setting is rural, and the heroine, like the lieutenant's
"chance acquaintance," exists as memory alone.

The plot is again deceptively simple. Mitya, a student in
Moscow, is in love with Katya, who is training to become an
actress. Although his love seems to be reciprocated, he is continually plagued by feelings of jealousy that threaten to destroy the relationship. They decide that a brief separation
would be beneficial, and on an early spring day Mitya leaves
for his home in the country. At first he feels a certain relief,
but as spring marches on and passes into summer, Katya becomes even more of an obsession in her absence than she was
in Moscow, and he begins to live solely for the arrival of her
letters. The arrival of the first, however, is followed by a long
silence, and in despair he seeks distraction from his anxiety in
the arms of the venal peasant girl Alenka. But the liaison
brings him little comfort, and on receiving from Katya shortly
afterward the news that she proposes to go away with the
director of the studio at which she is studying,[5] he shoots
himself.

This summary conveys some idea of the bare bones of
the tale, but few of Bunin's works demonstrate more clearly
than *Mitya's Love* how singularly unamenable they are to sum-
marization. Like "By the Road," it is ostensibly a story about a
fatal self-deception, but it is also much more, for the self-
deception is merely a reflection of the fundamental duality
of human nature, and this duality and its tragic implications
really constitute Bunin's subject. On the basis of the rather
trite plot summarized above, he succeeded in composing
one of the most moving and pessimistic works in twentieth-
century Russian literature.

In the figure of Mitya the human spirit receives its most
powerful and noble embodiment in the whole of Bunin's fic-

tion, but at the same time he is endowed with all the vitality and sensuality of a typical Bunin hero. He recognizes a single purpose in life—to discover a love in which the demands of spirit and body will be completely reconciled, and in his love for Katya he believes that he has found it. But the Katya whom Mitya loves is largely a phantom of his own creation. Or, more precisely, she is a creation of his ideal conception of love. Like every other character in the work apart from Mitya himself, she is exclusively a creature of instinct and impulse to whom the demands of the spirit are unknown. Shortly before he leaves Moscow she reproaches him with loving only her body, but the reproach is ironically most informative about Katya herself, for it highlights the truth to which Mitya remains blind—that this is the only kind of love she can recognize—and as discord follows discord, the breach between phantom and reality is progressively widened. The narrator comments: "Even then it often seemed that there were two Katyas: the one whom Mitya had begun to desire persistently and demand from the first moment of his acquaintance with her, and the other one—the real, ordinary Katya, who differed so excruciatingly from the first" (5:184). But the more the real Katya asserts herself, the more zealously Mitya clings to the phantom. He struggles to reconcile with his image of her the vulgar artificiality of the theatrical world to which she seems instinctively drawn, and the strain on them both becomes intolerable. The result is their separation, which they regard simply as a means of "clarifying their relationship." In reality, it is an escape from truth—from a truth that can no longer be reconciled with dream except at the cost of self-destruction. Only their separation can preserve the dream intact.[6]

But Mitya's departure for the country casts additional light on the irony that lies at the heart of this work, for the country offers the very opposite of what Mitya seeks. On the symbolic level, it is the domain of precisely that element which constitutes the real Katya's essential being—the element of amoral, capricious instinct. Though physically absent, therefore, from the second section of the tale, the real Katya continues to assert herself in the form of Mitya's rural environment, and in his relationship with this environment the conflict between reality and dream is eventually renewed. Initially, the separation has the anticipated beneficial results. In the absence of the real Katya, the contradictions are soon forgotten, and in everything Mitya contemplates he sees a reflection of the phantom's invisible presence. Almost everything he sees triggers off some cherished memory. But each association is simply another distortion of reality, another act of self-deception, for although the stimuli to recollection that he receives from his environment—for example, the naked legs of the maid Parasha and the eagle-owl's cry of sexual ecstasy[7]—are wholly in harmony with the nature of the real, sensual Katya, for Mitya they resurrect the Katya of his own creation.

Like Parashka's rejection of Nikanor in "By the Road," Mitya's idealization of Katya (and implicit rejection of the real Katya) is represented as a transgression of natural law. His love includes something foreign to nature, and it encounters a hostile response. On the night, for example, when he hears the screeching of the owl, he "shuddered and froze, and then carefully stepped down from the porch and entered the dark avenue that seemed to be keeping a hostile watch on him from all sides" (5:199). But nature is not only hostile; it is also a bewitching seductress. As it parades before Mitya's eyes the splendor of spring, it seems to be engaged in subtle and resolute combat with an alien invader. The peasant girls in the fields, the "languid song" of the nightingales, the "incessant, voluptuously drowsy buzzing" of the bees, the warm, honeyed air, even "the simple sensation of the earth beneath his back" (5:208)—all seem to be part of a grand conspiracy astutely mounted to undermine his "unnatural" love. And when the sirens are resisted and Mitya struggles to escape from "this happiness with which the world overwhelmed him but which lacked something of supreme importance" (5:215), nature delivers the coup de grace in the form of Katya's "double,"[8] the "natural," uninhibited Alenka.

Tormented by Katya's failure to write and by the weakening of his will before nature's relentless assault, Mitya finally succumbs to the bailiff's offer to arrange the fatal rendezvous. "He felt," we read, "like a sleepwalker subjected to someone's alien will, as if he were marching with increasing speed toward some fateful but irresistibly attractive abyss" (5:226). "To the devil with all this tragic poetry of love!" he now cries as he waits for the moment to arrive, and as he steps forth to make for the meeting place, the triumph of nature is reflected in the new sensations of his body: "As there was no dew, the smells of the evening garden were not particularly noticeable. But despite the unconscious nature of all his actions on this evening, it seemed to Mitya that never before in his life— except, perhaps, in early childhood—had he encountered such strong and varied smells as now" (5:231). But the spell is abruptly broken by the experience of intimacy. The narrator observes as he caresses Alenka: "The terrible force of physical desire failed to become spiritual desire, bliss, rapture, a languor pervading his entire being" (5:233). In the love of Alenka he finds the same deficiency as in the "happiness" of nature—a chilling incapacity to satisfy the demands of the spirit,[9] and the recognition denotes his liberation from nature's coils. Yet the episode, of course, is again ironic, for unwittingly in the figure of Alenka he had been confronted with the reality of Katya, and, as if to confirm the fact, he receives a few days later Katya's second letter. Even the letter, however, fails to convince him of his self-deception.

For Mitya, the surrender of Katya to the director is not a revelation of Katya's true self, but simply an additional proof of nature's irresistible power. He sees it as a parallel to his own surrender to Alenka. Her rejection, therefore, does not destroy his illusion. Indeed, after the debacle with Alenka he clings to it ever more fiercely. But equally fierce is the continuing antagonism of nature that now receives expression in the insidious violence of the summer rains.[10] In chapter XXVIII we read:

Increasing its force tenfold, the rain fell on the garden in the late afternoon with sudden crashes of thunder and finally drove him

into the house. . . . The noise of the rain was everywhere—on the
roof, around the house, and in the garden. There were two different
noises—one in the garden and the other by the house, where it was
accompanied by the constant babble and splashing of the gutters as
they poured the water into the puddles. And this stirred in Mitya,
who had instantly lapsed into a lethargic torpor, an inexplicable
alarm, and together with the fever with which his nostrils, breath,
and head were burning it seemed to plunge him into a state of
narcosis, to create a world that seemed different, another late afternoon in another house that seemed alien to him and that was filled
with a ghastly presentiment of something. [5:235]

As he gradually succumbs to the rain's hypnotic effect, he
manages to retain some awareness of the familiar sounds of
the house, of the voices of his mother, brother, and sister
down below, but ultimately he is "plunged" into the "alien
house" of his own subconscious, into the house of nature that
lies within him.

In his state of narcosis, Mitya is confronted with the
reality of his own subsconscious personality, with the threat
from within to the survival of his ideal. He sees himself as a
child being carried by the young nanny who had inspired his
childhood vision of a love "that human language cannot express" (5:197), and on looking into her face he briefly recognizes the features of Alenka. But the scene is abruptly
transferred to a dark classroom, where the nanny undergoes
her second metamorphosis. Now he sees her sitting before a
mirror in her undergarments and obviously waiting for someone. The door suddenly opens, and in strides a man in a
dinner jacket "with a pale shaven face and short, black, curly
hair" (5:236). With a disdainful air, he takes her by the waist
and meekly she submits to him. Such is the form in which
Mitya's imagination recreates the director's conquest of Katya.
But the source of his horror is not simply the seduction, but
his personal participation in it, the temporary merging of his
own personality with that of the director which is reflected
in the latter's physical appearance—in the pallor and black,
curly hair in which Mitya recognizes his own most conspicuous physical features. Fusing into a single, composite per-

sonality, the three women with whom his entire experience of love is associated—the nanny, Alenka, and Katya—the dream surrenders them all in its final scene to the dispensation of nature, and Mitya himself, in the "jacket" of the director, plays the part of nature's instrument.

The dream, therefore, induced by the hypnotic beating of the rain, is a culminating exposé of nature's power and of Mitya's own subordination to that power despite his unabating demands for a love that is no less spiritual than sensual. Its effect is finally to destroy his illusion that in a world governed by nature his conception of an ideal love is ever capable of realization. Far from renouncing his ideal, however, and acquiescing in the reality that he is compelled to acknowledge, he reacts by renouncing the world to which the ideal is alien. When he wakes from his dream, he is conscious only of an acute sense of estrangement from his surroundings, even from his family, and of the intolerable pain inflicted by Katya's surrender. Instinctively he opens the drawer of his bedside table, takes out his revolver, and placing the barrel in his mouth he pulls the trigger "with force and pleasure" (5:237).

Thus ends the story of a character who occupies a unique position in Bunin's gallery of fictional portraits. The theme is the underlying theme of all his major works—man's thralldom to the laws of nature. But never before had he portrayed a hero who responds to the evidence of his thralldom by taking his own life, a hero who prefers death to the prospect of living in a world that cannot satisfy the innermost demands of his personality. Mitya is Bunin's greatest rebel against the laws of nature, a Promethean champion of the unyielding human spirit, whose rejection of nature is a conscious gesture of defiance made in full awareness both of the bounty that nature offers and of the bounty that it cannot provide. It is not a moral gesture. Gorky's reference to the work, in a letter to the novelist Leonid Leonov, as a "copy" of Tolstoy's *The Kreutzer Sonata* [Kreytserova sonata][11] is totally devoid of foundation, and comparisons with the same author's *The Devil* [D'yavol][12] are equally inappropriate.[13] Mitya's rebellion is a condemnation not of nature or physical love as such, but of a world in which nature is omnipotent and man is constantly threatened by the forces of nature with the involuntary betrayal of his loftiest ideals.

Yet in the fictional universe of Bunin, it is a gesture that can have only one result—the self-destruction of the rebel. Rejection of nature, whatever the motives that prompt it, is a rejection of the sources of life. It is the mark of the degenerate, and in this sense the fate of Mitya is directly comparable to that of the loathsome Yegor in "A Gay Farmhouse." The story expresses the ironic paradox that heroic assertion of the demands of the human spirit is a self-destructive assertion of man's inherent degeneracy, and this grim conclusion offers a no less valid insight into Bunin's attitude to life than the ecstatic eulogies of *The Life of Arsen'yev*. The two works mark the extremes of attitude between which he never ceased to vacillate—grateful acceptance and horrified despair.

The greatest problem for the analyst of *Mitya's Love* is the customary one posed by Bunin's works of how to convey its meaning without giving an impression of excessive contrivance. The only really effective solution would be quotation on a scale that space does not permit—such is the difficulty of detaching the idea from the form in which it is expressed. In reality, one is never conscious when reading the work of inordinate striving for effect. Even Mitya's obsessive commitment to his ideal of love seems entirely plausible in the fictional world that Bunin creates for him. The symbolism is completely unobtrusive, for, like all Bunin's symbolism, it involves no distortion of the recognizable, physical reality of life. It is simply an aesthetic realization of the conviction expressed by Arsen'yev that "every movement in the air, however slight, is a movement in our own lives" (6:214). Not only every character, but even every microscopic detail woven into the exuberant landscapes seems to bear some relation to the struggle taking place in the hero's mind and to contribute, like the repeated allusions to death, to the atmosphere of foreboding that is introduced in the opening sentence.[14] The resultant impression of "sheer concentrated power"[15] explains the enthusiasm with which criticism has generally responded to the work. Nor does any loss of dramatic intensity result from the detailed recording of psychological processes, for here thoughts and emotions are merely part of the continuing dialogue between dream and reality conveyed by the evolving relationship between the hero and his environment. Without them the struggle could not exist except in the form of a single brief gesture like Parashka's act of violence.

Although, however, everything in the work is directly or obliquely related to the inner drama of the hero, this does not mean, as critics have tended to suggest,[16] that everything is seen through the hero's eyes. The active role played by nature is not a role imparted to it by the hero's imagination. It is a subtly contrived representation of the *real* power of nature over the human psyche. Had it been otherwise, Bunin would presumably have adopted the form of a first-person narrative, and it may reasonably be supposed that it was precisely his wish to stress the reality and extent of nature's influence on human behavior that chiefly explains the relative rarity of this type of narrative in his major fiction. The most cogent evidence in support of this argument is the generally inactive role of nature in the first-person narratives he did write, including "Ida" and "The Mordvinian Sarafan."

"Ida" is arguably Bunin's finest—and certainly his most poignant—first-person narrative, though, to be precise, it is rather a first-person narrative within a first-person narrative. The technique is reminiscent of Turgenev. The setting is the restaurant of a Moscow hotel where the narrator is dining with three companions, one of whom, a composer, feels a sudden compulsion to relate an episode involving a friend of his that had occurred some three years ago. The main character of his story is a friend of the "hero's" wife, the beautiful Ida, who at one time, we are told, was a regular visitor to his house. He never failed, the composer continues, to marvel at her beauty and sometimes even imagined the "sweet torment" of an embrace, but on each occasion his dedication to "some nonsense called art" deterred him from succumbing to the temptation. Suddenly her visits stopped, and though he was dimly conscious of a sense of loss, her disappearance made little impression on him. Two years later, however, he met her again, now married to a handsome and wealthy student, in the restaurant of a railway station. Curtly dismissing her husband, she took him by the arm, and as they walked together along the platform, she confessed to him that for five years she had loved him passionately. The effect of her words was shattering. Momentarily paralyzed by the sudden realization that unconsciously he had always loved her and that a unique chance of happiness had slipped from his grasp, he was unable to utter a word in reply. Understanding his silence, she kissed him and walked away, and the composer ends his tale with the cry: "Let us drink to all who have loved us, to all those whom we in our idiocy have not valued. Let us drink to all those with whom we have been happy and enjoyed bliss and with whom we have parted only to lose our way in life forever while still linked to them forever by the most awesome bond in the world!" (5:253).

The depth of feeling with which the story is told leaves little doubt that its hero is the composer himself. Even so, its tone is far from tragic, and in this respect "Ida" stands somewhat apart from the other love stories of 1924–25. No attempt is made here to probe the uncharted recesses of the human subconscious. The events are recounted with a kind of wistful humor, and tragedy is precluded from the start by the urbane *bonhomie* of the narrator, the interjections of his cheerful companions, and the general air of contentment in which the tale is told. Herein we perceive the importance of the frame of the work with its details of feasting and drinking and the raison d'être of the first narrator. The story of the composer is winnowed of its tragic implications by the frame in which it is set, and the work ends appropriately with the first narrator's salute to the rising sun as the revelers return to their homes in the early hours of the next morning. The reader, therefore, is left with the feeling that for all the sadness of missed opportunities, it is good to be alive in a world that offers such exquisite delights to the palate and the spectacle of such exquisite beauty as that of Ida. For the portrait of Ida, who seems almost an emanation of the sparkling winter background against which she is repeatedly projected, is itself a celebration of the feast with which life regales the senses of man, a feast which language is powerless to convey. Such is the import of the composer's description of her as she sits on the station platform:

What can I say to you, apart from banalities, about that raised face lit by the paleness of that special snow which falls after blizzards and about her delicate, indescribable complexion which also resembled that snow? In general, what can I say to you about the face of a delightful young woman who, after walking along breathing in the snowy air, suddenly declares her love for you and waits for your answer? What did I say about her eyes? Violet? Quite wrong, of course. And the half-open lips? And the expression—the expression of all these features together, the face, the eyes, and the lips? And the long sable muff in which her hands were hidden, and the knees which were outlined beneath a Scottish material in blue-green check? Heavens, can words convey even the remotest idea of all this? [5: 252–3]

It is clear, therefore, from this summary that in "Ida" nature is simply an element in the portrait of the heroine that is suggestive of the beauty of life in general. The reader may be conscious of the irony that had the hero of the composer's tale grasped the beauty and happiness that were within his grasp, the result, in accordance with Bunin's "grammar" of love, would almost certainly have been catastrophe. But the irony is absent from the story itself. Here there is no "flash" to blind the eye of reason, no submission to nature's seduction, and no anguish to distort the beauty of nature and woman as it is filtered through the haze of elegiac reminiscence. Very different is the situation in "The Mordvinian Sarafan."

Bunin's second first-person narrative of 1925 seems to have been conceived as an ironic contrast to his first. Creating in the person of the heroine a figure who contrasts with Ida in almost every conceivable respect, he asserts the power of even such a woman as this to exercise a no less irresistible attraction. His purpose is immediately apparent in the questions of the narrator that open the story: "Why am I going to see her, this strange and, moreover, pregnant woman? Why did I begin this unnecessary and even repugnant relationship and why do I keep it up?" (5:255). The heroine is yet another of Bunin's nameless characters, and in this case anonymity seems again to be an indicator of spiritual vacuity. Her demeanor, the furniture in her apartment, and every sentiment that she utters proclaim a creature of mindless and pathetic vulgarity. Like the pedestrians on Gogol's Nevsky Prospect, she lacks all identity save that bestowed by the contours of her body and the idiosyncrasies of her dress—above all, by the grotesque sarafan of her own creation which she proudly displays to the horrified hero. He describes it as follows:

There was something strange and dreadful in her hands: a long, shapeless garment made of the canvas used by peasants with stripes and embroidery in dark brown and indigo silk on the shoulders, the sleeves, the chest, and the hem of the skirt. . . . There was something somber, ancient, and seemingly deathly in this loose garment, and it aroused in me an eerie, unpleasant feeling connected with her pregnancy and unnatural gaiety. It occurred to me that she would probably die in childbirth. [5:257–58]

Even the vulgar incongruity, however, of this bizarre imitation of peasant attire in the setting of an urban apartment fails to detract from the lure of her physical charms, and succumbing meekly to her pitiful coquetry, he draws her to him with the resigned air of a prisoner being led to the scaffold.

The voluptuous body of the heroine may be viewed as the counterpart in this short tale of the richly detailed landscapes in *Mitya's Love*. It is both the main object of sensuous description[17] and the conqueror of the hero's will. But nature is not entirely absent from the work, and although it is confined exclusively to the frame—to the two brief portraits of a March night in Moscow inserted into the narrator's descriptions of his arrival at the apartment and his abrupt departure—its role is not only compositional. In a sense, it even contributes to the motivation of the hero's weakness, for the gloom and harsh wind of the opening scene evoke the image of an inhospitable universe from which even the apartment of the repugnant adulteress offers a welcome refuge. His relief, conversely, on reentering it at the end eloquently conveys his desire for escape from the force that holds him in thrall. In both landscapes nature is entirely inactive in the sense that it is not represented as an influence on the human subconscious, but they show that in the art of Bunin even an inactive nature cannot be dismissed as inconsequential.

Even so, its role in "The Mordvinian Sarafan" is plainly ancillary, and together with "Ida" the story presents additional evidence of Bunin's general reluctance to allocate to nature its customary role when entrusting his stories to fictional narrators. Nature becomes active in his fiction only when it is not seen through the prism of a clearly defined sensibility. Only thereby could he ensure that the activity of nature would not be mistaken for the activity of a narrator's imagination. Hence the inactivity of nature not only in his first-person narratives, but also in the stories with narrators who are simply chroniclers or observers of events in which they are personally not involved. One of his rare attempts at this type of work was written a month after the completion of "The Mordvinian Sarafan" (in August–September 1925)— the much longer *The Cornet Yelagin Affair*, which is devoid even of an inactive nature.

The exclusion not only makes this tale virtually unique among Bunin's works; it is also perhaps one of the reasons for its relative weakness, for it is certainly one of his least successful works. Its weakness is mainly attributable, however, not so much to the exclusion of nature as to the cause of its exclusion, that is, to the intrinsic limitations of its theme, for as in the dénouement of "The Son," Bunin again attempts the impossible. Once more his attention is focused on the complexity of human nature as revealed in the experience of love, but now this complexity is related to the influence on man of his biological or genetic heritage. It is important to note that the story was written at the time when he was working on "Night," and it may be regarded, in part, as an attempt to translate into a work of fiction one of its main philosophical propositions. But the difficulties were obviously immense, and the attempt ended in complete implausibility. Although Bunin made some minor adjustments to the work a few months before his death, it is clear that he considered it a failure.[18]

The Cornet Yelagin Affair is the most conspicuous example in Bunin's fiction of a narrative constructed on the model of a court case, and the reason, of course, is self-evident: as indicated earlier, it was actually based on a trial that had been widely publicized in the Russian press—the trial in Warsaw in February 1891 of a junior officer named Bartenev in a hussar regiment, who was charged with the murder of the Polish actress Maria Wisnowska. After confessing to the crime, Bartenev was sentenced to eight years' hard labor, but was released, partly through the intervention of influential relatives, before the sentence had hardly begun. It was a mystifying case in many respects, and its curious features have been summarized by L. Nikulin:

Bartenev was an aristocrat from an old noble family. He did not kill Wisnowska out of jealousy. It seems that some agreement existed between them, for it was impossible for him, a hussar and an officer, to marry her in the conditions of that time. But after shooting his mistress, Bartenev did not kill himself. He presented himself to the court which examined the case without a jury. In his appearance and conduct both before the murder and after he showed himself to be a degenerate young man of limited ability, and his victim was also a woman of strange habits. The conditions in which the murder was committed, the behavior of Wisnowska before her death—everything indicated that Bartenev had killed his mistress at her insistence. In everything that happened there was a certain theatricality. A note left by the murdered woman stated: "In killing me this man is acting justly. He is justice."[19]

Each of the points noted by Nikulin is reproduced in Bunin's account of the enigmatic relationship between the cornet Yelagin and the actress Sosnovskaya, the fictional counterparts of Bartenev and Wisnowska, but his main object is to suggest an interpretation of the affair with the aid of one of his most cherished convictions. At the same time, he was obviously anxious to avoid any impression of forcing the facts into the straitjacket of his thesis—an impression to which the unusual and contentious nature of the thesis could easily have given rise. He wished merely to present the reader with the evidence and with the judgments expressed at the trial, to pinpoint the deficiencies of these judgments, and to order his presentation in such a way that the only valid judgment would suggest itself without being actually formulated. These would seem to be the considerations that prompted him to introduce as narrator and as a dispassionate commentator on the evidence submitted an inhabitant of the town in which Yelagin's trial took place. As an eyewitness of the trial, this worthy citizen is entrusted with the task of freeing the author from the charge of distorting the facts to suit his case. He simply reproduces the evidence as he heard it, exposes the flaws in the arguments of the prosecuting counsel, and replaces a chronological exposition of the events with an order that seems to him most conducive to a just verdict.

Thus, in effect, the story begins at the end with Yelagin's confession to his fellow officers and their discovery of Sosnovskaya's body in her apartment. These are the main events of the first three chapters. Thereafter, the narrator's method is basically the same throughout—to adduce statements made at the trial and then to subject them to his personal analysis. While chapter IV, for example, is wholly devoted to the arguments of the prosecutor, chapter V introduces the narrator's rejoinder, and in chapter VI he almost assumes the role of defending counsel, listing in response to the prosecutor's observations the points he would have stressed in his client's favor. In order to justify his doubts and reservations about the prosecutor's conclusions, he then passes, in chapter VII, to the evidence of Yelagin's character witnesses, subjecting it to the same painstaking scrutiny. The procedure, therefore, is essentially one of cross-examining both counsel and witnesses after the trial has actually taken place, and by the end of chapter VII the narrator's picture of Yelagin, as distinct from the picture of him presented at the trial as a calculating murderer and congenital criminal, is virtually complete. After employing the same methods, in chapters VIII and IX, in the characterization of Sosnovskaya, the narrator turns in the last five chapters to the last fatal meeting of the defendant and his victim and to the events that directly preceded it as described (in chapters X, XIII, and XIV) by Yelagin himself and (in chapter XII) by Sosnovskaya's maid, while in chapter XI he interpolates his remarks on Yelagin's evidence and his reflections on a number of points that at the trial had been completely ignored. His reexamination of the case is thus completed, and formulation of the final judgment is left to the reader.

Since the case of Bartenev seems to have fascinated Bunin from the time it was first publicized,[20] one may reasonably ask why he allowed thirty-four years to elapse before attempting his imaginative reconstruction of it. The reason already suggested is that his memories of the case may well have been resuscitated by the issues that preoccupied him in "Night." But it is also conceivable that his interest in it had been indirectly rekindled by his work on *Mitya's Love*, specifically, by the question that could well have occurred to him in the course of its composition of the possible consequences of such an "unnatural" love as Mitya's if it were truly to be reciprocated. In other words, what might have been the outcome if the real Katya had proved to be the personification of her lover's ideal? It is certainly undeniable that Mitya's elevated conception of love is shared both by Yelagin and by Sosnovskaya—who, incidentally, like Katya, is an actress—and an approach to *The Cornet Yelagin Affair* from this angle seems to offer the most reliable insight into Bunin's intended meaning.

Like Mitya, Yelagin and Sosnovskaya are rebels against nature, but their rebellion takes the different form of an antipathy to their families and backgrounds—the form of an aspiration to "withdraw from the chain." The prosecutor's description of Yelagin as a "degenerate" (5:272) is entirely apt, but in a sense of which the prosecutor himself is quite unaware. Again the term is invested here by Bunin with its primary etymological meaning of "one who departs from his race or kind," and herein we see the reason for the narrator's intriguing interest in Yelagin's parents and ancestry. He is the scion, we are informed, of a rich and noble family that could boast ten generations of army officers before him. His mother —"an extremely excitable woman" (5:272)—had died when he was very young, and he had spent his entire childhood and youth in dread of his domineering father. In an attempt to blacken his character, the prosecutor cited this fact at the trial as evidence of his cowardice, but the narrator takes issue with him. He comments: "Yes, Yelagin grew up in fear and trembling before his father. But trembling is not cowardice, especially before one's parents and in a man endowed with a keen sense of the entire heritage that links him with all his fathers, grandfathers, and forefathers" (5:272). The implication seems to be that Yelagin's "fear and trembling" were an expression of his instinctive rejection of his father and of the "entire heritage" his father seemed to him to represent—a heritage that had borne down on him with particular intensity after the premature removal of his mother's alleviating influence. In support of his point, the narrator introduces the subject of Yelagin's appearance. He states: "Yes, the appearance of Yelagin is not the classical appearance of a hussar, but I see in this one of the proofs of his exceptional nature. Look a little more attentively, I would say to the prosecutor, at his reddish hair, his round shoulders, and his thin legs, and you see almost with awe how far from insignificant this freckled face is with its small, greenish eyes (which avoid looking at you)" (5:272–73). It is clear that for the narrator Yelagin's appearance, which differs so markedly from that of the typical hussar and, implicitly, from the bearing of his military ancestors, is a physical or biological expression of his rebellion. It is the visual emblem of his degeneracy. And in harmony with this physical contrast is the contrast of temperament between Yelagin and his fellow officers, his inability to rest content with the everyday pattern of a young officer's life in which they seem to find complete self-fulfillment. "He is a man of strong passions," one of them observes at the trial, "but he always seemed to be waiting for something real and unusual" (5:274). When he met Sosnovskaya, his waiting evidently came to an end.

Although Sosnovskaya hails from a lower social class, her background displays significant affinities with that of her lover. She also, we are told, was brought up by a single parent, having lost her father at the age of three, and throughout her life she was schooled in strict observance of the bourgeois standards to which her mother was a living monument. From an early age, she sought refuge in books, and her rebellion expressed itself in the many extracts she copied down from them. Among the examples quoted by the narrator are the statements: " 'Not to be born is the first happiness, while the second is to return with all speed to nonexistence.' 'The world is tedious, terribly tedious, but my soul aspires to something unusual' " (5:276). Disregarding her mother's protests, she later attempted to realize this aspiration in the world of the theater, but disenchantment came rapidly. Her notes reveal her abhorrence of the lustful eyes that followed her movements on the stage. "They all demand my body," she laments, "not my soul" (5:277). Repelled by this experience, she resolved to devote her life to the search for a love capable of satisfying the demands of body and soul alike, and to her astonishment she ultimately found it in her relationship with the unsightly hussar.

The two portraits, therefore, show obvious similarities of background, temperament, and aspiration. Both Yelagin and Sosnovskaya are rebels against their biological and social heritage with which their spiritual needs are as incompatible as those of Mitya with the love of Alenka, and in their love for one another they discover the answer to their needs for which Mitya looks in vain to Katya. But from what we know of the laws that govern the world of Bunin's fiction it is clear that they cannot but share his fate. Once more the truth is affirmed that rejection of nature is a rejection of life and that a love based on this rejection, like any other form of degeneracy, can end only in death. Such is the import of the suicide pact—of the decision of the two lovers to seek an eternal refuge[21] and a state of blissful nirvana[22] in a world that lies beyond nature's reach. Their estrangement from life and from all that is "natural" is conveyed by the room in which Sosnovskaya's body is later discovered: "In the right-hand wall of the corridor there was a small entrance leading into the next room which was also quite dark, lit by the sepulchral light of an opal lamp that hung from the ceiling beneath an enormous shade of black silk. All the walls of this completely sealed, windowless room were also covered from top to bottom in something black" (5:264). The windowless room is the revealing symbol that links Yelagin and Sosnovskaya with the gentleman from San Francisco and the cloistered citizens of Streletsk in "The Cup of Life."

It is true that Yelagin, like Emile in "The Son," omits to take the final step, but the similarity goes no further. Indeed, it is plain that in every other respect they are sharply contrasting figures. The murderer of Sosnovskaya experiences no temporary insanity after committing his crime. He fails to fulfill his promise, in his own words, because he "simply forgot about it" (5:296). He concludes his statement: "I could not but keep the promise I gave her that after killing her I would kill myself, but I was overwhelmed by complete indifference. . . . And with the same indifference I now regard the fact that I am alive" (5:296). Yelagin's crime is not intended to signify, like Emile's, a dramatic confrontation with an unsuspected reality. It is an expression of his conscious renunciation of life. It is entirely consistent, therefore, that having killed the one person in whom he found an escape from life he should remain totally indifferent to his continuing existence.

The differences between the two murderers are paralleled by equally salient differences between their victims, for although they meet death in an identical manner, the superficial similarity conceals a fundamental contrast. Mme Marot is no rebel against nature. On the contrary, her death is an allegory of her complete submission, of her victory over the final impediment to her reintegration with nature. Hence the contrast between the symbolic lightness of the death scene in "The Son"[23] and the oppressive gloom in which death comes to Sosnovskaya. Diametrically opposed attitudes to nature are symbolically represented by two identical forms of death, the first of which signifies surrender, and the second rejection. The only really significant feature the dénouements of the two works have in common is that neither can prevail on the reader to suspend his disbelief, and the evidence suggests that Bunin was aware of the fact.

10. The Last Volume

Bunin's stories of the twenties not only offer further evidence of the remarkable inspirational power of his distinctive approach to the theme of love; they also confirm that in emigration his art continued to develop. The same comment may justifiably be made on his stories of the next two decades. The theme of love continues to predominate, and no major change may be detected in the principal ingredients of his tales, but the spirit of experimentation continues to reveal itself in this last period in an intensified pursuit of brevity. The beginning of this final stage in the evolution of his art is marked by the cycle of forty-one "miniatures" entitled *Short Tales* [Kratkiye rasskazy] that he wrote in 1930. Varying in length from a few lines to three pages, they reflect a common aesthetic purpose: to achieve an indissoluble fusion of form and meaning in a multifaceted revelation of the mystery of life and human nature. As usual, meaning is primarily conveyed in these tales not by sequential or cumulative description, but by the diffuse reverberations that are triggered off by the relation of the parts to the whole—by the galvanizing effect on the whole of individual words, phrases, or details. The innovation is the increased power of these reverberations that results from the extreme compression.[1]

The method is clearly illustrated by "The Eve" [Kanun], which consists of two short paragraphs and a one-sentence coda. The setting is urban, and the vantage point of the narrator is that of a passenger in a cab on its way to the local station. The first paragraph lists the sights that catch his eye on the journey: a bridge over a stream; a tramp standing with hunched shoulders beneath the bridge and devouring a kind of stuffing from a dirty rag; and the "terrible boots," the enormous size, the red hair, and the red shirts of the peasants on the carts that pass him by. In the second paragraph, attention is switched to the interior of the train boarded by the narrator—to the broad shoulders, cropped hair, gold spectacles, and evident self-confidence of a traveler in the same compartment and to the array of handsome suitcases he is constantly checking. The final sentence reads: "But it was already the autumn of 1916" (5:457). The effect of this statement is to prompt a reassessment of every detail—not only of the contrast between the bourgeois and the doglike tramp, but also of the "terrible boots" that are implicitly transformed into potential instruments of social change.

In this tale, therefore, the final statement retroactively fuses a succession of disparate details into a coherent, meaningful whole, and this procedure is the one most commonly adopted in the cycle. Occasionally, however, the pattern is reversed. A single example will suffice—"The Calf's Head" [Telyach'ya golovka], which ends with a description of the splitting of a calf's head by a butcher's chopper. There is no direct comment on the act. It acquires its force and meaning solely from its juxtaposition with the preceding reactions to the butcher's shop and its contents of a mother and child whose dinners the head will eventually provide—from the contrast between the child's awe and wonder at the sight of the suspended carcasses and the mother's single-minded devotion to haranguing the butcher. Implicitly apprehended from these two contrasting viewpoints, the mutilation of the head is suggestive, on the one hand, of the horror and sensuous delight with which man is "naturally" accustomed to react to the primitive brutality of life and, on the other, of the weakening of man's sentient responsiveness to the wonder of existence that comes to him with "maturity"—the "maturity" that is the subject of the colonel's lament in "The Brothers." The contrast between the implied reactions highlights the degeneracy of modern man.

The impression conveyed by the *Short Tales* is that they were conceived as a series of experiments in which Bunin sought to test the expressive potentialities of the narrative technique he had evolved over the previous two decades. More particularly, in the context of the development of his art, they may be seen as a preparation for his last volume of stories, *Dark Avenues*, in which the same pursuit of brevity is repeatedly in evidence. Between 1930 and 1937, he wrote very little apart from the last book of *The Life of Arsen'yev* and *The Emancipation of Tolstoy*, but in November 1937 he began the cycle of tales on which he was intermittently to expend his creative energies for the next twelve years. The most productive periods were the autumn of 1940 and the spring and summer of 1944, and there can be little doubt that in a very real sense they represented for him, in Baboreko's words, "a kind of refuge from nightmarish reality"[2]—an escape from the hardships of life in Grasse under the German yoke. The first edition, a limited edition of six hundred copies containing only eleven stories, came out in New York in 1943. This was followed in 1946 by an edition containing thirty-eight stories which was published in Paris. Bunin intended to add two more stories to the volume—"In Spring in Judaea" [Vesnoy v Iudeye] (1946) and "Lodging for the Night" [Nochleg] (1949)[3]—but the Paris edition still remains the most complete. In the latest Soviet edition of Bunin's works, the original cycle of thirty-eight tales is reduced to thirty-five by the exclusion of "The Guest" [Gost'] (1940), "Miss Klara" [Baryshnya Klara] (1944), and "Iron Wool" [Zheleznaya sherst'] (1944), presumably on the grounds that the descriptions of physical intimacy in them are excessively frank.[4] The same charge has been leveled at several other stories in the volume.

The theme of the volume is briefly summarized in Bunin's own reference to it as "a book about love."[5] Since only one of the forty tales—"Vengeance" [Mest'] (1945)—has an ending that can positively be termed happy, it might perhaps be thought that "a book about tragic love," as suggested by the epithet in the title,[6] would be a more fitting description. The qualification, however, would not only be inappropriate; it would be seriously misleading, for love in these tales is almost invariably a source of joy, an initiation into an unsuspected intensity of experience that transforms all preconceived notions of life and its meaning, "Is there really such a thing as unhappy love?" asks the heroine of "Natalie" (1941) (7:170), and almost every tale prompts a negative reply. The recurrent source of tragedy is not love but life as Bunin conceived it, and "a book about life" would perhaps be the most apt definition of the volume. Love ends tragically because the life of man is itself tragic—such is the repeated implication of these unusual stories in which Bunin's tendency to absolve his characters of all responsibility for the motivation of events is displayed more starkly than ever before.

The story "In Paris" [V Parizhe] (1940), for example, portrays two lonely, middle-aged Russian émigrés who meet in a Paris restaurant—a former general and a waitress. They arrange to meet, go to the cinema, and after making love in his apartment decide to live together. Both are rejuvenated by the relationship. "I feel," exclaims the general, "as if I were twenty years old" (7:119). The next short paragraph reads: "On the third day of Easter he died in a carriage of an underground train. While reading a newspaper he suddenly threw back his head against the back of the seat and rolled his eyes" (7:120). The reader is given no warning of this climax. It is totally unprepared by the preceding development of the tale, and in this respect it differs sharply from the climax of "The Gentleman from San Francisco." Death in this context does not denote the confrontation of a degenerate with reality; it is simply a stark manifestation of the blind, indiscriminate cruelty of life, just as the chance meeting in the restaurant is a manifestation of its indiscriminate beneficence.

"In Paris" is an exceptional work in the cycle only in the sense that it is unequivocally set in the "present"—in the Paris of the Russian émigrés. In general, the "present" is avoided by Bunin,[7] and the reason has already been suggested. Since his theme imposed no constraints of time and place, it was natural that he should pluck his characters and settings from the land and period that had never ceased to dominate his thoughts. In a remarkable variety of prerevolutionary settings —the houses of provincial gentry, the smallholdings of peasants, metropolitan hotels and provincial inns, Volga steamers, the bohemian quarter of Odessa—the same kind of drama is

reenacted by an equally remarkable variety of prerevolutionary character types. In almost every story we encounter the
same sequence of ecstatic joy and sudden disaster, the same
spectacle of human dependence on the whims of fate, and
again the punished are usually innocent of all sin. And it is
noticeable that even when guilt does exist, the catastrophe
that follows is completely unrelated to it.

The point is illustrated by "Natalie," the hero of which,
Meshchersky, bears a certain superficial resemblance, as M.
Iof'yev has observed, to Sanin in Turgenev's *Spring Waters*
[Veshniye vody] (1871).[8] Though deeply in love with Natalie,
Meshchersky allows himself to be seduced by the charms of
his cousin Sonya and is ultimately caught with her by Natalie
in a compromising situation. But the heroine's indignant departure does not mark the end of the story. Had it done so,
the entire emphasis would have fallen, as it does in Turgenev's tale, on the hero's weakness of will and personal responsibility for the course of events. The story continues, in fact,
for another twelve pages, in which hero and heroine, after
having been parted for three years, are finally brought together again and Meshchersky's sins are forgiven. Yet no
sooner have they declared their undying love for one another
than the story ends with the cold, factual statement: "In December she died in premature childbirth on Lake Geneva"
(7:172). Thus a dénouement that would have been fully motivated is replaced by one that is simply appended, and it is
precisely this lack of motivation, which is Bunin's aesthetic
correlative of irremediable human impotence, that strikes the
note of horror.

Although death is by no means the only obstacle in the
cycle to the prolongation of happiness, the force or implication of the various other stumbling blocks is identical to
that of death in "Natalie" and "In Paris." In "Dark Avenues"
(1938), the story that gives the volume its title, the obstacle is
social—the difference of class that thirty years before the
events described had prevented the marriage of the hero, a
high-ranking officer, to the woman whom he now meets again
by chance in a wayside inn. The intensity of the affair had

made it impossible for the woman ever to marry anyone else, and even the hero remembers it as the only experience that had ever brought him happiness. Yet he still does not question the rightness of his decision to abandon her and take a wife from his own class, even though he himself was later betrayed and abandoned in his turn. The obstacle presented by social circumstance, he concludes, was simply insuperable. And we may confidently assume that even if he had allowed his heart to rule his head, the idyll would soon have been interrupted. As if to confirm the fact, Bunin depicts in "Tanya" (1940) an affair between a landowner and a peasant girl that survives every threat to its continuation only to have the death sentence pronounced on it in another brief coda: "This took place in February of the terrible year 1917. He was visiting the village for the last time in his life" (7:109).

History similarly intervenes in "A Cold Autumn," in the form of World War I, to deprive a young girl of her fiancé. But the apparent hostility of life to enduring happiness also expresses itself in less exalted forms—in the possessiveness of a mother ("Rusya" [1940]), in the moral indignation of a protective relative ("Antigona" [1940]), or in the jealousy of a rival ("Heinrich" [Genrikh] [1940]). It might perhaps be thought that these obstacles differ from those mentioned above in the sense that in each case the relationship between hero and heroine seems to bring them into being. The obstacles exist because the relationships exist, and with the cessation of the relationships they would instantly disappear. But the crucial point, of course, is that the causal connections are completely arbitrary. Bunin was not obliged by the nature of the relationships portrayed in these stories to end them as he does. In effect, he takes the formula A + B = C, or D, or E, or F and reduces it consistently to A + B = C. Thereby he contrives to express a truth about life which A + B = D, or E, or F would only obscure. Like death in "Natalie" and "In Paris," the principles or emotions that destroy the relationships in "Rusya," "Antigona," and "Heinrich" are forces that irrupt from without. They are totally beyond the control of the lovers themselves. They are part of human nature, and human nature is a no less disruptive force in the brutal world in which Bunin's lovers laugh and weep than death and the wars of nations. And since the lovers themselves are as subject to the dictates of their unpredictable natures as anyone else, it follows that the destructive obstacle can equally arise from within their relationship—from the natural ebb and flow of passion, for example, that drives Galya Ganskaya, in the eponymous story of 1940, to suicide and the hero of "Muza" (1938) to the verge of madness, or from the disenchantment with the "present" that impels the enigmatic heroine of "The First Monday in Lent" to seek refuge in a nunnery and in restored spiritual contact with Russia's ancient past.[9]

The stories of *Dark Avenues* resemble Bunin's love stories of the twenties in many obvious respects. It is already apparent that love is again repeatedly depicted as a blinding "flash," as a kind of "sunstroke" yielding to sudden and agonizing "eclipse." Again the heroines are usually seen through the eyes of the heroes, and the latter generally retain the ability to articulate their emotions that differentiates Bunin's lovers of the twenties from their prerevolutionary predecessors. It is equally clear, however, that in these later stories the contrasts are dramatically sharpened, and it is here perhaps that the effects of his experiments in the *Short Tales* are most noticeable. The psychological dramas of "rebels" now recede from view to be replaced by man's wholly conscious and uncomprehending experience of life's polar extremes, the heights of bliss and the depths of despair; the middle ground between the extremes is now completely excluded. The characters, who are often nameless, seem to have no existence outside their pursuit of love and the relationships that reward their efforts.[10] Their professions may be indirectly conveyed, like that of the artist in "Galya Ganskaya," whose narrative reflects his sensitivity to color,[11] but essentially they are little more than a means of individualization, and their relevance to the fiction is usually negligible. Prised from the routine of their normal lives, the heroes of these tales exist only to experience the most fundamental contrasts of the human condition as magnified in the experience of love.

The concentration of attention on these critical experiences is most commonly effected with the aid of a more extensive use than ever before of the simple expedient that had served Bunin so well in the past—the motif of travel. With few exceptions, the heroes of these stories are portrayed in motion. "Antigona," for example, begins: "In June a student set off from his mother's estate to see his aunt and uncle" (7:58). The hero of "Tanya" remarks: "I have no home, Tanya. I have spent my whole life traveling from one place to another" (7:104). And in "Heinrich" the writer Glebov embarks on a trip abroad for the simple reason, as he puts it, that "it always seems as if somewhere there will be some happy experience or meeting" (7:130). The common feature of almost all Bunin's protagonists is that their contact with the relatively stable and predictable reality of their individual private worlds is temporarily severed, and their dependence on the vagaries of fate is correspondingly enhanced. Regardless of differences of personality and temperament, they are transformed by the very situations in which they find or place themselves into helpless recipients of life's blessings and blows.

The motif of travel, therefore, enables Bunin to eliminate everything that is irrelevant to his central concern. His heroes simply travel, love, and die or suffer torment. Almost all of them complete the same three-stage course. Yet despite the repetitiveness, even those who are left nameless are endowed with a distinct, recognizable identity, for the element of generalization inherent in the repetitive plot does not produce a schematic type of narrative in which everything is pared down to an algebraic transparency. On the contrary, all the familiar elements of Bunin's mature narrative technique are continually in evidence—not least his habit of placing his heroes in settings that veritably bombard their senses with the most varied stimuli and the superficially digressive but subtly suggestive style of writing in which his poetic genius had always most brilliantly displayed itself. The powerful element of contrast in the plot offered unlimited scope for the kind of allusive interplay between the landscapes and the experience of the characters he had always relished. Thus the rotation of

the seasons vividly chronicled in the backdrop to the romance
in "Tanya" acquires a totally unsuspected relevance in the
light of the coda, while the impassivity of a radiant spring day
and the ubiquitous signs of nature's stirring life convey more
expressively than any direct statement the grief and solitude
of the heroine of "In Paris" as she returns from her lover's
funeral. In general, nature enjoys its customary prominence
in the volume. It stimulates the senses of the characters, it
impels them into passionate embraces, and coldly it observes
the outcome, and, in combination with the drastic economy
that is the dominant stylistic feature of the tales, its interventions create an even more striking impression than usual
of that intermittent "extravagance" generally characteristic of
Bunin's art.[12]

The story in the cycle that is perhaps most illustrative of
this "extravagance" is "Rusya" which, although it is a third-
person narrative, consists mainly of the hero's recollections of
a romantic episode that occurred in his youth. His memory is
suddenly jolted when the train on which he is traveling with
his wife stops at a small country station not far from the house
where the episode took place during his service there as a
young tutor. The temporal distance thus established between
the time of narration and the events of the narrative determines and motivates the distinctive features of the work's
style, in particular, the combination of vague, "poetic" impressions and individual striking details that have embedded
themselves in the narrator's memory.

Through the mists of time the setting of his romance
with Rusya, his pupil's sister, emerges in his recollections as a
green, hot, steamy, almost tropical locality situated near a
swamp. Introduced from the very beginning by a reference
to the "damp smell of a swamp" that enters the train's windows (7:44), the setting plainly alludes to the heat of passion
and evokes the conception of love as a fever that takes complete possession of body and soul. The atmosphere created by
the proximity of the swamp is sustained throughout the story
by colorful descriptions of the ceaseless, seething activity of
nature and by the repetition of a small number of individual

concrete details that acquire the force of motifs. Thus a constant sound accompaniment to the events is provided by the
whining of gnats and the beating of dragonflies' wings, and
the lurking presence of these insects instills a subtle element
of menace that is powerfully reinforced by the other repeated
details of nature, by the numerous references to frogs, grass
snakes, leeches, and moths. We read: "And everywhere there
was always something rustling, crawling, threading its way"
(7:51). Equally prominent is the flora of the setting, above all,
the huge rushes and water lilies of the swamp that, like the
gnats and dragonflies, are invariably paired and similarly
convey a vague sense of foreboding. The explanation of the
"extravagance," in short, is apparent almost from the outset.
Dispensing with explicit statements, Bunin contrives to create
simply by means of repetition and accumulation the atmosphere of tension between the lovers and their environment
that augurs the outcome, and, as the narrative unfolds, the
active participation of nature in the drama is progressively
intensified, finally expressing itself in the irruption into the
house of a sinister black cock at the precise moment when the
hero and heroine are enjoying their first embrace (7:47).[13] In
this tale nature as a whole appears to be endowed with a
malicious intelligence and almost to be in league with Rusya's
mother, who savagely brings the romance to an end.[14]

It should be added, however, that the sense of foreboding is created not only by the extravagant descriptions
of nature. We have seen that in "Light Breathing" Bunin
achieved a similar effect by a different means—by introducing, through the reference to the schoolboy Shenshin, the
suggestion of an ending that, though tragic, contrasts with
the actual ending. The same device is used in "Rusya." When
the hero's wife asks him early in the tale why he did not marry
the girl, he replies solemnly: "Well, because I shot myself and
she stabbed herself with a dagger" (7:46). The jest makes little
impression, but it clearly refers to a dénouement in which the
affair may well have culminated. In "Light Breathing" the
actual dénouement is even more tragic than the "decoy"; the
fact that in "Rusya" the reverse is the case in no way dimin-

ishes the effectiveness of the device as a means of reinforcing the atmosphere that pervades the work.

Further variations of this device are encountered in "Heinrich" and "The Caucasus" [Kavkaz] (1937). As the heroine of the former tale,[15] for example, speeds southward to Austria in the arms of the writer Glebov, she muses on the reaction she can expect from her waiting Austrian lover to her decision to terminate the relationship. "He is a cautious man," she concludes, "and he will agree to a peaceful separation" (7:133). A few pages later, however, she recalls her last meeting with him when she attempted to make her attitude clear and the hatred that suddenly glared at her from his contorted features. Thus the question is implicitly raised: which of the two contrasting images of the Austrian will she meet on her arrival? In this case, as the reader senses in advance, the "peaceful" conclusion turns out to be the "decoy." Heinrich is unwittingly speeding to her death.

The possibility of a violent conclusion is similarly foretold in "The Caucasus," but here Bunin plays with our expectations by creating a false impression of the likely victim of the violence. Having given her husband two addresses at which she allegedly proposes to spend her Caucasian holiday, the heroine sets off from Moscow with her lover for a different destination. She knows that in a few days' time her husband will follow and endeavor to track them down, but she regards even a violent death as preferable to her normal existence. "Better death," she remarks, "than this torment" (7:14). Resigned to the inevitability of retribution, the lovers are rewarded in the few days left to them with a happiness neither of them has ever known before, and their idyll is described in considerable detail. But a few lines before the end, the narrative abruptly switches direction, and after a pause the brief paragraph is appended: "He sought her in Gelendzhik, in Gagry, and in Sochi. The day after his arrival in Sochi he bathed in the sea in the morning, then shaved, put on clean underwear and a snow-white jacket, breakfasted in his hotel on the restaurant terrace, drank down a bottle of champagne followed by coffee and chartreuse and slowly smoked a cigar.

Returning to his room, he lay down on the sofa and shot himself in the temples with two revolvers" (7:16). Thus the idyll is indeed brought to an end by death, but paradoxically by the death of the one who threatened it.

Although most of the longer stories in the volume provide similar evidence of Bunin's concern with the creation of atmosphere, it is by no means the sole explanation of his occasionally puzzling extravagance. Since the long description, for example, of the idyll in "The Caucasus" temporarily disrupts the atmosphere that prevails in the rest of the tale, it must plainly have been dictated by quite different considerations. The abrupt insertion of this static, lavishly detailed descriptive section is intelligible only as a characteristic variation of the tempo of the narrative designed partly to convey the narrator's absorption in his memories of the episode and partly to offset the unexpected dénouement. In general, variations of this kind play a more conspicuous role in the stories of *Dark Avenues* than in Bunin's tales of any other period, and it is noticeable that the stories that are most dependent on them for their effect are usually, like "The Caucasus," first-person narratives. The reason is self-evident. In this kind of work the form of the narrator's tale is obviously determined by his personal involvement in the events, and the elements of the tale are ordered and the accents placed in accordance with his emotional responses to each recollected experience. At the same time, it is clear that the pace at which the narrative flows may itself be determined by his reactions and thus add substantially to our understanding of his state of mind. It is difficult to think of any Russian writer who has been more attentive than Bunin to the opportunities afforded by the first-person narrative form for oblique psychological characterization of this kind, and the alternations of "economy" and "extravagance" in the tales of *Dark Avenues* may frequently be attributed to the use he makes of them. As this aspect of his technique cannot be illustrated without detailed analysis, the survey will be confined to an examination of the six-page story "Muza."

   The sequence of events can be briefly recounted. After a leisurely opening, the heroine, whose Christian name forms the title, suddenly presents herself to the hero in his apartment on the Arbat, informs him of the favorable impression he had made on her at a concert the previous day, and announces her desire for a closer acquaintance. The rest of the story traces the development of their relationship and describes the happiness they enjoy before Muza suddenly abandons him for his neighbor Zavistovsky. Immediately striking is the apparent irrelevance of the opening to the main events of the narrative. The detailed information in the first two paragraphs (186 words) about the art course on which the hero embarks and about the artist who teaches him is totally unrelated to the events that follow. Indeed, the fictional life of the artist, with whom the narrator is momentarily so preoccupied that his attention even extends to the "dirty gray color" of his spats (7:30), is confined to this introductory section. His momentary concern, however, with an object distinguished by the color "gray" perhaps discloses the explanation of this seemingly unjustified prolixity. If we take it in conjunction with the two references in these two paragraphs to the overwhelming boredom of the narrator's life at the recollected time, the thought suggests itself that here prolixity and irrelevance may be consciously employed as an objective correlative of his state of mind and lethargic existence. This impression is reinforced by the two references to time in these paragraphs—one direct, the other indirect. The first appears in the opening sentence: "Abandoning my estate in the province of Tambov, I spent the winter in Moscow" (7:30), and the second in the penultimate sentence of the second paragraph: "My memory has retained the image of snow falling constantly outside the windows and of the muffled roar and ringing of horse-drawn trams on the Arbat" (7:31). Thus the prelude to the story is framed by two general indications of time, and in both cases the time is the same. The generalization "winter" and its positioning at the beginning and end of the two introductory paragraphs create an impression of

burdensome stasis that, like winter itself, clearly harmonizes
with the mood the narrator is seeking to evoke at this point
and also provides a basis for expressive contrast.

With the unheralded appearance of the heroine in the
third paragraph at the door of the hero's apartment, the
stasis of the opening two paragraphs is terminated. Time is
set in motion. The disruption of the introductory tempo is
anticipated in the first sentence by the *specific* indication of
time and the reference to the passing of winter: "But one
day in March while I was sitting at home at work with my pen-
cils—the dampness of wet snow and rain borne in through
the ventilation windows of the double frames was no longer
wintry, the clattering of hooves along the road had lost its
wintry sound, and the ringing of the trams seemed more
musical—someone knocked at the door in my hall" (7:31).
Thus the triple transition—from winter to spring, from stasis
to motion, and from tedium to exhilaration—is linked in
a single complex syntactic structure with the appearance of
Muza, who emerges immediately as the very embodiment of
movement and vitality. Into the timeless, lifeless world of the
hero Muza brings quickness of thought, word, and action,
vividly conveyed by the syntactic transparency—the sequence
of short, simple clauses—of the passage that describes her
actions on entering the apartment and by the clipped, decisive
character of her statements in the ensuing dialogue.

Initially, the contrast between these syntactic forms and
the more protracted and complex structures that record the
impressions of the startled hero appears to perpetuate the
contrast between stasis, associated with the hero, and motion,
associated with the heroine, but by degrees the psychological
implications of the contrast change significantly. From a reflection of her instinctive spontaneity and self-assurance the
uncomplicated syntax of Muza evolves into an expression of
her impetuous and uninhibited surrender to her infatuation.
The hero, conversely, seeks to restrain her impetuousness,
to arrest the flow of time, to hang onto the passing moment
of exhilaration that contrasts so sharply with his foregoing
wretchedness. Previously the turgid flow of time was a source

of pain to him; now he actively strives to hold it back. Displaying his usual preference for indirect methods of communication, Bunin substitutes syntax for explicit statements as the main indicator of the feelings of his characters. The syntax itself expresses the two conflicting attitudes to time.

Entranced by Muza, the hero abandons his art course and moves "in May" to a dacha on the outskirts of Moscow. But hardly has the flow of time resumed than it is immediately interrupted, for this briefly stated forward movement of the plot gives way abruptly to a lengthy description of the dacha, its situation, and the weather. Like the protracted description of the "idyll" in "The Caucasus," the accumulation of details at this juncture can be related only to the narrator's intoxication with the recollected moment and to his reluctance to release it from his memory, and the scene portrayed is itself devoid of change or development. Emphasis on constant or repeated features alternates with generalizations that exclude variation or movement: "It rained constantly. There were pine forests all around. . . . Everything was wet, lush and mirrorlike . . . , and the twilight of the west lingered and lingered in the motionless, silent moonlight which was also motionless and bewitched" (7:33). The duplication of the verb in the third sentence is reminiscent of the attitude to time expressed by the duplicated imperatives in the second quatrain of Tyutchev's lyric "The Last Love" [Poslednyaya lyubov'] (1853):

Do not hasten, do not hasten, evening light,
Linger, linger, enchantment![16]

The frozen, crystallized character of the landscape itself seems to reflect the narrator's disinclination to advance to the painful dénouement.

Toward the end of the descriptive passage he suddenly switches from generalizations to the particular, and the poetic, time-consuming landscape begins to disintegrate under the pressure of more specific recollections. The sequence of events is reactivated. His memory of falling asleep one night at the station after seeing off Muza is followed by that of his impatient wait for the next evening to arrive, expressively conveyed by three short sentences, each beginning—in a manner reminiscent of the description of Ignat's nocturnal vigil—with a statement of time: "In the morning. . . . Toward midday. . . . Just before sunset" (7:34).[17] He meets her off the train, they dine, and peace, silence, and stability are momentarily restored. Again the landscape interrupts the flow of events. But now the interlude is brief. The undercurrent of time swiftly gathers momentum. The following short paragraph, consisting of only sixty-four words, covers a seven-month period, and noticeable once more is the sharp change of syntax—the rarity of subordination and the impression of quickened time produced by the succession of main clauses. Three of the first four sentences begin with statements of time, and now the periods embraced are significantly enlarged. They take us successively into June, into autumn, and, in the fourth sentence, into winter. The intervening third sentence introduces the figure of the neighboring landowner Zavistovsky, whose name itself, while deceptive,[18] seems to imply a no less potent threat to the continuation of the happy affair than the conspicuous acceleration of time. Together with the increasing frequency of Zavistovsky's visits, the quickened passage of time reinforces the reader's presentiments of impending crisis. The impression is created that the narrator is no longer capable of resistance, that he has surrendered to the magnetic pull of the climax.

The next paragraph introduces the events that immediately precede the dénouement and maintains the tendency toward more specific statements of time. After the opening statement ("Just before Christmas . . . " [7:34]) they follow one another in ominous succession. At seven o'clock on the decisive day the hero returns from town to find the house empty. Initially he suspects nothing and, exhausted by his journey, he falls asleep. An hour later, however, he wakes with the distinct feeling that Muza has left him. After a vain search at the station, he sets out for Zavistovsky's estate. His journey there on foot, the surrounding scene, and the approach to his neighbor's house are all described in some detail, as if he is seizing every pretext to delay the climactic moment. The interval between his decision to visit Zavistovsky and his arrival in the dark entrance hall of the latter's house is described in 114 words—almost double the number used to describe the period from June to December. But again, of course, the resistance collapses. He enters the house to find his suspicions confirmed.

The analysis illustrates, therefore, the tension in this story, created by variations of narrative tempo, between an actual, objective succession of events and a superimposed set of temporal relations. On one level, this tension may be seen as a reflection of the hero's reinterpretation of the recollected episode, that is, of the processes of emphasis and selectivity that are inseparable from the workings of memory, particularly when the emotions are deeply involved. On another level, it alludes to one of the central themes of the entire volume— not simply to man's slavery to time but to his heightened sensitivity to this slavery at moments of intense happiness. In particular, we observe once more the contribution of descriptive digressions to the creation of this tension. Quite apart from their more conventional "poetic" role, they are closely connected in each case with the narrator's attitude to time, reflecting either his indifference to time before the appearance of Muza or his subsequent attempts to arrest its flow at moments of recollected delight and again, at the very last moment, in the face of the inexorable dénouement. This use of descriptive passages corresponds on the compositional level to the retarding effect of accumulated descriptive elements in individual sentences. The alternation of short sentences, composed almost entirely of main clauses, and more diffuse, rambling sentences with repeated subordination reflects the contrast between time in motion and superimposed stasis. In conjunction, these two stylistic procedures—the insertion of descriptive interludes and the syntactic complication of the individual sentence—convey indirectly the narrator's vain resistance to the ineluctable passage of time that

foredooms his escape from the apathy evoked in the first
two paragraphs. Disregard for these aspects of the style and
structure of the story does not preclude, of course, a correct
understanding of its theme, but it may well distort our judgment of Bunin as an artist and prompt unmerited reservations about his reputed sensitivity to the force of every syllable
and mark of punctuation.[19] In "Muza" form and structure do
not simply reflect the content; they are an inalienable part
of the content. Bunin's recurrent tendency to interrupt the
tempo of his narratives, for which he was often severely
criticized before the Revolution, becomes in this story a vital
ingredient of the total artistic structure, contributing significantly to the development and dramatic interest of the theme.

Expressive variations of narrative tempo or rhythm similar to those perceived in "Muza" can be found in most of Bunin's later stories. The sequence of slow beginning, abounding
in descriptive detail, and terse, clipped ending is encountered
repeatedly. But even in this respect there are striking differences between one tale and another. "Every story," Bunin
often remarked to his wife, "has its own rhythm."[20] In "Muza"
the transition from happiness to disaster involves, in simple
terms, a gradual, if interrupted, acceleration of tempo accompanied by the narrator's sharpening sensitivity to the passage of time. In other stories, as we have seen, the transition is
effected much more abruptly. Thus almost the entire action
of the first-person narrative "Three Roubles" [Tri rublya]
(1944)[21]—the development of the relationship between the
hero-narrator and the nameless girl who visits him in his hotel
room for the purpose of earning the pittance that provides
the title—is confined to a single night. Exchanges of dialogue
alternate regularly with long descriptive interludes that appear to carry the same psychological implications as their
counterparts in "Muza." This section of the narrative embraces all but the last ninety-seven words. The first forty-nine
words of the final section embrace almost a year, and this
dramatic quickening of time is again accompanied by a characteristic simplification of the syntax: "She stayed in the hotel.

I made a short trip into the country, and the next day we left together for Mineral'nyye Vody. We wanted to spend the autumn in Moscow, but we spent both the autumn and winter in Yalta. She became feverish and began to cough. Our rooms began to smell of creosote. . . . In the spring I buried her" (7:318). In this story, therefore, the tension between narrative time and actual time is much more acute than in "Muza." The protracted rapture of one night is savagely contrasted with the incomparably swifter, year-long descent to disaster.

Even in "Three Roubles," however, the collision between the two sections of the plot with their contrasting stylistic features is not effected by direct juxtaposition. The process of transition, though briefly delineated, is nevertheless included. It has been noted already that this is not the case, for example, in "Natalie," in which the intervening events are omitted and the tragic dénouement is simply appended after a break in the text. Here, as in the majority of the longer third-person narratives, the collision is maximally sharpened by the reduction of the temporal interval to zero and the simple insertion of a transitional silence. It is a procedure that reminds one of the last two lines of Bunin's poem "Rhythm" [Ritm], written in August 1912:

Everything is rhythm and haste. Aimless striving!
But terrible is the moment when the striving ceases. [1:353]

In his last stories the "terrible pause" becomes a major ingredient of his narrative technique. Nor is its role restricted to sharpening the transition from joy to catastrophe. "The Caucasus" and "Heinrich," for instance, both contain six examples of the device. Short bursts of narrative and dialogue are isolated and abruptly terminated before yielding to protracted descriptive digressions, and in the intervening lacunae we sense the invisible working of those primitive forces that finally reveal themselves in the violent dénouements. The pauses—particularly those that isolate the dénouement from the foregoing narrative—are in no sense intended as signals of deducible logical processes. They are not inserted to mask or abbreviate a rational motivation of the events. They reflect the author's attempts to achieve in his last volume of stories a closer correlation between structure and content than ever before, to make the form itself expressive of his lifelong belief in man's complete subservience, however strong his resistance, to the blind, irrational forces of nature.

Concluding Remarks

Perhaps the most frequently encountered cliché of Bunin criticism is the assertion that he was, above all else, a meticulous stylist, a sharply discriminating and fastidious practitioner of his craft. The judgment, of course, is intended less as a tribute than as a criticism. It implies a certain narrowness of outlook, an excessive preoccupation with formal perfection that allegedly explains the impression of coldness his fiction tends to convey. One of the main purposes of this study has been to expose the limitations of this view. The underlying argument throughout has been the contention that in the art of Bunin, as in that of any major writer, form and content are closely interdependent and that the most distinctive features of his style, including its alleged chill, are attributable neither to a lack of significant content nor indeed to a lack of concern for the human condition, but rather to a particular conception of the human condition that is found in the works of no other Russian writer. Certainly some readers of this book will regret that his style (in the narrow sense of the term) has not been more extensively discussed and illustrated, but there is already no shortage of critical literature on this subject. What critics have consistently failed to provide is an examination of his style, and more generally of the most characteristic formal and structural features of the typical Bunin short story, in relation to the content of his fiction. The relationship between content and style is the central issue in the assessment of any writer's art, and it has been posed as the central issue in this study of Bunin.

In order to assess this relationship, it is obviously necessary first to establish the precise nature of the content. Here the term refers, of course, not so much to the events, scenes, and characters that a writer describes as to the general view of life that determines both the choice of such events, scenes, and characters and his particular approach to them. Understood in this sense, the content clearly does not have to be distinguished by its newness or originality in order to inspire works of art that merit our attention, even though the view of life reflected in the art of Bunin is quite distinctive in the Russian context. We do not turn to works of art solely for intellectual stimulation, and the intellectual stimulation that we do derive from them is provided less often by the novelty of the artist's insights than by the manner his insights are expressed. What we do demand of a major writer is the ability to highlight significant aspects of the human condition in imaginative structures that, however contentious his view of life may be, contrive to win our sympathy and to prompt a reappraisal of our convictions by virtue of their truthfulness or aesthetic integrity. This demand, it is submitted, is fully met by the art of Ivan Bunin. Perhaps it will be argued that there is much more in his art than the view of life that has been attributed to him in this study, and it must obviously be conceded that not every aspect of his fiction has been exhaustively covered. But there are two valid rejoinders to this argument. The first is that the questions the study has attempted to answer are questions that must be answered before any aspect of his art may be properly judged. And the second is that the view of life that has been recognized as the main premise of his fiction, far from being narrow and restrictive, embraces, as we have seen, the most fundamental questions of human existence that have inspired artists over the ages: the questions of freedom and necessity, body and spirit, reason and the irrational, man's relation to God and to the world about him. To relate the most notable and conspicuous features of Bunin's art in its entirety to such a conception of life is not to convey a misleadingly limited impression of its range, but, on the contrary, to accord it the sustained breadth and significance critics have often tended to deny it.

The emphasis has been placed in the study on the evolution of the artistic embodiment of this conception. We have observed that he begins by stressing in his early fiction its relevance to the development of Russian society in the postreform era. In the accelerated decline of the Russian rural economy that followed the emancipation of the serfs he perceived a symbolic justification of his belief that in rejecting nature man condemns himself to degeneration and self-destruction. Hence the concept of "social" or "cultural degeneracy" that formed the premise of his interpretation of the decline that culminated in the events of 1917. The sentence he passes on Russian society is then extended to Western civilization as a whole, in the rationalism and materialism of which he saw evidence of a comparable degeneracy and the omens of a similar disaster. Again the oppressive solitude of his heroes and their capacity solely for destructive activity are implicitly ascribed to a crippling loss of sensitivity to the nonrational forms of experience that are acclaimed as an expression of the laws of nature working through man and thus as an inalienable prerequisite of significant human achievement. But from 1915 onward the philosophical impersonalism that inspired Bunin's deterministic view of history expresses itself less commonly in fictional studies of social evolution than in studies of man as an individual. From the penalty of self-destruction that societies incur by their rejection of nature his attention is transferred to the pain to which man is unalterably condemned by his dual existence as part of the unity of nature and as an individual endowed with a profound sense of his personal identity. The victims of this pain are the heroes and heroines of the long succession of love stories that ends with his final volume. In the tales of *Dark Avenues* it remained merely to summarize his conclusions with the aid once more of the theme that served to illuminate most vividly the impermanence of everything on earth and the inescapable truth of man's alternately ecstatic and horrendous slavery.

It is not only, however, for thematic reasons that these stories mark a fitting end to Bunin's career as an artist. We may miss in them the powerful and sustained "solidity" of "A Gay Farmhouse," "Ignat," and "The Gentleman from San Francisco," the polyphonic complexity of *Sukhodol*, or the cumulative tension of *Mitya's Love*, but it is evident from our survey that Bunin devised in them a medium that is singularly appropriate to his tragic theme—a highly flexible medium capable of conveying with startling effect a sense of the mystery, the irrationality, and the strident contrasts of man's ephemeral existence. "Perhaps in my old age I will write something worthwhile," he had remarked many years before to his nephew Pusheshnikov.[1] The stories of *Dark Avenues* seem to have represented for him a fulfillment of the prophecy. His reference to the volume, in a letter to Teleshov of 1 April 1947, as "the best and most original work" that he had ever written[2] may be taken to denote his satisfaction with the relationship between form and content that he had achieved after more than sixty years of creative endeavor.

Notes

Preface

1. K. Zaytsev, *I. A. Bunin*.
2. Cf. his volume of essays entitled *Vstrechi*, pp. 87–122.
3. "Na smert' Bunina."
4. Of particular importance in this regard are the materials assembled by A. K. Baboreko in his *I. A. Bunin: Materialy dlya biografii (s 1870 po 1917)* and those published in commemoration of the centenary of Bunin's birth in *Literaturnoye nasledstvo. Tom 84. Ivan Bunin*, 2 vols. These sources are referred to hereafter as *Materialy* and *Literaturnoye nasledstvo*.
5. Cf. V. N. Afanas'yev, *I. A. Bunin*; O. N. Mikhaylov, *Ivan Alekseyevich Bunin*; and A. A. Volkov, *Proza Ivana Bunina*.
6. S. Kryzytski, *The Works of Ivan Bunin*.
7. I. A. Bunin, *Sobraniye sochineniy*, 9 vols.

Chapter 1

1. Cf. V. Zenzinov, "Ivan Alekseyevich Bunin," p. 293.
2. Cf. V. N. Muromtseva-Bunina, *Zhizn' Bunina, 1870–1906*, p. 121.
3. Bunin's father had been a contemporary of Leskov at the Voronezh *gimnaziya* and had met Tolstoy during the Crimean War (cf. *Materialy*, p. 7).
4. The works concerned are "Nefedka," "Two Wanderers" [Dva strannika], and the poems "Over the grave of S. Ya. Nadson" [Nad mogiloy S. Ya. Nadsona] and "A Country Beggar" [Derevenskiy nishchiy], which appeared during the years 1887–88 in the St. Petersburg weekly *Rodina* [The motherland]. "Two Wanderers," which was later entitled "God's People" [Bozh'i lyudi], has recently been republished in *Literaturnoye nasledstvo*, 1:139–45. In 1914 it formed the basis of Bunin's story "A Spring Evening" [Vesenniy vecher].
5. Bunin was one of eight children, four of whom died in infancy or early childhood.
6. Cf. Muromtseva-Bunina, *Zhizn' Bunina*, p. 23.
7. By this time Yevgeniy, the most practical member of the family, had taken over the management of Ozerki, and Bunin's par-

ents and sister had moved to the estates of relatives (cf. *Materialy*, p. 35).

8. Cf. *Sobr. soch.*, 9:261.

9. The enduring success of the translation is indicated by the ten Soviet editions that came out before 1958 (cf. S. L. Gol'din, "K voprosu o literaturnykh svyazyakh I. A. Bunina s A. P. Chekhovym i A. M. Gor'kim," p. 55).

10. Cf. A. K. Baboreko, "Chekhov i Bunin," p. 395.

11. On the subject of Bunin's early relations with Bryusov and Bal'mont, cf. V. N. Afanas'yev, "I. A. Bunin i russkoye dekadentstvo 90-kh godov. (V poryadke postanovki voprosa)," pp. 175–81, and S. L. Gol'din, "K voprosu o literaturnykh svyazyakh V. Bryusova i I. Bunina," pp. 168–84.

12. Vasil'yevskoye was the country seat of Bunin's relatives the Pusheshnikovs.

13. Cf. his letter to Bunin of April 1899 in *Gor'kovskiye chteniya, 1958–1959*, p. 11.

14. Cf. A. A. Ninov, ed., "Perepiska s V. Ya. Bryusovym, 1895–1915," *Literaturnoye nasledstvo*, 1:421–70; "Perepiska," p. 3; and V. Bryusov, *Dnevniki 1891–1910*, p. 106.

15. "Black Earth" incorporated two narratives—"Dreams" [Sny] and "The Gold Mine" [Zolotoye dno]—which are now usually printed separately.

16. The title of the tale was later changed to "Birds of Heaven" [Ptitsy nebesnyye].

17. The circulation of the volumes in 1905–6 had reached 65,-000 copies. Thereafter it steadily declined until by 1913, the last year of the publishing house's existence, it stood at only 8,000 (cf. A. A. Polikanov, Z. V. Udonova, and I. T. Trofimov, *Russkaya literatura kontsa XIX–nachala XX vv.*, p. 126).

18. In 1908–9 he served briefly as editor of the literary sections of the journal *Severnoye siyaniye* [Northern lights] and the *Zemlya* [The earth] miscellanies published by Moskovskoye knigoizdatel'stvo [The Moscow publishing house]. He also had close ties with the St. Petersburg publishing house Shipovnik [The wild briar], which published a series of almanacs between 1907 and 1917.

19. Cf. A. Sedykh, *Dalyokiye, blizkiye*, p. 201.

20. It took Gorky, it seems, a long time to recognize this mercenary streak in Bunin's character. He refers to it only in a note of the mid-twenties, written some years after their relationship had come to an end (cf. *Gor'kovskiye chteniya*, p. 92).

21. Cf., for example, his reaction to the death of his sister Nadya (6:43–44).

22. Cf. *Materialy*, p. 149.

23. Letter to I. A. Belousov of late December 1911 in *Arkhiv A. M. Gor'kogo*, 7:103.

24. Cf. Gol'din, "K voprosu o literaturnykh svyazyakh I. A. Bunina," p. 73.

25. Cf. Zenzinov, "Ivan Alekseyevich Bunin," p. 289.

26. G. Kuznetsova, *Grasskiy dnevnik*, p. 26.

27. He had been mentioned in the press as a possible candidate in each of the preceding three years, and his name had first been canvassed as early as 1922 by Romain Rolland, who had himself received the prize in 1915 (cf. *Materialy*, p. 215).

28. Cf. V. A. Aleksandrova, "I. A. Bunin," p. 176.

29. New English translations that appeared in the wake of the award are indicated in the Bibliography.

30. A. K. Baborekov and A. N. Teleshov, "Pis'ma I. A. Bunina N. D. Teleshovu (1941–1947)," p. 160.

31. Although no prisoners of war, it seems, used his hospitality as a means of escape, he did offer shelter to a number of fugitives, including the pianist Aleksandr Liberman and his wife (cf. A. K. Baboreko, "Posledniye gody I. A. Bunina. [Novyye materialy]," p. 253).

32. Cf. A. V. Bakhrakh, "Po pamyati, po zapiskam (II)," p. 283–84.

33. Cf. Sedykh, *Dalyokiye, blizkiye*, pp. 217–18.

34. *Vtoroy Vsesoyuznyy s'yezd sovetskikh pisateley. Stenograficheskiy otchot*, p. 503.

35. Cf. M. A. Aldanov, "O Bunine," p. 133.

36. The first of many Soviet collections of Bunin's works published in the late fifties and early sixties was a volume entitled *Tales* [Rasskazy], which came out in Moscow in 1955 with an introduction by L. Nikulin. These were his first works to be published in Russia since 1928.

Chapter 2

1. "In general," he remarked in 1910, "I love the east and eastern religion. India interests me as the cradle of mankind and religion" (*Literaturnoye nasledstvo*, 1:363).

2. Cf. I. A. Bunin, "Nedostatki sovremennoy poezii," p. 737.

3. G. Kuznetsova, *Grasskiy dnevnik*, p. 98.

4. Cf. his remark in one of the preparatory notes to Book II of *The Life of Arsen'yev*: "Throughout my life I have never understood how one can seek the meaning of life in work, housekeeping, politics, profit, or the family" (9:352).

5. Kuznetsova, *Grasskiy dnevnik*, p. 24. Cf. Bunin's remarks on his story "Stepa" (1938) in *Sobr. soch.*, 9:373.

6. F. Stepun, "Literaturnyye zametki. (I. A. Bunin: Po povodu 'Mitinoy lyubvi')," pp. 329–30.

7. One of the rough drafts of the story indicates that Bunin took these words, which originally formed its epigraph, from the Chinese philosopher and traveler Fâ-Hien (cf. *Literaturnoye nasledstvo*, 1:97, 107, 119).

8. V. Ya. Grechnev, "Proza Ivana Bunina," p. 223.

9. In only one, for example, of the stories of *Dark Avenues* which are set in Russia is the theme inconceivable in any other setting—in "The First Monday in Lent" [Chistyy ponedel'nik] (1944).

10. Explicit identification of God with the contrasts of nature is repeatedly encountered in Bunin's poetry. In "Giordano Bruno" (1906), for example, he writes: "The world is an abyss of abysses. And every atom in it is imbued with God—with life and beauty" (1:271). A poem of 1915, by contrast, contains the following reference to the stars: "In the iron frost flourish and burn the unsated, wolfish eyes of God" (1:380).

11. "In Turgenev," he wrote in a letter to the émigré academic P. Bitsilli, "there are vivid descriptions, but in my works and—forgive me!—in those of Tolstoy there is the 'sensuality' which you illustrate with quotations from 'Arsen'yev'" (A. Meshchersky, ed., "Neizvestnyye pis'ma I. A. Bunina," p. 155).

12. Cf. V. Zenzinov, "Ivan Alekseyevich Bunin," p. 301.

13. In reference to Bunin's methods of characterization, cf. L. M. Granovskaya, "Iz nablyudeniy nad yazykom I. A. Bunina. (O nekotorykh osobennostyakh upotrebleniya opredeleniy-prilagatel'nykh)," p. 254; N. I. Volynskaya, "Vzglyady I. A. Bunina na khudozhestvennoye masterstvo," pp. 59–60; and M. A. Aldanov, "O Bunine," p. 131.

14. Cf. his speech on the fiftieth anniversary of the Moscow newspaper *Russkiye vedomosti* [The Russian gazette] in *Literaturnoye nasledstvo*, 1:318.

15. Letter of 23 August 1951. Quoted from L. Rzhevsky, "Pamyati I. A. Bunina," p. 3.

16. "I am not an ambitious man," he once remarked, "but I am very conceited" (Zenzinov, "Ivan Alekseyevich Bunin," p. 296).

17. Cf. *Literaturnoye nasledstvo*, 1:318.

18. Ibid., p. 319.

19. Cf. his letter of 23 January 1910 to N. S. Klestov in A. K. Baboreko, "Iz perepiski I. A. Bunina," p. 210.

20. Cf. *Literaturnoye nasledstvo*, 1:290–96, and *Sobr. soch.*, 9:502–6.

21. Cf. his remarks on this subject in an interview of 1910 in *Sobr. soch.*, 9:535.

22. Cf., for example, the writer Artsybashev's reaction to Bunin's speech on the fiftieth anniversary of *Russkiye vedomosti* in *Literaturnoye nasledstvo*, 1:324.

23. Cf., for example, A. A. Blok, *Sobraniye sochineniy*, 5:141.

24. Cf. Kuznetsova, *Grasskiy dnevnik*, p. 214; M. V. Vishniak, "*Sovremennyye zapiski.*" *Vospominaniya redaktora*, p. 129; and Zenzinov, "Ivan Alekseyevich Bunin," p. 301.

25. Like Tolstoy, Bunin showed little enthusiasm for Chekhov's plays, though his cool response may perhaps be seen as a reflection of his general distaste for the theater to which he gives vent in *The Life of Arsen'yev* (6:216–18). Cf. also G. V. Adamovich, *Odinochestvo i svoboda*, p. 111. At the same time his interest in the expressive potentialities of drama was considerable (cf. *Materialy*, pp. 179–80), and in 1902, it seems, he even attempted to write a play (cf. his letter of 29 June 1902 to I. A. Belousov in I. S. Gazer, ed., "Pis'ma L. Andreyeva i I. Bunina," p. 177). Evidently he did not succeed.

26. Cf. Teleshov's letter to Bunin of 14 January 1912 in *Literaturnoye nasledstvo*, 1:606.

27. H. S. Canby, *The Short Story in English*, p. 303.

28. Cf. *Sobr. soch.*, 9:172.

29. Cf. his remarks on this subject quoted in R. Spivak, "'Zhivaya zhizn'' I. Bunina i L. Tolstogo. (Nekotoryye storony estetiki Bunina v svete traditsiy L. Tolstogo)," p. 92.

30. It is not surprising to learn in this connection that the story of Chekhov that made the most powerful impact on Bunin was "In the Ravine" [V ovrage] (1900), in which the gentle doctor's inhibitions are perhaps least in evidence (cf. *Sobr. soch.*, 9:226).

31. Quoted from A. K. Baboreko, "Bunin o Tolstom," pp. 131–32.

32. Cf. his remarks in a letter of 20 July 1938 to M. V. Karamzina: "What is there in common between Tolstoy and myself? He is close to me not only as an artist and great poet, but also as a religious spirit" (*Literaturnoye nasledstvo*, 1:670).

33. Cf. in this connection, I. A. Il'in, *O t'me i prosvetlenii*, p. 33.

34. J. Bayley, *Tolstoy and the Novel*, p. 73.

35. K. I. Zaytsev, *I. A. Bunin*, p. 243.

36. Cf. his poem "Giordano Bruno" (1:271).

37. Cf. *Sobr. soch.*, 6:126–27.

38. Quoted from Zenzinov, "Ivan Alekseyevich Bunin," p. 302.

Chapter 3

1. "At the age of seven," he wrote in 1915, " a life began for me which is closely associated in my memories with the fields and peasant huts" (9:256). Cf. V. N. Muromtseva-Bunina, *Zhizn' Bunina, 1870–1906,* p. 47.

2. *Materialy,* p. 161.

3. Cf. *Literaturnoye nasledstvo,* 1:372.

4. I. A. Bunin, "Poet-gumanist. (Po povodu 50-letnego yubileya literaturnoy deyatel'nosti A. M. Zhemchuzhnikova)," p. 80.

5. D. S. Mirsky, *A History of Russian Literature,* pp. 391–92.

6. Cf. Muromtseva-Bunina, *Zhizn' Bunina,* p. 37.

7. O. N. Mikhaylov, *Ivan Alekseyevich Bunin,* p. 41.

8. When first published in 1900–1901 the two works bore the subtitles "From the Book 'An Epitaph'" and "Pictures from the Book 'An Epitaph'" (cf. *Sobr. soch.,* 2:504, 508). For further discussion of Bunin's early cycles, cf. Ye. A. Polotskaya, "Vzaimoproniknoveniye poezii i prozy u rannego Bunina," p. 418.

9. Cf. K. D. Muratova, ed., "I. A. Bunin," p. 136.

10. When the work first appeared in 1901, it bore the title "Ore" [Ruda].

11. Cf., for example, I. D. Bazhinov, "Rasskaz I. A. Bunina 'Antonovskiye yabloki.' (K stoletiyu so dnya rozhdeniya I. A. Bunina)," p. 24, and N. M. Kucherovsky, "O kontseptsii zhizni v liricheskoy proze I. A. Bunina," p. 101.

12. Cf. Kucherovsky, "O kontseptsii zhizni," pp. 101–2.

13. Hence, presumably, the replacement of the title that he first gave the work—"The Protection of the Mother of God" [Pokrov Bogoroditsy].

14. Cf. Muromtseva-Bunina, *Zhizn' Bunina,* p. 80, and T. M. Bonami, *Khudozhestvennaya proza I. A. Bunina (1887–1904),* p. 43.

15. It might be noted, however, that "In Foreign Parts" belongs to the traditional genre of the "Easter story," which specifically required the sentimental treatment of a contemporary social problem.

16. Cf. P. V. Zavelin, "Syuzhet i stil' v pervykh rasskazakh I. A. Bunina," p. 167.

17. The original title of "In the Field" was "Lazybones" [Baybaki].

18. L. V. Krutikova, "'Na kray sveta'—pervyy sbornik rasskazov I. A. Bunina," pp. 77–79.

19. I. A. Bunin, *Rasskazy,* p. 268, 1902 edition.

20. Muromtseva-Bunina, *Zhizn' Bunina,* p. 91.

21. A. A. Ninov, "'Derevnya' Bunina i russkaya literatura," p. 72.

22. L. V. Krutikova, "Iz tvorcheskoy istorii 'Derevni' I. A. Bunina," p. 131.

23. Cf. A. A. Volkov, *Proza Ivana Bunina*, p. 88, and Ninov, "'Derevnya' Bunina," p. 70.

24. Cf. A. Tvardovsky, "O Bunine," p. 20.

25. S. Kryzytski, *The Works of Ivan Bunin*, p. 67.

26. N. M. Kucherovsky, "Esteticheskaya sushchnost' filosofskikh iskaniy I. A. Bunina (1906–1911 gg.)," p. 26. Cf. V. N. Afanas'yev, *I. A. Bunin*, p. 80.

27. A desyatina is equivalent to 2.7 acres.

28. This process is admirably described in N. M. Kucherovsky, "Povest' I. A. Bunina 'Vesyolyy dvor,'" p. 135.

29. Cf. chapter 1, note 4.

30. Cf. Muromtseva-Bunina, *Zhizn' Bunina*, p. 166.

31. Cf. Krutikova, "Iz tvorcheskoy istorii 'Derevni,'" p. 143.

32. N. M. Kucherovsky, "Istoriya Durnovki i yeyo 'Myortvyye dushi.' (Povest' I. A. Bunina 'Derevnya')," p. 115.

33. "Again," we read, "Seryy spent the whole summer at home awaiting favors from the Duma" (3:102).

34. Like the two Krasovs, the two Bunins had little in common, and Bunin's preoccupation in his early fiction with the disintegration of the family may well have been influenced to some extent by the harsh indifference of Yevgeniy to his parents' struggles, as Muromtseva-Bunina testifies (*Zhizn'Bunina*, p. 161).

35. It has been suggested that Bunin may have deliberately sought to combine in the figures of the two brothers the contrasting types of temperament and personality that Turgenev embodies in his peasants Khor' and Kalinych (cf. R. Poggioli, "The Art of Ivan Bunin," p. 267). The suggestion is by no means implausible, though if the parody was indeed intended, due attention should obviously be paid to the purpose that presumably inspired it—the desire to show the effects on the types of peasant portrayed by Turgenev of subsequent social change. The same point is equally relevant to the fairly transparent parody of Turgenev's "Bezhin Meadow" [Bezhin lug] (1851) in "A Nocturnal Conversation."

36. A Soviet critic has suggested that the name of this peasant might have been selected by Bunin as an allusion by contrast to the Karatayevlike hero of Tolstoy's play *The Power of Darkness* [Vlast' t'my] (1886) (Ninov, "'Derevnya' Bunina," p. 70).

37. The inability of Tikhon to beget an heir is one of the several features that he shares with Yevgeniy Bunin, who eventually succeeded only in old age with the aid of a housemaid.

38. Cf. Fedosevna's reaction to the hut: "The dark hut seemed to her to resemble a low tomb or cellar" (2:364).

39. Cf., for example, S. Kastorsky, "Gor'kiy i Bunin," p. 147; Afanas'yev, *I. A. Bunin*, p. 80; and A. A. Volkov, *Russkaya literatura XX veka*, pp. 194–95.

40. Cf., for example, his letter to Gorky of 20 August 1910, written shortly after the completion of *The Village*, in *Gor'kovskiye chteniya, 1958–1959*, p. 49.

41. Cf. L. V. Krutikova, "'Derevnya' I. Bunina," p. 171.

42. A. M. Gor'kiy, *Sobraniye sochineniy*, 2:404.

43. Ye. A. Koltonovskaya, "Bunin, kak khudozhnik-povestvovatel'," p. 333.

44. Cf., for example, V. Muyzhel's *The Dacha* [Dacha] (1908), N. Oliger's *An Autumn Song* [Osennyaya pesnya] (1909), and I. Rodionov's *Our Crime* [Nashe prestupleniye] (1908).

45. Ye. A. Koltonovskaya, *Kriticheskiye etyudy*, p. 277.

46. Bunin's increasingly determined attempts to exculpate the government and ruling classes are clearly shown in Krutikova's comparative study of the different redactions of *The Village* ("Iz tvorcheskoy istorii 'Derevni,'" pp. 141–42).

47. *Literaturnoye nasledstvo*, 1:372. Cf. in this connection, his scathing portrait of the Populist writer Zlatovratsky, ibid., p. 389.

48. Cf. N. P. Smirnov-Sokol'sky, "Poslednyaya nakhodka," p. 219.

49. Quoted from V. Zenzinov, "Ivan Alekseyevich Bunin," p. 303.

50. Cf. *Literaturnoye nasledstvo*, 1:366–67.

51. *Gor'kovskiye chteniya*, p. 92.

52. L. V. Krutikova, "'Sukhodol,' povest'-poema I. Bunina," p. 50.

53. Cf. *Materialy*, p. 165.

54. Sukhodol was apparently based on the Bunin estate Kamenka in the province of Oryol (cf. Muromtseva-Bunina, *Zhizn' Bunina*, pp. 21–22, and A. K. Baboreko, "Tipy i prototipy. [Neizvestnyye materialy o I. A. Bunine]," p. 254).

55. Cf., for example, Poggioli, "The Art of Ivan Bunin," pp. 271, 275, and G. Struve, "The Art of Ivan Bunin," p. 427.

56. Cf. the final words of chapter VII: "And since the *sukhodol'tsy* love to play a part, to instill in themselves the belief that what apparently must be is unalterable, even though the conception of what must be is their own invention, so Natal'ya also assumed a role" (3:171).

57. I. A. Bunin, *Sukhodol*, p. 13.

58. Krutikova, "'Sukhodol,'" p. 50.

Chapter 4

1. V. N. Afanas'yev, *I. A. Bunin*, p. 77. Cf. L. V. Krutikova's criticism of his interpretation in her review "Prochitan li Bunin?" p. 185.

2. Cf. his poem of 1916 "St. Prokopiy" (1:387).

3. Letter of 1 June 1901 in K. D. Muratova, ed., "I. A. Bunin," p. 132.

4. Quoted from *Problemy realizma i khudozhestvennoy pravdy*, 1: 169.

5. A. K. Baboreko, "Bunin na Kapri. (Po neopublikovannym materialam)," p. 246. Cf. his letter to Teleshov of 18 June 1899 in which he wrote: "To blazes with plots! Invention is unnecessary. Simply describe what you have seen and what you enjoy recalling" (quoted from V. N. Afanas'yev, "I. A. Bunin i russkoye dekadentstvo 90-kh godov. [V poryadke postanovki voprosa]," p. 179).

6. This explanation of the choice of epigraph is supported by his decision in 1912 to give the same title to the fourth edition of his stories of the period 1892–1902.

7. Cf. his remark in a letter of 21 January 1896 to S. N. Kukshina, the daughter of a contemporary music critic: "In my soul I must be a vagrant, but I feel the lure of the valley, the peaceful valley" (A. K. Baboreko, ed., "Neopublikovannyye pis'ma I. A. Bunina," p. 178).

8. Cf. A. K. Baboreko, "Chekhov i Bunin," p. 396.

9. Cf. the similar symbolic opposition of night and day in the last two quatrains of Bunin's poem "Ormuzd" (1903–5) (1:232).

10. The story did not appear in its present form and with its present title until 1926, when it was published in Paris, but this version was merely an abridgment of a story written in 1909 with the title "The Same Old Story" [Staraya pesnya].

11. Since, as N. M. Kucherovsky has observed, the descriptions of the hero's domestic life in the last two chapters of the original merely provide a background for his "spiritual insights" ("Esteticheskaya sushchnost' filosofskikh iskaniy I. A. Bunina (1906–1911 gg.)," p. 33), it is difficult to accept A. A. Volkov's contention that their deletion deprived the work of its "important social implications" (*Proza Ivana Bunina*, p. 60).

12. Cf. Job, 39:18–25.

13. It seems that before this he had thought of calling them *Fields of the Dead* [Polya myortvykh] after the cemeteries of Constantinople (cf. *Sobr. soch.*, 3:453).

14. In the first volume of the Petropolis edition of his works (1934), he went back to the original title *The Shrine of the Sun*, but *The Shadow of the Bird* was reinstated in 1953.

15. "On the Donets" [Na Dontse] was the original title of the work.

16. Cf. the second stanza of Bunin's poem of 1903 "An Inscription on a Cup" [Nadpis' na chashe]: "Only the sea, the limitless sea, and the sky are eternal. Only the sea, the earth, and its beauty are eternal. Only that is eternal which links with an invisible bond the soul and heart of the living and the dark soul of graves" (1:190).

17. F. D. Batyushkov, "Iv. A. Bunin," p. 348.

18. Cf., for example, O. N. Mikhaylov, *Ivan Alekseyevich Bunin*, p. 77.

19. Cf. Tikhon Krasov's remark in *The Village* to the postmaster Sakharov: "Our Palestines are completely desolate" (3:42).

20. V. N. Muromtseva-Bunina, *Zhizn' Bunina, 1870–1906*, p. 146.

21. Cf. Kucherovsky, "Esteticheskaya sushchnost'," p. 27.

22. Spengler's work did not become well known in Russia till 1921.

Chapter 5

1. Cf., for example, the five chapters that comprise the five-page tale "In Autumn."

2. R. Jakobson, "The Prose of the Poet Pasternak," p. 144. The article was first published in German in 1935.

3. Cf. the reaction of A. A. Davydova, editor of the journal *Mir Bozhiy* [God's world], to the sketch "In the Forests" [V lesakh] (1893–95), which Bunin unsuccessfully submitted to her: "It is regrettably unsuitable for us. It is very fragmentary, my friend—forgive my frankness—and I formed the impression that the work is incomplete" (*Literaturnoye nasledstvo*, 1:63).

4. E. Auerbach, *Mimesis*, p. 479.

5. Yu. Aykhenval'd, *Siluety russkikh pisateley*, p. 201.

6. Cf. *Sobr. soch.*, 9:539, and A. K. Baboreko, "Bunin o Tolstom," p. 132.

7. A. K. Baboreko, "Bunin na Kapri. (Po neopublikovannym materialam)," p. 246.

8. A. P. Chekhov, *Sobraniye sochineniy*, 12:429.

9. The term is taken from Sean O'Faolain, *The Short Story*, p. 187.

10. Quoted from N. M. Kucherovsky, "O kontseptsii zhizni v liricheskoy proze I. A. Bunina," p. 86.

11. The story was initially entitled "A Meeting" [Svidaniye].

12. It is possible, in fact, that only "Hope," as V. M. Muromtseva-Bunina claims (*Zhizn' Bunina, 1870–1906*, p. 150), was written dur-

ing this year, as the dating of "Dawn Throughout the Night" is based solely on the date of its first publication (cf. *Sobr. soch.*, 2:515).

13. "Lodging for the Night" was itself a repetition of a section of an earlier work entitled "The Cuckoo" [Kukushka] (1903).

14. Cf. J. Bayley, *Tolstoy and the Novel*, p. 123.

15. Letter of 1 June 1901 in K. D. Muratova, ed., "I. A. Bunin," p. 132.

16. Quoted from Baboreko, "Bunin o Tolstom," p. 132.

17. Cf. I. Dzhonson, "Krasivoye darovaniye," p. 58.

18. Cf. N. Å. Nilsson, *Studies in Čechov's Narrative Technique*, pp. 63–64.

19. Cf. his remarks on this story to Pusheshnikov quoted in A. K. Baboreko, "Chekhov i Bunin," p. 406.

20. Baboreko records his statement: "In his best works Chekhov began to change his form. He made remarkable progress. He was a very great poet. Yet has any critic said a single word about the form of his last stories? Not one!" ("Bunin na Kapri," p. 247).

21. R. Spivak, "Yazyk prozy I. A. Bunina i traditsiya L. N. Tolstogo," p. 29.

22. F. Stepun, *Vstrechi*, p. 92.

23. Quoted from Baboreko, "Bunin na Kapri," p. 248.

24. David Daiches, *A Study of Literature for Readers and Critics*, pp. 35–36.

25. Cf. G. Kuznetsova, *Grasskiy dnevnik*, p. 194.

26. Letter to Bunin of 27 October 1910 in *Gor'kovskiye chteniya, 1958–1959*, p. 50.

27. Cf. ibid., p. 51.

28. Cf. G. V. Adamovich, *Odinochestvo i svoboda*, p. 100. His irritation on learning of Gide's praise of the work is recalled in A. V. Bakhrakh, "Po pamyati, po zapiskam (II)," p. 287.

29. He had revised it previously in 1915 for a six-volume edition of his works published as a supplement to the Petrograd journal *Niva* [The cornfield] and in 1934 for the Petropolis edition.

30. Quoted from A. A. Ninov, "'Derevnya' Bunina i russkaya literatura," p. 72.

31. Quoted from I. S. Gazer, "O nekotorykh khudozhestvennykh osobennostyakh povesti I. A. Bunina 'Derevnya,'" pp. 98–99.

32. V. Weidle, "Na smert' Bunina," p. 88.

33. L. Gurevich, *Literatura i estetika*, p. 145.

34. Cf. the titles of his stories "The Last Meeting" [Posledneye svidaniye] (1912) and "The Last Day" [Posledniy den'] (1913).

35. Cf. L. M. Granovskaya, "Iz nablyudeniy nad yazykom I. A. Bunina. (O nekotorykh osobennostyakh upotrebleniya opredeleniy-prilagatel'nykh)," p. 264. Typical examples are the repeated references to the long, dark eyelashes of Molodaya in *The Village* and

the general emphasis on "length" in the iconlike portrait of the heroine of "Aglaya" (1916).

36. "There was an insane expression on the tear-stained face of the peasant which was barely visible in the dark" (4:254).

37. "'Give it to me!' he said in a voice that had suddenly become hoarse" (ibid.).

38. "For a long time the peasant was silent" (4:255).

39. "Then a crunch was heard—evidently he was tearing a stone from the foundations" (ibid.).

40. F. D. Batyushkov, "Iv. A. Bunin," p. 363.

Chapter 6

1. Cf. *Sobr. soch.*, 3:54.

2. These words from Revelation 18:10 initially formed the epigraph of "The Gentleman from San Francisco." They were removed only in the final redaction of 1951.

3. The story was not completed until October 1915.

4. Quoted from V. Zenzinov, "Ivan Alekseyevich Bunin," p. 303.

5. G. Kuznetsova, *Grasskiy dnevnik*, p. 213. The remark may be linked with the comments on Russian Orthodoxy that he made two years earlier in a discussion of the Russian character with I. I. Fondaminsky: "People talk about our radiant, joyous religion. It is a lie. Nothing is so dark, terrible, and cruel as our religion. Remember those black icons, those terrible arms and legs" (ibid., p. 102).

6. I. A. Bunin, *Sobraniye sochineniy*, 10:196, 1934–36 edition.

7. "Behold the brothers fighting one another. I wish to speak of sorrow" (4:256).

8. *Materialy*, pp. 196–97.

9. He had mentioned in an interview two years earlier (1912) that he was attracted by the idea of writing a tragedy about the Buddha's life (cf. *Literaturnoye nasledstvo*, 1:375).

10. At the time of writing the story, Bunin was editing a collection of the works of Kipling.

11. R. Poggioli, "The Art of Ivan Bunin," p. 260.

12. Cf. the captain's remark to him as he develops his arguments: "It is Ceylon that has had this effect on you" (4:276). The colonel instantly agrees.

13. Cf. Muromtseva-Bunina's remark in a letter to Baboreko of 15 May 1957: "The feelings of his Englishman in 'The Brothers' were autobiographical" (*Materialy*, p. 158).

14. W. C. Booth, *The Rhetoric of Fiction*, pp. 3–20.

15. The physical portrait of Iordansky was apparently based on Bunin's contemporary Leonid Andreyev (cf. Kuznetsova, *Grasskiy*

dnevnik, p. 239), and it may not be coincidental that in temperament he has much in common with the priest who is the central figure of Andreyev's story "The Life of Vasiliy Fiveysky" [Zhizn' Vasiliya Fiveyskogo] (1903).

16. Herein presumably lies the reason for the title "The House" [Dom] that Bunin gave the work in manuscript. "The Cup of Life" was actually his third title. The second was "In Streletsk" (cf. *Materialy*, p. 190).

17. The adjective belongs to Iordansky (4:211).

18. Cf. *Literaturnoye nasledstvo*, 2:106.

19. Extracts from these manuscripts are quoted in *Sobr. soch.*, 4:492–94.

20. Cf., for example, Ye. A. Koltonovskaya, "Garmoniya kontrastov," pp. 96–97, and V. N. Afanas'yev, *I. A. Bunin*, p. 253.

21. Cf. Afanas'yev, *I. A. Bunin*, pp. 252–53.

22. Cf. ibid., p. 248.

23. The polemic was implicit in one of Bunin's original titles for the work, "Without Punishment" [Bez nakazaniya] (cf. *Literaturnoye nasledstvo*, 2:118), which plainly alludes to Dostoyevsky's novel.

24. The detail of Korol'kova's ill-fitting clothes, and particularly that of her large, grotesque hat (4:394), may well be a direct allusion to Sonya's bizarre attire.

25. Afanas'yev, *I. A. Bunin*, p. 247.

26. Cf. also, for example, Yu. Aykhenval'd, *Siluety russkikh pisateley*, pp. 195–96, and A. A. Volkov, *Proza Ivana Bunina*, pp. 251–52.

27. I. S. Gazer, ed., "Pis'ma L. Andreyeva i I. Bunina," p. 193.

28. V. Katayev, "Trava zabven'ya," p. 322. Katayev actually used the phrase in reference to "The Dreams of Chang."

29. Cf. *Literaturnoye nasledstvo*, 1:32.

30. Cf. the original title of the work, "Death on Capri" [Smert' na Kapri].

31. Yu. Olesha, *Ni dnya bez strochki*, p. 245.

32. Cf. Bunin's comments on the work to Katayev shortly before he left Russia for the last time: "The main thing is what I developed in 'The Gentleman from San Francisco'—the symphonic quality that is inherent in the highest degree in any universal soul. I mean not so much a logical as a musical structuring of prose with changes of rhythm, variations, transitions from one musical key to another—in short, the kind of counterpoint that Lev Tolstoy, for example, made some attempt to apply in *War and Peace*: Bolkonsky's death and so on" (Katayev, "Trava zabven'ya," p. 312).

33. Cf. A. A. Achatova, "Rabota I. Bunina nad rasskazom 'Gospodin iz San-Frantsisko,'" p. 61.

34. S. L. Gross, "Nature, Man, and God in Bunin's 'The Gentleman from San Francisco,'" p. 155.

35. Cf., for example, A. B. Derman, "Pobeda khudozhnika. ('Gospodin iz San-Frantsisko')," p. 26, and F. M. Borras, "A Common Theme in Tolstoy, Andreyev and Bunin," pp. 230–35.

Chapter 7

1. Quoted from A. A. Ninov, "K avtobiografii I. Bunina," p. 226.
2. "He strode firmly, evenly, and briskly. . . . The field was empty, lifeless, and silent."
3. Cf. Yu. Aykhenval'd, *Siluety russkikh pisateley*, p. 200.
4. "The Main Road" [Bol'shaya doroga] was the first title that Bunin gave the story.
5. The name is derived from Bunin's Christian name and patronymic—Ivan Alekseyevich.
6. V. V. Krasnyansky, "Tri redaktsii odnogo rasskaza," p. 62.
7. Cf. *Sobr. soch.*, 9:369.
8. K. Paustovsky, *Blizkiye i dalyokiye*, p. 265.
9. Cf. G. Kuznetsova, *Grasskiy dnevnik*, p. 104.
10. Cf. *Sobr. soch.*, 9:369.
11. "Above a fresh clay mound in the cemetery stands a new oak cross—strong, heavy, smooth."
12. In reference to the episode on Capri, Bunin wrote: "I encountered a grave with a cross that bore the photograph of a young girl with unusually lively, joyful eyes on a convex porcelain medallion" (9:369).
13. Kuznetsova, *Grasskiy dnevnik*, p. 104.
14. A. Tvardovsky, "O Bunine," p. 24.
15. Although it is conveyed indirectly, the nonphysical character of her marital relationship emerges clearly (cf. *Sobr. soch.*, 4:335). In the early drafts of the tale it was revealed explicitly (cf. N. I. Volynskaya, "Vzglyady I. A. Bunina na khudozhestvennoye masterstvo," p. 65).
16. K. Zaytsev, who argues that Mme Marot is, in fact, quite capable of controlling her passion but yields to it simply out of pity for Emile (*I. A. Bunin*, p. 180), makes no reference to either of the two "lapses" of the heroine's will.
17. Cf., for example, G. V. Adamovich, *Odinochestvo i svoboda*, p. 98; V. Weidle, "Na smert' Bunina," p. 92; and M. Aldanov, "I. A. Bunin," p. 385.

Chapter 8

1. K. Zaytsev, *I. A. Bunin*, p. 201.
2. See chapter 4, note 5.
3. Cf. his remarks to Pusheshnikov, chapter 4.
4. Letter of 10 August 1917 in *Gor'kovskiye chteniya, 1958–1959*, p. 91.
5. Bunin took the phrase *nesrochnaya vesna* from Boratynsky's poem "Desolation" [Zapusteniye] (1834). Boratynsky not only coined the phrase; he also invented the epithet. On the question of its meaning, cf. N. S. Avilova, "'Nesrochnaya vesna,'" p. 67.
6. The term "Elysium" [Elizey] in this phrase was also taken by Bunin from Boratynsky's "Desolation."
7. N. P. Smirnov-Sokol'sky, "Poslednyaya nakhodka," p. 219.
8. *Literaturnoye nasledstvo*, 1:87.
9. Cf. Bunin's letter to P. M. Bitsilli of 17 May 1931 in A. Meshchersky, ed., "Neizvestnyye pis'ma I. Bunina," p. 154.
10. Kryzytski observes in this connection: "Nechaev's outward appearance is 'pleasant' which would probably not be the case if Bunin had written about this sort of peasant in his 'period of gloom'" (*The Works of Ivan Bunin*, p. 188). The remark reveals his complete misunderstanding of Bunin's treatment of the peasantry. Nechayev's appearance would have been "pleasant" regardless of the period in which Bunin had portrayed him, for "pleasantness" of appearance is one of the most consistent features of his "trees of God" from the very beginning. Cf., for example, the portraits of Meliton (2:204) and Mitrofan (2:213) as well as his comments on "the reapers of Ryazan'" (5:69).
11. According to V. N. Muromtseva-Bunina (*Zhizn' Bunina, 1870–1906*, p. 90), the story was inspired by a conversation that had taken place between Bunin and A. N. Bibikov on 1 May 1918, a few hours after the death of Varvara Pashchenko.
12. Bunin used this term in reference to the work in a letter to A. Sedykh of 10 June 1926 (cf. A. Sedykh, *Dalyokiye, blizkiye*, p. 203).
13. *Literaturnoye nasledstvo*, 1:382.
14. Cf. chapter 2.
15. Cf. ibid.
16. This implied contrast is particularly evident in "The Blind Man," which contains the statement: "Do not concern yourselves with equality in ordinary, mundane life with its envy, hatred, and vicious rivalry. Equality cannot exist there. It has never existed, and it will never come about" (5:148).
17. This story, which Bunin began on Capri in 1914, is dated 1918 in the latest edition of his works. It acquired its present form and title only in 1920, however. In 1918, when it appeared in the

Kievan monthly *Rodnaya zemlya* [Native land], it bore the title "The End" [Konets] and accordingly expressed a different view of death.

18. Quoted from V. N. Afanas'yev, *I. A. Bunin*, p. 159.

19. *Literaturnoye nasledstvo*, 1:386.

20. This appropriate designation (*mechtaniye*) is taken from I. A. Il'in, *O t'me i prosvetlenii*, p. 36.

21. Letter of 16 May 1936 in Meshchersky, ed., "Neizvestnyye pis'ma I. Bunina," p. 155. Cf. his letter of 3 September 1938 to M. V. Karamzina in *Literaturnoye nasledstvo*, 1:673.

22. A. V. Bakhrakh, "Po pamyati, po zapiskam (II)," p. 273.

23. B. Zaytsev, "Pamyati Ivana i Very Buninykh," p. 138.

24. K. Paustovsky, "Ivan Bunin," p. 14.

25. Cf. I. A. Bunin, *Zhizn' Arsen'yeva: Yunost'*. New York, 1952.

26. *Literaturnoye nasledstvo*, 1:381.

27. Cf. Bunin's note in the manuscript of Books I–IV in *Sobr. soch.*, 6:326.

28. "It is perhaps true," he remarked, "that there is much in *The Life of Arsen'yev* that is autobiographical, but it is not the business of *artistic* criticism to talk about this" (quoted from Bakhrakh, "Po pamyati," p. 280).

29. The term *povest'* is used by Paustovsky in his "Ivan Bunin," p. 14.

30. The death of Lika is perhaps the most obvious indication of the element of invention in her portrait, for Varvara Pashchenko, as we have already observed, lived for more than twenty years after her break with Bunin and marriage to A. N. Bibikov.

31. Cf. Arsen'yev's comments on his brother's Populist associates: "In general, they were all rather narrow, single-minded, and intolerant and professed a rather simple outlook: 'By "the people" we mean only ourselves and various "insulted and injured"; everything bad is on the right and everything good is on the left; everything virtuous is to be found in the people, in their "time-honored customs and aspirations"; all calamities have their source in the system of government and in bad rulers (whom they even considered a special breed); and salvation lies only in revolution, a constitution, or a republic'" (6:167–68).

32. Cf. Arsen'yev's reflections on the subject matter of his early writings: "The main thing was always my own life and personality. However intensely I might have observed them, was I really interested at that time in other people?" (6:236).

33. Cf., for example, Afanas'yev, *I. A. Bunin*, pp. 344, 346, and the introductory comments of O. N. Mikhaylov in *Sobr. soch.*, 6:313, 318–19.

34. G. Kuznetsova, *Grasskiy dnevnik*, p. 9.

35. Ibid., p. 178.

Chapter 9

1. Bunin's first title for the tale was "A Chance Acquaintance" [Sluchaynoye znakomstvo].
2. Cf. V. N. Afanas'yev, *I. A. Bunin*, p. 309, and R. Poggioli, "The Art of Ivan Bunin," p. 253.
3. It may be deduced from the second title that Bunin considered for the story, "Kseniya," that the heroine at least was initially given a name.
4. G. Kuznetsova, *Grasskiy dnevnik*, p. 24.
5. According to Afanas'yev, the shadowy figure of the director had a real-life prototype in the person of A. I. Adashev, an actor at the Moscow Art Theater and the founder of one of Moscow's private schools of acting. Shortly before World War I, apparently, he was charged by the press and public opinion with the moral corruption of his female pupils and compelled to take refuge in the provinces (*I. A. Bunin*, pp. 296–97).
6. F. Stepun's view—that Mitya's jealousy and the "temporary" separation are directly consequent on the increasingly sexual nature of their relationship ("Literaturnyye zametki. (I. A. Bunin: Po povodu 'Mitinoy lyubvi')," p. 335)—is totally unsupported by the text, which states quite clearly (in chapter IV): "In books and in life everyone seemed to agree once and for all to speak only of a love that was almost incorporeal or only of that which is called passion or sensuality. His love differed from them both" (5:188).
7. It will be recalled that the cry of the eagle-owl (*filin*) had been similarly used as a symbol of the primitive, irrational forces of nature in *Sukhodol* (3:142). Cf. also "The Eternal Spring" (5:122).
8. Cf. the reference to Mitya's first sight of Alenka: "It suddenly struck him . . . that there was, or seemed to be, something in common between Alenka and Katya" (5:220).
9. G. Adamovich's reference to the episode of Mitya's experience with Alenka as "a masterful turning, almost at the last moment, to the salutary bosom of mother nature" (*Odinochestvo i svoboda*, p. 98) suggests a complete misunderstanding of the work.
10. In the early stages of writing the work, Bunin conceived the idea of publishing as a separate tale under the title "Rain" [Dozhd'] the material that was later included in the last two chapters of the final version.
11. A. M. Gor'kiy, *Sobraniye sochineniy*, 29:413.
12. Cf. V. Shklovsky, "'Mitina lyubov'' Ivana Bunina," p. 43, and P. Bitsilli, "Bunin i Tolstoy," p. 280.
13. Strangely enough, Bunin claimed that he had never read Tolstoy's story (cf. A. Meshchersky, ed., "Neizvestnyye pis'ma I. Bunina," p. 155).

14. "The ninth of March was Mitya's last happy day in Moscow" (5:181).

15. G. Struve, "The Art of Ivan Bunin," p. 427.

16. Cf., for example, Afanas'yev, *I. A. Bunin*, p. 294.

17. Bunin claimed that he had written words "about the female bosom" in this tale which no one had used before him (Kuznetsova, *Grasskiy dnevnik*, p. 24).

18. Cf. *Sobr. soch.*, 5:527.

19. L. Nikulin, *Chekhov, Bunin, Kuprin*, pp. 227–28.

20. Cf. ibid., p. 228.

21. The early title of the work was *Nevertheless Forever* [Vsyo zhe naveki].

22. Cf. the reference by Sosnovskaya's doctor at the trial to her assiduous study of Schopenhauer (5:281).

23. Emile recollected in his evidence: "Despite the blind it was light in the room" (4:340).

Chapter 10

1. Cf. in this connection F. Stepun, "Ivan Bunin. 'Bozh'ye drevo,'" p. 489.

2. A. K. Baboreko, "Posledniye gody I. A. Bunina. (Novyye materialy)," p. 254. Cf. A. V. Bakhrakh, "Po pamyati, po zapiskam (II)," p. 282.

3. Cf. the note left by Bunin in his personal copy of the Paris edition in *Literaturnoye nasledstvo*, 2:486. The story "Lodging for the Night" referred to here should not be confused with the tale with the same title that he wrote in 1903 (see chapter 5, note 13).

4. "Iron Wool" has recently been published for the first time in the Soviet Union in *Literaturnoye nasledstvo*, 1:127–29.

5. Cf. A. Sedykh, *Dalyokiye, blizkiye*, p. 210.

6. The title was taken from a line in a poem by Nikolay Ogaryov entitled "An Ordinary Story" [Obyknovennaya povest'] (1842).

7. Only one other story in the volume—"Vengeance"—has Russian émigrés as its principal characters, though the heroine of "A Cold Autumn" [Kholodnaya osen'] (1944) is also portrayed after her emigration.

8. Cf. M. Iof'yev, *Profili iskusstva*, p. 282.

9. On the complex symbolism of this story, which Bunin valued highly (cf. Muromtseva-Bunina's letter to P. L. Vyacheslavov of 19 September 1960 in I. A. Bunin, *Povesti. Rasskazy. Vospominaniya*, p. 627), cf. the excellent analysis in L. K. Dolgopolov, "O nekotorykh osobennostyakh realizma pozdnego Bunina. (Opyt kommentariya k rasskazu 'Chistyy ponedel'nik')," pp. 93–109.

10. Cf. the remark of the hero of "In Paris": "From one year to another, from day to day, one secretly waits for only one thing—a happy love affair. Essentially one lives only in the hope of this affair, and nothing ever comes of it" (7:113).

11. Cf. in this respect "Vengeance," the narrator of which is also an artist.

12. Cf. Iof'yev, *Profili iskusstva*, p. 318.

13. A similar hint of menace is conveyed by the bat that flies into Meshchersky's face as he enters his bedroom in the first chapter of "Natalie" (7:147–48).

14. A. A. Volkov's typically sociological interpretation of the mother's intervention as an attempt to arrest the decline of her ailing estate is interesting (*Proza Ivana Bunina*, p. 334).

15. "Heinrich" is the pen name of the heroine, who is a professional translator.

16. F. I. Tyutchev, *Polnoye sobraniye sochineniy*, p. 123.

17. The unusual frequency in the volume generally of sentences beginning with temporal phrases has been indicated in I. A. Figurovsky, "O sintaksise prozy Bunina," p. 64.

18. It is deceptive in the sense that Zavistovsky does not experience "envy" (*zavist'*) himself but provokes it in the hero.

19. Cf. M. V. Vishniak, *"Sovremennyye zapiski." Vospominaniya redaktora*, p. 128, and A. A. Achatova, "Iz tvorcheskoy laboratorii I. A. Bunina," p. 57.

20. *Literaturnoye nasledstvo*, 2:371.

21. For some reason, Bunin did not include this story in *Dark Avenues*.

Concluding Remarks

1. A. K. Baboreko, "Bunin na Kapri. (Po neopublikovannym materialam)," p. 246.

2. A. K. Baboreko and A. N. Teleshov, "Pis'ma I. A. Bunina N. D. Teleshovu (1941–1947)," p. 165.

Bibliography

I. Editions of Bunin's Works

A. Russian

Stikhotvoreniya: 1887–1891 gg. [Poems: 1887–1891]. Oryol, 1891.

"Na kray sveta" i drugiye rasskazy ["To the Edge of the World" and Other Stories]. St. Petersburg, 1897.

Pod otkrytym nebom: Stikhotvoreniya [Beneath an Open Sky: Poems]. Moscow, 1898.

Stikhi i rasskazy [Poetry and Stories]. Moscow, 1900.

Listopad: Stikhotvoreniya [The Fall of the Leaves: Poems]. Moscow, 1901.

Novyye stikhotvoreniya [New Poems]. Moscow, 1902.

Sobraniye sochineniy [Collected Works]. 5 vols. St. Petersburg, 1902–9.

Derevnya [The Village]. Moscow, 1910.

Pereval: Rasskazy, 1892–1902 g. [The Pass: Stories, 1892–1902]. Moscow, 1912.

Rasskazy i stikhotvoreniya, 1907–1910 gg. [Stories and Poems, 1907–1910]. Moscow, 1912.

Stikhotvoreniya [Poems]. Moscow, 1912.

Sukhodol: Povesti i rasskazy, 1911–1912 gg. [Sukhodol: Stories and Tales, 1911–1912]. Moscow, 1912.

Ioann Rydalets: Rasskazy i stikhi, 1912–1913 gg. [Ioann the Weeper: Stories and Poetry, 1912–1913]. Moscow, 1913.

Izbrannyye rasskazy [Selected Stories]. Moscow, 1914.

Zolotoye dno: Rasskazy, 1903–1907 gg. [The Gold Mine: Stories, 1903–1907]. Moscow, 1914.

Polnoye sobraniye sochineniy [Complete Collected Works]. 6 vols. Petrograd, 1915.

Chasha zhizni: Rasskazy, 1913–1914 gg. [The Cup of Life: Stories, 1913–1914]. Moscow, 1915.

Gospodin iz San-Frantsisko: Proizvedeniya, 1915–1916 gg. [The Gentleman from San Francisco: Works, 1915–1916]. Moscow, 1916.

Khram solntsa [The Shrine of the Sun]. Petrograd, 1917.

Gospodin iz San-Frantsisko [The Gentleman from San Francisco]. Paris, 1920.

Chasha zhizni [The Cup of Life]. Paris, 1921.

251

Derevnya [The Village]. Paris, 1921.
Krik [The Cry]. Berlin, 1921.
Nachal'naya lyubov' [First Love]. Prague, 1921.
Roza Iyerikhona [The Rose of Jericho]. Berlin, 1924.
Mitina lyubov' [Mitya's Love]. Paris, 1925.
Mitina lyubov' [Mitya's Love]. Leningrad, 1926.
Posledneye svidaniye [The Last Meeting]. Paris, 1926.
Delo korneta Yelagina [The Cornet Yelagin Affair]. Khar'kov, 1927.
Sny Changa: Izbrannyye rasskazy [The Dreams of Chang: Selected Stories]. Moscow-Leningrad, 1927.
Solnechnyy udar [Sunstroke]. Paris, 1927.
Khudaya trava [Thin Grass]. Moscow-Leningrad, 1928.
Grammatika lyubvi: Izbrannyye rasskazy [The Grammar of Love: Selected Stories]. Belgrade, 1929.
Izbrannyye stikhi (1900–1925) [Selected Poetry (1900–1925)]. Paris, 1929.
Zhizn' Arsen'yeva: Istoki dney [The Life of Arsen'yev: The Well of Days]. Paris, 1930.
Bozh'ye drevo [The Tree of God]. Paris, 1931.
Ten' ptitsy [The Shadow of the Bird]. Paris, 1931.
Sobraniye sochineniy [Collected Works]. 11 vols. Berlin, 1934–36.
Osvobozhdeniye Tolstogo [The Emancipation of Tolstoy]. Paris, 1937.
Lika [Lika]. Paris, 1939.
Tyomnyye allei [Dark Avenues]. New York, 1943.
Tyomnyye allei [Dark Avenues]. Paris, 1946.
Vospominaniya [Memoirs]. Paris, 1950.
Zhizn' Arsen'yeva: Yunost' [The Life of Arsen'yev: Youth]. New York, 1952.
Mitina lyubov'. Solnechnyy udar [Mitya's Love. Sunstroke]. New York, 1953.
Vesnoy v Iudeye. Roza Iyerikhona [In Spring in Judaea. The Rose of Jericho]. New York, 1953.
Petlistyye ushi i drugiye rasskazy [Gnarled Ears and Other Stories]. New York, 1954.
O Chekhove: Nezakonchennaya rukopis' [About Chekhov: An Unfinished Manuscript]. New York, 1955.
Rasskazy [Stories]. Moscow, 1955.
Izbrannyye proizvedeniya [Selected Works]. Moscow, 1956.
Sobraniye sochineniy [Collected Works]. 5 vols. Moscow, 1956.
Stikhotvoreniya [Poems]. Leningrad, 1956.
Rasskazy [Stories]. Moscow, 1957.
Gospodin iz San-Frantsisko [The Gentleman from San Francisco]. Moscow, 1959.
Povesti. Rasskazy. Vospominaniya [Stories. Tales. Memoirs]. Moscow, 1961.

Stikhotvoreniya [Poems]. Leningrad, 1961.
Rasskazy [Stories]. London, 1962.
Sobraniye sochineniy [Collected Works]. 9 vols. Moscow, 1965–67.
Izbrannoye [Selected Works]. Moscow, 1970.
Literaturnoye nasledstvo: Tom 84. Ivan Bunin [Literary Inheritance: Vol.
    84. Ivan Bunin]. Volume 1. Moscow, 1973.
Okayannyye dni [The Accursed Days]. London, Ontario, 1973.
Pod serpom i molotom [Beneath the Hammer and Sickle]. Edited by S.
    P. Kryzytski. London, Ontario, 1975.

B. English

The Gentleman from San Francisco and Other Stories. Translated by D. H.
    Lawrence et al. 1922; 2d ed. London, 1934.
The Village. Translated by Isabel F. Hapgood. 1923; 2d ed. New
    York, 1933.
The Dreams of Chang and Other Stories. Translated by B. G. Guerney.
    1923; 2d ed. New York, 1935.
Fifteen Tales. Translated by Isabel F. Hapgood. London, 1924.
Mitya's Love. Translated from the French by Madelaine Boyd. New
    York, 1926.
The Gentleman from San Francisco and Other Stories. Translated by B. G.
    Guerney. New York, 1933.
The Well of Days. Translated by G. Struve and H. Miles. 1933; 2d ed.
    London, 1946.
Grammar of Love. Translated by J. Cournos. London, 1935.
The Elaghin Affair and Other Stories. Translated by B. G. Guerney. New
    York, 1935.
Dark Avenues and Other Stories. Translated by R. Hare. London, 1949.
Memories and Portraits. Translated by Vera Traill and R. Chancellor.
    London, 1951.
Shadowed Paths. Translated by Ol'ga Shartse. Moscow, n.d.
The Gentleman from San Francisco and Other Stories. With an introduc-
    tion by William Sansom. London, 1975.

II. Letters, Memoirs, and Other Primary Sources

Arkhiv A. M. Gor'kogo [The Archive of A. M. Gorky], 7:103. Moscow,
    1959.
Baboreko, A. K. "Iz perepiski I. A. Bunina" [From I. A. Bunin's Cor-
    respondence]. *Novyy mir* 32, no. 10 (1956): 197–211.
_____. "Bunin o Tolstom" [Bunin about Tolstoy]. In *Yasnopolyanskiy*

sbornik: Stat'i i materialy. *God 1960–y*, edited by A. I. Popovkin et al., pp. 129–46. Tula, 1960.

————. "Bunin na Kapri. (Po neopublikovannym materialam)" [Bunin on Capri. (According to Unpublished Materials)]. In *V bol'shoy sem'ye*, pp. 238–53. Smolensk, 1960.

————. "Chekhov i Bunin" [Chekhov and Bunin]. *Literaturnoye nasledstvo* 68 (1960): 395–416.

————. "Tipy i prototipy. (Neizvestnyye materialy o I. A. Bunine)" [Types and Prototypes. (Unknown Materials about I. A. Bunin)]. *Voprosy literatury* 4, no. 6 (1960): 254–55.

————. "Bunin i Ertel' " [Bunin and Ertel']. *Russkaya literatura* 4, no. 4 (1961): 150–51.

————, ed. "Neopublikovannyye pis'ma I. A. Bunina" [Unpublished Letters of I. A. Bunin]. *Russkaya literatura* 6, no. 2 (1963): 177–83.

————. "Posledniye gody I. A. Bunina. (Novyye materialy)" [The Last Years of I. A. Bunin. (New Materials)]. *Voprosy literatury* 9, no. 3 (1965): 253–56.

————. "Neopublikovannoye pis'mo Romena Rollana. (O tvorchestve I. Bunina)" [An Unpublished Letter of Romain Rolland. (About the Works of I. Bunin)]. *Voprosy literatury* 9, no. 6 (1965): 255.

————. *I. A. Bunin: Materialy dlya biografii (s 1870 po 1917)* [I. A. Bunin: Materials for a Biography (from 1870 to 1917)]. Moscow, 1967.

————. "I. A. Bunin: Pis'ma D. L. Tal'nikovu" [I. A. Bunin: Letters to D. L. Tal'nikov]. *Russkaya literatura* 17, no. 1 (1974): 170–79.

————, and Teleshov, A. N. "Pis'ma I. A. Bunina N. D. Teleshovu (1941–1947)" [Letters of I. A. Bunin to N. D. Teleshov (1941–1947)]. *Istoricheskiy arkhiv* 27, no. 2 (1962): 156–67.

Bakhrakh, A. V. "Po pamyati, po zapiskam (II)" [From Memory, from Notes (II)]. *Mosty* 12 (1966): 272–97.

Bryusov, V. *Dalyokiye i blizkiye* [Far Ones and Near Ones], pp. 154–56. Moscow, 1912.

————. *Dnevniki 1891–1910* [Diaries 1891–1910]. Moscow, 1927.

Bunin, I. A. "Nedostatki sovremennoy poezii" [The Shortcomings of Modern Poetry]. *Rodina* 28 (1888): 737.

————. "Poet-gumanist. (Po povodu 50-letnego yubileya literaturnoy deyatel'nosti A. M. Zhemchuzhnikova)" [A Humanitarian Poet. (On the Occasion of the Fiftieth Anniversary of A. M. Zhemchuzhnikov's Literary Activity)]. *Vestnik vospitaniya*, no. 3 (1900), p. 80.

Chekhov, A. P. *Sobraniye sochineniy* [Collected Works]. 12 vols. 12: 429. Moscow, 1960–64.

Gazer, I. S., ed. "Pis'ma L. Andreyeva i I. Bunina" [Letters of L. Andreyev and I. Bunin]. *Voprosy literatury* 13, no. 7 (1969): 175–93.

Gor'kovskiye chteniya, 1958–1959 [Gorky Readings, 1958–1959], pp. 3–126. Moscow, 1961.

Katayev, V. "Trava zabven'ya" [The Grass of Oblivion]. *Sobraniye sochineniy* [Collected Works]. 9 vols. 9:249–446. Moscow, 1968–72.

Kuznetsova, G. *Grasskiy dnevnik* [Grasse Diary]. Washington, 1967.

Literaturnoye nasledstvo: Tom 84. Ivan Bunin [Literary Inheritance: Vol. 84. Ivan Bunin]. 2 vols. Moscow, 1967.

Meshchersky, A., ed. "Neizvestnyye pis'ma I. Bunina" [Unknown Letters of I. Bunin]. *Russkaya literatura* 4, no. 4 (1961); 152–58.

Muratova, K. D., ed. "I. A. Bunin: Pis'ma k V. S. Mirolyubovu (1899–1904)" [I. A. Bunin. Letters to V. S. Mirolyubov (1899–1904)]. *Literaturnyy arkhiv* 5 (1960): 128–41.

Muromtseva-Bunina, V. N. *Zhizn' Bunina, 1870–1906* [The Life of Bunin, 1870–1906]. Paris, 1958.

————. "Iz literaturnogo nasledstva I. A. Bunina" [From the Literary Legacy of I. A. Bunin]. *Novyy zhurnal* 59 (1960): 127–56; 60 (1960): 166–78; 62 (1960): 147–75; 63 (1961): 173–203; 64 (1961): 205–20.

Na rodnoy zemle: Literaturno-khudozhestvennyy sbornik [In the Homeland: A Collection of Belles-lettres], pp. 272–310, 383–97. Oryol, 1956.

"Perepiska" [Correspondence]. *Literaturnaya Rossiya* 51 (20 December 1963): 3.

Problemy realizma i khudozhestvennoy pravdy [Problems of Realism and Artistic Truth]. 1:161–74. L'vov, 1961.

Rzhevsky, L. "Pamyati I. A. Bunina" [To the Memory of I. A. Bunin]. *Grani* 20 (1953): 3–8.

Sedykh, A. [pseudonym of Ya. M. Tsvibak.] "I. A. Bunin." *Novyy zhurnal* 65 (1961): 151–97.

————. *Dalyokiye, blizkiye* [Far Ones, Near Ones], pp. 189–246. New York, 1962.

Smirnov-Sokol'sky, N. P. "Poslednyaya nakhodka" [The Latest Find]. *Novyy mir* 41, no. 10 (1965): 213–21.

————. "V. N. Muromtseva-Bunina: Bunin i Chekhov (1901–1902 gg. Vospominaniya)" [V. N. Muromtseva-Bunina: Bunin and Chekhov (1901–1902. Memoirs)]. *Novyy mir* 46, no. 10 (1970): 195–203.

Ustami Buninykh [From the Lips of the Bunins], edited by M. Green. Vol. 1. Frankfurt-am-Main, 1977.

Vesna prishla [Spring Has Come], pp. 208–41. Smolensk, 1959.

256   Bibliography

Vishniak, M. V. "Sovremennyye zapiski." Vospominaniya redaktora ["Con-
temporary Notes." An Editor's Reminiscences]. Indiana Uni-
versity Publications, Slavic and East European Series. Vol. 7.
Bloomington, 1957.
Zaytsev, B. "Pamyati Ivana i Very Buninykh" [To the Memory of
Ivan and Vera Bunin]. In his Dalyokoye [The Distant Past], pp.
137–43. Washington, 1965.
Zenzinov, V. "Ivan Alekseyevich Bunin." Novyy zhurnal 3 (1942):
288–304.
Zurov, L. F. "Pis'ma N. D. Teleshova k I. A. Buninu" [Letters of N.
D. Teleshov to I. A. Bunin]. Novyy zhurnal 85 (1966): 129–40.

III. Criticism

Abramovich, N. Ya. "Estetizm i erotika" [Aestheticism and Sen-
suality]. Obrazovaniye 17, no. 4 (1908): 103–6.
————. "I. A. Bunin, kak khudozhnik" [I. A. Bunin as an Artist].
Novaya zhizn', no. 12 (1915), pp. 161–68.
Achatova, A. A. "Detal' v povesti I. Bunina Derevnya" [Details in Bu-
nin's Short Novel The Village]. Uchonyye zapiski Tomskogo
gosudarstvennogo universiteta im. V. V. Kuybysheva 42 (1962):
58–67.
————. "Peyzazh v dorevolyutsionnykh rasskazakh I. A. Bunina"
[The Landscape in the Prerevolutionary Stories of I. A.
Bunin]. Uchonyye zapiski Tomskogo gosudarstvennogo universiteta
im. V. V. Kuybysheva 45 (1963): 93–103.
————. "Rabota I. Bunina nad rasskazom Gospodin iz San-Frantsisko:
Po materialam rukopisey" [I. Bunin's Work on the Story The
Gentleman from San Francisco: According to Manuscript Mate-
rials]. Uchonyye zapiski Tomskogo gosudarstvennogo universiteta im.
V. V. Kuybysheva 48 (1964): 61–78.
————. "Iz tvorcheskoy laboratorii I. A. Bunina" [From I. A. Bunin's
Creative Laboratory]. Uchonyye zapiski Tomskogo gosudarstven-
nogo universiteta im. V. V. Kuybysheva 50 (1965): 56–65.
Adamovich, G. V. Odinochestvo i svoboda [Solitude and Freedom], pp.
79–125. New York, 1955.
Afanas'yev, V. N. "Ot 'Derevni' k 'Gospodinu iz San-Frantsisko'"
[From "The Village" to "The Gentleman from San Francis-
co"]. Uchonyye zapiski Moskovskogo pedagogicheskogo instituta im.
V. I. Lenina 222 (1964): 5–158.
————. I. A. Bunin: Ocherk tvorchestva [I. A. Bunin: A Survey of His
Works]. Moscow, 1966.
————. "I. A. Bunin i russkoye dekadentstvo 90-kh godov. (V
poryadke postanovki voprosa)" [I. A. Bunin and the Russian

Decadence of the Nineties. (By Way of Posing a Question)].
Russkaya literatura 11, no. 3 (1968): 175–81.

————. "O nekotorykh chertakh pozdney liricheskoy prozy Bunina"
[Concerning Certain Features of the Later Lyrical Prose of
Bunin]. *Izvestiya Akademii Nauk SSSR: Seriya literatury i yazyka*
29, no. 6 (1970): 534–37.

Aldanov, M. A. "Iv. Bunin: 'Zhizn' Arsen'yeva: Istoki dney'" [Iv.
Bunin: "The Life of Arsen'yev: The Well of Days"]. *Sovremennyye zapiski* 42 (1930): 523–25.

————. "I. A. Bunin: 'Lika.' Izdaniye 'Petropolis'" [I. A. Bunin:
'Lika.' The 'Petropolis' Edition]. *Sovremennyye zapiski* 69 (1939):
385–87.

————. "O Bunine" [About Bunin]. *Novyy zhurnal* 35 (1953): 130–34.

————. "Predisloviye" [Foreword]. In I. A. Bunin, *O Chekhove:
Nezakonchennaya rukopis'* [About Chekhov: An Unfinished
Manuscript], pp. 7–20. New York, 1955.

Aleksandrova, V. A. "I. A. Bunin." *Novyy zhurnal* 12 (1946): 168–78.

————. "Ivan Bunin: 'Tyomnyye allei'" [Ivan Bunin: "Dark Avenues"]. *Novyy zhurnal* 15 (1947): 295–96.

Avilova, N. S. "'Nesrochnaya vesna'" ["The Eternal Spring"].
Russkaya rech' 4, no. 5 (1970): 63–67.

Aykhenval'd, Yu. *Siluety russkikh pisateley* [Silhouettes of Russian
writers]. 3 vols. 3:176–203. Berlin, 1923.

Batyushkov, F. D. "Iv. A. Bunin." In S. A. Vengerov, ed., *Russkaya
literatura XX veka* [Russian Literature of the Twentieth Cen-
tury]. 3 vols. 2:342–65. Moscow, 1915.

Bazhinov, I. D. *Dooktyabr'skaya proza I. A. Bunina* [The Pre-October
Prose of I. A. Bunin]. Kiev, 1963.

————. "Rasskaz I. A. Bunina 'Antonovskiye yabloki.' (K stoletiyu so
dnya rozhdeniya I. A. Bunina)" [I. A. Bunin's Story "Antonov
Apples." (For the Centenary of I. A. Bunin's Birth)]. *Voprosy
russkoy literatury* 14, no. 2 (1970): 22–27.

Bedford, C. H. "The Fulfilment of Ivan Bunin." *Canadian Slavonic
Papers* 1 (1956): 31–44.

Berzups, J. *Ivan A. Bunin and the Soviet Regime*. Ann Arbor, 1976.

Bitsilli, P. "Iv. Bunin: 'Ten' ptitsy'" [Iv. Bunin: "The Shadow of the
Bird"]. *Sovremennyye zapiski* 47 (1931): 493–94.

————. "Bunin i Tolstoy" [Bunin and Tolstoy]. *Sovremennyye zapiski*
60 (1936): 280–81.

Blok, A. A. *Sobraniye sochineniy* [Collected Works]. 8 vols. 5:141–4.
Moscow-Leningrad, 1960–63.

Bonami, T. M. *Khudozhestvennaya proza I. A. Bunina (1887–1904)*
[The Fiction of I. A. Bunin (1887–1904)]. Vladimir, 1962.

Borras, F. M. "A Common Theme in Tolstoy, Andreyev and Bunin."
Slavonic and East European Review 32 (1953): 230–35.

Buninsky sbornik [A Bunin Miscellany]. Edited by A. I. Gavrilov et al. Oryol, 1974.

Chukovsky, K. "Ranniy Bunin" [The Early Bunin]. *Voprosy literatury* 12, no. 5 (1968): 83–101.

Colin, A. G. "Ivan Bunin in Retrospect." *Slavonic and East European Review* 34 (1955–56): 156–73.

Croisé, J. "Ivan Bunin (1870–1953)." *Russian Review* 13 (1954): 146–51.

Derman, A. B. "I. Bunin." *Russkaya mysl'* 35, no. 6 (1914): 52–57.

————. "Pobeda khudozhnika. ('Gospodin iz San-Frantsisko')" [The Triumph of an Artist. ("The Gentleman from San Francisco")]. *Russkaya mysl'* 37, no. 5 (1916): 23–27.

Dolgopolov, L. K. "O nekotorykh osobennostyakh realizma pozdnego Bunina. (Opyt kommentariya k rasskazu 'Chistyy ponedel'nik')" [About Certain Features of the Later Bunin's Realism. (An Attempted Commentary on the Story "The First Monday in Lent")]. *Russkaya literatura* 16, no. 2 (1973): 93–109.

Dzhonson, I. [pseudonym of I. I. Ivanov.] "Krasivoye darovaniye" [A Beautiful Gift]. *Obrazovaniye* 11, no. 12 (1902): 51–62.

Figurovsky, I. A. "O sintaksise prozy Bunina: Sintaksicheskaya dominanta 'Tyomnykh alley'" [Concerning the Syntax of Bunin's Prose: The Dominant Syntactic Feature of "Dark Avenues"]. *Russkaya rech'* 4, no. 5 (1970): 63–66.

Foster, L. A. "O kompozitsii *Tyomnykh alley* Bunina" [Concerning the Composition of Bunin's *Dark Avenues*]. *Russian Literature* 9 (1975): 55–65.

Gazer, I. S. "O nekotorykh khudozhestvennykh osobennostyakh povesti I. A. Bunina 'Derevnya'" [Concerning Certain Artistic Features of I. A. Bunin's Short Novel "The Village"]. *Visnik L'viv'skogo ordena Lenina derzhavnogo universitetu im. Iv. Franka: Seriya filologichna*, no. 3 (1965), pp. 98–104.

————. "O svoyeobrazii lirizma v novellakh Bunina" [Concerning the Distinctive Lyricism of Bunin's Short Stories]. *Voprosy russkoy literatury* 16, no. 1 (1971): 59–67.

Geydeko, V. *A. Chekhov i Iv. Bunin* [A. Chekhov and Iv. Bunin]. Moscow, 1976.

Gol'din, S. L. "O literaturnoy deyatel'nosti I. A. Bunina kontsa vos'midesyatykh—nachala devyanostykh godov. (Zabytyye i neizvestnyye stranitsy)" [Concerning I. A. Bunin's Literary Activity in the Late Eighties and Early Nineties. (Forgotten and Unknown Pages)]. *Uchonyye zapiski Orekhovo-Zuyevskogo pedagogicheskogo instituta* 9 (1958): 3–38.

————. "K voprosu o literaturnykh svyazyakh I. A. Bunina s A. P. Chekhovym i A. M. Gor'kim" [On the Subject of I. A. Bunin's

Literary Connexions with A. P. Chekhov and A. M. Gorky].
Uchonyye zapiski Orekhovo-Zuyevskogo pedagogicheskogo instituta 9
(1958): 53–75.

————. "K voprosu o literaturnykh svyazyakh V. Bryusova i I.
Bunina" [On the Subject of the Literary Connexions of V.
Bryusov and I. Bunin]. In *Bryusovskiye chteniya 1962 goda*
[Bryusov Readings of 1962], pp. 168–84. Yerevan, 1963.

Gor'kiy, A. M. *Sobraniye sochineniy* [Collected Works]. 30 vols. Moscow,
1949–55.

Granovskaya, L. M. "Iz nablyudeniy nad yazykom I. A. Bunina. (O
nekotorykh osobennostyakh upotrebleniya opredeleniy-
prilagatel'nykh)" [Some Observations on I. A. Bunin's Language. (Concerning Certain Features of His Use of Adjectives)]. *Uchonyye zapiski Azerbaydzhanskogo pedagogicheskogo instituta yazykov im. M. F. Akhundova: Seriya filologicheskaya* 9
(1961): 253–66.

Grechnev, V. Ya. "Proza Ivana Bunina" [The Prose of Ivan Bunin].
Russkaya literatura 13, no. 4 (1970): 221–26.

Gross, S. L. "Nature, Man, and God in Bunin's 'The Gentleman from
San Francisco.'" *Modern Fiction Studies* 6, no. 2 (1960): 153–63.

Gurevich, L. *Literatura i estetika: Kriticheskiye opyty i etyudy* [Literature
and Aesthetics: Critical Essays and Sketches], pp. 144–46.
Moscow, 1912.

Il'in, I. A. *O t'me i prosvetlenii* [Concerning Darkness and Enlighten-
ment], pp. 27–77. Munich, 1959.

Iof'yev, M. *Profili iskusstva* [Profiles of Art], pp. 277–319. Moscow,
1965.

Kastorsky, S. "Gor'kiy i Bunin" [Gorky and Bunin]. *Zvezda* 33, no. 3
(1956): 144–53.

Koltonovskaya, Ye. A. "I. Bunin: 'Derevnya'" [I. Bunin: "The Village"]. *Vestnik Yevropy*, no. 1 (1911), pp. 395–96.

————. *Kriticheskiye etyudy* [Critical Studies], pp. 96–99, 273–80. St.
Petersburg, 1912.

————. "Bunin, kak khudozhnik-povestvovatel'" [Bunin as a Narrative Artist]. *Vestnik Yevropy*, no. 5 (1914), pp. 327–41.

————. "Garmoniya kontrastov" [A Harmony of Contrasts]. *Russkaya
mysl'* 38, no. 2 (1917): 90–103.

Kotlyar, L. V. *Khudozhestvennaya proza I. A. Bunina (1917–1953)* [The
Fiction of I. A. Bunin (1917–1953)]. Moscow, 1967.

Krasnyansky, V. V. "Tri redaktsii odnogo rasskaza" [Three Editions
of One Story]. *Russkaya rech'* 4, no. 5 (1970): 57–62.

Kravchenko, A. A. "K voprosu o realizme I. Bunina. (Tvorcheskaya
istoriya rasskaza 'Gospodin iz San-Frantsisko')" [On the Subject of I. Bunin's Realism. (The History of the Creation of the
Story "The Gentleman from San Francisco")]. In *Kazanskoye*

zonal'noye ob'yedineniye kafedr literatury gruppy pedagogicheskikh institutov: Doklady i soobshcheniya (po materialam I i II nauchnykh konferentsiy). 1:267–95. Kazan'-Cheboksary, 1963.

Krutikova, L. V. "O sobranii sochineniy I. A. Bunina" [Concerning I. A. Bunin's Collected Works]. *Russkaya literatura* 1, no. 2 (1958): 215–22.

———. "Iz tvorcheskoy istorii 'Derevni' I. A. Bunina" [From the History of the Creation of I. A. Bunin's "The Village"]. *Russkaya literatura* 2, no. 4 (1959): 130–45.

———. " 'Derevnya' I. Bunina" [I. Bunin's "The Village"]. *Uchonyye zapiski Leningradskogo gosudarstvennogo universiteta: Seriya filologicheskikh nauk* 295 (1960): 169–88.

———. " 'Na kray sveta' - pervyy sbornik rasskazov I. Bunina" ["To the Edge of the World" - I. Bunin's First Collection of Stories]. *Vestnik Leningradskogo universiteta* 20 (1961): 77–88.

———." 'Sukhodol,' povest'-poema I. Bunina" [I. Bunin's Poetic Story "Sukhodol"]. *Russkaya literatura* 9, no. 2 (1966): 44–59.

———. "Prochitan li Bunin?" [Has Bunin Been Read?]. *Russkaya literatura* 11, no. 4 (1968): 182–92.

———. "Vernost' prizvaniyu" [Loyalty to One's Calling]. In I. A. Bunin, *Izbrannoye* [Selected Works], pp. 5–36. Moscow, 1970.

Kryzytski, S. *The Works of Ivan Bunin*. The Hague-Paris, 1971.

Kucherovsky, N. M. "Brat'ya Buniny. (Nachalo literaturnoy deyatel'nosti I. A. Bunina)" [The Bunin Brothers. (The Beginning of I. A. Bunin's Literary Activity)]. In *Iz istorii russkoy literatury XIX veka* [From the History of Nineteenth-Century Russian Literature], pp. 85–109. Kaluga, 1966.

———. "Mundir tolstovstva. (Molodoy I. A. Bunin i tolstovstvo)" [A Uniform of Tolstoyism. (The Young I. A. Bunin and Tolstoyism)]. In *Iz istorii russkoy literatury XIX veka* [From the History of Nineteenth-Century Russian Literature], pp. 110–31. Kaluga, 1966.

———. "O kontseptsii zhizni v liricheskoy proze I. A. Bunina. (Vtoraya polovina 90-kh–nachalo 900-kh godov)" [Concerning the Conception of Life in the Lyrical Prose of I. A. Bunin. (The Second Half of the Nineties and the Beginning of the 1900's)]. In *Russkaya literatura XX veka. (Dooktyabr'skiy period): Sbornik statey* [Russian Literature of the Twentieth Century. (The Pre-October Period): A Collection of Articles], pp. 80–106. Kaluga, 1968.

———. "Esteticheskaya sushchnost' filosofskikh iskaniy I. A. Bunina (1906–1911 gg.)" [The Aesthetic Nature of I. A. Bunin's Philosophical Searchings (1906–1911)]. *Filologicheskiye nauki*, no. 6 (1969), pp. 25–35.

———. "Istoriya Durnovki i yeyo 'Myortvyye dushi.' (Povest' I. A. Bunina 'Derevnya')" [The History of Durnovka and Its "Dead Souls." (I. A. Bunin's Short Novel "The Village")]. In *Russkaya literatura XX veka. (Dooktyabr'skiy period): Sbornik vtoroy* [Russian Literature of the Twentieth Century. (The Pre-October Period): The Second Collection], pp. 107–54. Kaluga, 1970.

———. "Povest' I. A. Bunina 'Vesyolyy dvor'" [I. A. Bunin's Story "A Gay Farmhouse"]. *Russkaya literatura* 13, no. 4 (1970): 128–39.

L'vov-Rogachevsky, V. *Snova nakanune* [Again on the Eve], pp. 3–28. Moscow, 1913.

———. *Noveyshaya russkaya literatura* [The Latest Russian Literature], pp. 73–79. Moscow, 1927.

Lyatsky, Ye. "Voprosy iskusstva v sovremennykh yego otrazheniyakh" [Questions of Art in Its Modern Reflections]. *Vestnik Yevropy*, no. 3 (1907), pp. 281–97.

Marullo, T. G. "Bunin's *Dry Valley*: The Russian Novel in Transition from Realism to Modernism." *Forum for Modern Language Studies* 14, no. 3 (1978): 193–207.

Mikhaylov, O. N. "Proza Bunina" [Bunin's Prose]. *Voprosy literatury* 1, no. 5 (1957): 128–55.

———. "I. A. Bunin." In I. A. Bunin, *Gospodin iz San-Frantsisko* [The Gentleman from San Francisco], pp. 3–12. Moscow, 1959.

———. *Ivan Alekseyevich Bunin: Ocherk tvorchestva* [Ivan Alekseyevich Bunin: A Survey of His Works]. Moscow, 1967.

———. "Put' Bunina-khudozhnika" [The Path of Bunin the Artist]. In *Literaturnoye nasledstvo: Tom 84. Ivan Bunin* [Literary Inheritance: Vol. 84. Ivan Bunin]. 2 vols. 1:7–56. Moscow, 1973.

———. *Strogiy talant. Ivan Bunin: Zhizn', sud'ba, tvorchestvo* [An Austere Talent. Ivan Bunin: His Life, Fortune and Works]. Moscow, 1976.

Mirsky, D. S. *A History of Russian Literature*, pp. 389–94. New York, 1960.

Nikulin, L. "I. A. Bunin." In I. A. Bunin, *Sobraniye sochineniy* [Collected Works]. 5 vols. 1:3–30. Moscow, 1956.

———. "Kuprin i Bunin" [Kuprin and Bunin]. *Oktyabr'* 34, no. 7 (1958): 204–18.

———. "O chom govoryat rukopisi Bunina" [What Bunin's Manuscripts Reveal]. *Moskva* 3, no. 7 (1959): 200–210.

———. *Chekhov, Bunin, Kuprin: Literaturnyye portrety* [Chekhov, Bunin, Kuprin: Literary Portraits], pp. 171–264. Moscow, 1960.

Ninov, A. A. "Bunin v 'Znanii'" [Bunin in "Znaniye"]. *Russkaya literatura* 7, no. 1 (1964): 184–201.

———. "K avtobiografii I. Bunina" [Towards I. Bunin's Autobiography]. *Novyy mir* 41, no. 10 (1965): 222–30.

———. "'Derevnya' Bunina i russkaya literatura" [Bunin's "The Village" and Russian Literature]. *Voprosy literatury* 14, no. 10 (1970): 56–78.

———. *M. Gor'kiy i Iv. Bunin* [M. Gorky and Iv. Bunin]. Leningrad, 1973.

Olesha, Yu. *Ni dnya bez strochki* [Not a Day without a Line], pp. 245–47. Moscow, 1965.

Paustovsky, K. "Ivan Bunin." In I. A. Bunin, *Povesti. Rasskazy. Vospominaniya* [Stories. Tales. Memoirs], pp. 3–18. Moscow, 1961.

———. *Blizkiye i dalyokiye* [Near Ones and Far Ones]. Moscow, 1967.

Poggioli, R. "The Art of Ivan Bunin." *Harvard Slavic Studies* 1 (1953): 249–77.

Polotskaya, Ye. A. "Vzaimoproniknoveniye poezii i prozy u rannego Bunina" [The Interpenetration of Prose and Poetry in the Works of the Early Bunin]. *Izvestiya Akademii Nauk SSSR: Seriya literatury i yazyka* 29, no. 5 (1970): 412–18.

Red'ko, A. Ye. "Iz literaturnykh vpechatleniy. ('Nochnoy razgovor')" [Literary Impressions. ("A Nocturnal Conversation")]. *Russkoye bogatstvo* 37, no. 4 (1912): 137–43.

Richards, D. J. "Memory and Time Past: A Theme in the Works of Ivan Bunin." *Forum for Modern Language Studies* 7, no. 2 (1971): 158–69.

———. "Bunin's Conception of the Meaning of Life." *Slavonic and East European Review* 50 (1972): 153–72.

Sansome, W. "Ivan Bunin: The Harpstring Broken." *London Magazine* 1, no. 2 (1954): 64–68.

Sazonova, Yu. "'Zhizn' Arsen'yeva': Pervoye polnoye izdaniye" ["The Life of Arsen'yev": The First Complete Edition]. *Novyy zhurnal* 30 (1952): 287–90.

———. "I. A. Bunin: 'Vesnoy v Iudeye' i 'Mitina lyubov'" [I. A. Bunin: "In Spring in Judaea" and "Mitya's Love"]. *Novyy zhurnal* 33 (1953): 298–99.

Shklovsky, V. "'Mitina lyubov'' Ivana Bunina" [Ivan Bunin's "Mitya's Love"]. *Novyy Lef* 1, no. 4 (1927): 43–45.

Slivitskaya, O. V. "O kontseptsii cheloveka v tvorchestve I. A. Bunina. (Rasskaz 'Kazimir Stanislavovich')" [Concerning the Conception of Man in the Works of I. A. Bunin. (The Story "Kazimir Stanislavovich")]. In *Russkaya literatura XX veka. (Dooktyabr'skiy period): Sbornik vtoroy* [Russian Literature of the Twentieth Century. (The Pre-October Period): The Second Collection], pp. 155–62. Kaluga, 1970.

Spivak, R. "'Zhivaya zhizn'" I. Bunina i L. Tolstogo. (Nekotoryye storony estetiki Bunina v svete traditsiy L. Tolstogo)" [The "Living Life" of I. Bunin and L. Tolstoy. (Certain Aspects of Bunin's Aesthetics in the Light of the Traditions of L.

Tolstoy)]. *Voprosy izucheniya russkoy literatury XIX - nachala XX vekov: Uchonyye zapiski* 155 (1967): 87–128.

———. "Yazyk prozy I. A. Bunina i traditsiya L. N. Tolstogo" [The Language of I. A. Bunin's Prose and the Tradition of L. N. Tolstoy]. *Filologicheskiye nauki*, no. 3 (1968), pp. 23–33.

———. "Printsipy khudozhestvennoy konkretizatsii v tvorchestve L. Tolstogo i I. Bunina: Detal'" [Principles of Artistic Concretization in the Works of L. Tolstoy and I. Bunin: Details]. In *Literaturovedeniye: Uchonyye zapiski Permskogo ordena Krasnogo znameni gosudarstvennogo universiteta im. A. M. Gor'kogo* 193 (1968): 247–77.

———. "Russkaya derevnya v izobrazhenii I. A. Bunina i L. Tolstogo" [The Russian Village in the Depiction of I. A. Bunin and L. Tolstoy]. *Vestnik Moskovskogo universiteta: Filologiya* 24, no. 3 (1969): 41–48.

Stepun, F. "Literaturnyye zametki. (I. A. Bunin: Po povodu 'Mitinoy lyubvi')" [Literary Notes. (I. A. Bunin: Apropos "Mitya's Love")]. *Sovremennyye zapiski* 27 (1926): 323–45.

———. "Ivan Bunin. 'Bozh'ye drevo'" [Ivan Bunin. "The Tree of God"]. *Sovremennyye zapiski* 46 (1931): 486–89.

———. "Ivan Bunin." *Sovremennyye zapiski* 54 (1934): 197–211.

———. *Vstrechi* [Meetings], pp. 87–122. Munich, 1962.

Sterlina, I. D. *Ivan Alekseyevich Bunin*. Lipetsk, 1960.

Strelsky, N. "Bunin: Eclectic of the Future." *South Atlantic Quarterly* 35 (1936): 273–81.

Struve, G. "The Art of Ivan Bunin." *Slavonic and East European Review* 11 (1932–33): 423–36.

Tarasenkov, A. "O zhizni i tvorchestve I. A. Bunina" [Concerning the Life and Works of I. A. Bunin]. In I. A. Bunin, *Izbrannyye proizvedeniya* [Selected Works], pp. 3–25. Moscow, 1956.

Tsetlin, M. "Ivan Bunin: 'Roza Iyerikhona'" [Ivan Bunin: "The Rose of Jericho"]. *Sovremennyye zapiski* 22 (1924): 449–51.

Tvardovsky, A. "O Bunine" [About Bunin]. In I. A. Bunin, *Sobraniye sochineniy* [Collected Works]. 9 vols. 1:7–49. Moscow, 1965–67.

Vantenkov, I. P. *Bunin-povestvovatel' (rasskazy 1890–1916 gg.)* [Bunin the Narrator (Stories 1890–1916)]. Minsk, 1974.

Volkov, A. A. *Russkaya literatura XX veka* [Russian Literature of the Twentieth Century]. Moscow, 1957.

———. *Russkaya literatura XX veka: Dooktyabr'skiy period* [Russian Literature of the Twentieth Century: The Pre-October Period]. Moscow, 1964.

———. *Proza Ivana Bunina* [The Prose of Ivan Bunin]. Moscow, 1969.

Volynskaya, N. I. "Vzglyady I. A. Bunina na khudozhestvennoye masterstvo" [The Views of I. A. Bunin on Artistic Craftsmanship]. *Uchonyye zapiski Vladimirskogo gosudarstvennogo pedagogicheskogo instituta im. P. I. Lebedeva-Polyanskogo: Seriya "russkaya i zarubezhnaya literatura"* 1 (1966): 54–66.

Voronsky, A. K. "Vne zhizni i vne vremeni. (Russkaya zarubezhnaya khudozhestvennaya literatura)" [Outside Life and Outside Time. (Foreign Russian Belles-lettres)]. *Prozhektor*, no. 13 (1925), pp. 18–20.

Vtoroy Vsesoyuznyy s'yezd sovetskikh pisateley. Stenograficheskiy otchot [The Second All-Union Congress of Soviet Writers. A Stenographic Report]. Moscow, 1956.

Weidle, V. "Na smert' Bunina" [On the Death of Bunin]. *Opyty* 3 (1954): 80–93.

Winner, T. "Some Remarks about the Style of Bunin's Early Prose." In *American Contributions to the Sixth International Congress of Slavists*. 2 vols. 1:369–81. The Hague-Paris, 1968.

Woodward, J. B. "Eros and Nirvana in the Art of Bunin." *Modern Language Review* 65, no. 3 (1970): 576–86.

———. "The Evolution of Bunin's Narrative Technique." *Scando-Slavica* 16 (1970): 5–21.

———. "Narrative Tempo in the Later Stories of Bunin." *Die Welt der Slaven* 16, no. 4 (1971): 383–96.

———. "Structure and Subjectivity in the Early 'Philosophical' Tales of Bunin." *Canadian Slavic Studies* 5, no. 4 (1971): 508–23.

———. "The Thematic Unity of Bunin's Peasant Fiction." *Forum for Modern Language Studies* 10, no. 1 (1974): 45–56.

Zavelin, P. V. "Syuzhet i stil' v pervykh rasskazakh I. A. Bunina" [Plot and Style in the First Stories of I. A. Bunin]. *Trudy Irkutskogo gosudarstvennogo universiteta im. A. A. Zhdanova: Seriya literaturovedeniya i kritiki* 33, no. 4 (1964): 165–81.

———. *Khudozhestvennyy stil' v proze I. A. Bunina o derevne* [Artistic Style in I. A. Bunin's Prose about the Countryside]. Tomsk, 1966.

Zaytsev, K. *I. A. Bunin: Zhizn' i tvorchestvo* [I. A. Bunin: Life and Works]. Berlin, n.d.

IV. Miscellaneous

Auerbach, E. *Mimesis: Dargestellte Wirklichkeit in der abendländischen Literatur*. Bern, 1946.

Bayley, J. *Tolstoy and the Novel*. London, 1966.

Booth, W. C. *The Rhetoric of Fiction*. Chicago, 1961.

Canby, H. S. *The Short Story in English*. New York, 1909.

Daiches, D. *A Study of Literature for Readers and Critics*. London, 1948.

Jakobson, R. "The Prose of the Poet Pasternak." In D. Davie and A.

Livingstone, eds., *Pasternak: Modern Judgements*, pp. 135–51. London, 1969.

Nilsson, N. Å. *Studies in Čechov's Narrative Technique*: "The Steppe" and "The Bishop." Uppsala, 1968.

O'Faolain, S. *The Short Story*. London, 1948.

Polikanov, A. A., Udonova, Z. V., and Trofimov, I. T. *Russkaya literatura kontsa XIX*–nachala XX vv. [Russian Literature of the Late Nineteenth and Early Twentieth Century]. Moscow, 1965.

Tyutchev, F. I. *Polnoye sobraniye sochineniy* [Complete Collected Works]. St. Petersburg, 1913.

Index